The Invention of Nature

Thomas Bargatzky
Rolf Kuschel
(Eds.)

# The Invention of Nature

PETER LANG
Frankfurt am Main · Berlin · Bern · New York · Paris · Wien

Die Deutsche Bibliothek - CIP-Einheitsaufnahme

The invention of nature / Thomas Bargatzky ; Rolf Kuschel (Hrsg.). - Frankfurt am Main ; Berlin ; Bern ; New York ; Paris ; Wien : Lang, 1994
ISBN 3-631-45369-8

NE: Bargatzky, Thomas [Hrsg.]

ISBN 3-631-45369-8
© Verlag Peter Lang GmbH, Frankfurt am Main 1994
All rights reserved.

All parts of this publication are protected by copyright. Any utilisation outside the strict limits of the copyright law, without the permission of the publisher, is forbidden and liable to prosecution. This applies in particular to reproductions, translations, microfilming, and storage and processing in electronic retrieval systems.

Printed in Germany 1 2 3 4  6 7

# PREFACE

The ecological crisis has taught us that "nature always sides with the hidden flaw", as yet another variant of Murphy's law correctly formulates it. There must be a flaw in the reconstruction of the concept of Nature underlying our behavior toward the natural environment which makes us destroy the very foundations on which life on earth is based. Just what is wrong with our concept of Nature, however, is not easy to say, because it is so elusive. This becomes the more obvious when we confront Western with Non-Western concepts of Nature, because Non-Western people conceive Nature in ways that are very different from the modern Western one. *What* then *is* Nature, and is there a common denominator at the bottom of all the different Western and Non-Western concepts? An interdisciplinary approach is required to deal with the problems involved.

This was the aim of a conference which took place during *The Fifth Biennial Meeting of the Society for the Study of Human Ideas on Ultimate Reality and Meaning (URAM)* in Toronto, Canada, August 1989. A sequel to this conference was convened in the following year at *The Third European Congress of URAM Society* in Leuven, Belgium. Participants[*] were invited to present papers on topics such as: ultimate reality and meaning of the concept of Nature; origin and history of the concept of Nature in Western thought and its representation in art, literature, and poetry; the impact of the concept of Nature on Western ethnic stereotypes; Non-Western concepts of Nature; the concept of Nature and its role in the 'New

---

[*] The following scholars attended the URAM-conferences of Toronto and Leuven: Myrdene Anderson (Purdue University, West Lafayette, USA), Thomas Bargatzky (University of Bayreuth, Germany), Gerhold Becker (Hong Kong Baptist College), Ulrich Berner (University of Bayreuth, Germany), A. Martin Byers (Vanier College, Saint-Laurent, Canada), Marc E. Carvallo (University of Groningen, The Netherlands), Franz Faust (University of München, Germany), Jörn Greve (Marburg, Germany), Antonio Guerci (University of Genova, Italy), Thomas Hölscher (University of München, Germany), Rolf Kuschel (University of Copenhagen, Denmark), Catherine E. Martin (California State University at Los Angeles, USA), Balaji Mundkur (University of Connecticut, Storrs, USA), Patricia J. O'Brien (Kansas State University, Manhattan, USA), Robert Rotenberg (De Paul University, Chicago, USA), Antonio Santangelo (Milano, Italy), Oscar Torretta (University of Genova, Italy), M. Estellie Smith (State University of New York, Oswego, USA), Maria Ester Grebe Vicuña (Santiago, Chile), and Fred W. Voget (Southern Illinois University at Edwardsville, USA).

Romanticism' prevailing in contemporary Western society. Scholars providing a wide interdisciplinary background (anthropology, archaeology, biology, philosophy, and art history) from Canada, Chile, Denmark, Germany, Hong Kong, Italy, The Netherlands and the United States presented papers.

Only a selection of these papers are published in the present volume, since some papers have already been published elsewhere. However, one article (Spittler) which was not presented at the URAM conferences is included because it is significant to the theme of the present volume.

We mention with gratitude the hospitality offered us by the University of Toronto at the request of Professor Tibor Horvath, S.J., and the Catholic University of Leuven at the request of Dr. Raymond Macken. With gratitude the editors mention Maria Böhnisch, Beate Sauter-Köder, Monika Schecklmann, Trevor Petney, Mark R. Manzo and Fabian Pfitzenmaier for their editorial assistance. We would also like to acknowledge the help of Marion Jepsen of The Peter Lang Verlag for her editorial advices and her encouragement to go ahead with the production of this book.

Thomas Bargatzky, Rolf Kuschel

March, 1993

# CONTENTS

*Thomas Bargatzky, Rolf Kuschel*
Preface   5

*Thomas Bargatzky*
Introduction   9

*Ulrich Berner*
Concepts of nature in Greek religion and philosophy   27

*Gerhold K. Becker*
The divinization of nature in early modern thought   47

*Catherine E. Martin*
Ecology, dualism, and utilitarianism: Attitudes toward nature
in American society   63

*Rolf Kuschel*
The Bellonese attitude toward nature   83

*Gerd Spittler*
The desert, the wild, and civilization - as seen by the Kel Ewey   103

*Fred W. Voget*
Were the Crow Indians conservationists?   125

*Patricia J. O'Brien*
Pawnee views of nature in the Central Plains: The historic
and prehistoric data   137

*A. Martin Byers*
The action-constitutive meaning of Newark: The forms that count   159

*Franz X. Faust*
What 'Nature' means for a south-west Colombian Indian   201

*Antonio Santangelo*
Culture, technology and the relation between man and nature   211

*Antonio Guerci and Oscar Torretta*
Phylogenesis: Reflections on evolution  225

*Jörn Greve*
The theory of inner entropy - its relations to genetic engineering and the concept of nature  237

*Thomas Hölscher*
Art, nature, artificiality: The artificiality of nature in Western art  255

Contributors  279

# INTRODUCTION

Thomas Bargatzky

### I. Physis and the reconstruction of nature in myth and science

The opposition between nature and culture has become an integral part of Western science and metaphysics. We conceive nature as something external and independent of ourselves. According to contemporary treatises on economic theory, nature is all that is not attributable to human work and achievement. Generations of leading cultural anthropologists, e.g., Franz Boas, Alfred Louis Kroeber, Claude Lévi-Strauss, and Leslie A. White have considered culture to be unique to humans. Lévi-Strauss would even argue that the contrast of nature and culture should be seen as an artificial creation of culture, necessary to assert its uniqueness (1969:xxix) and ultimately dependent on the capacity of the human mind to conceptualize reality in terms of binary oppositions.

What is at issue here is not the relatively well thought-out conjecture that binary oppositions are vital to human thought. Humans need to create order and meaning in a seemingly chaotic world by transforming randomness into patterns of assumed stability (cf. Kuschel and Santangelo, this volume) and binary oppositions are apt to achieve this. We should rather be concerned with the allegedly universal meanings given to category nouns in binary oppositions such as nature/culture, since neither the concept of nature nor that of culture can be free from the biases and traditions of the culture in which they were constructed (MacCormack, 1980:5). Anthropologists studying non-Western people mostly agree that these people conceive nature and culture in ways which are very different from ours. One can even go as far and say that, in many cases, they do not have a concept of nature which can be compared to the contemporary Western one. This finding invites us to rethink our own concepts. Western ideas, however, are not easy to unravel since they have changed considerably in the course of time. The modern Western concept of nature was developed partly in the age of Enlightenment (Horigan, 1988; cf. Becker, this volume), but it came into being, essentially as it stands today, about the turn of the 18th century. Hence, it has its roots in European civil society and was fully developed during the decades following the industrial revolution (Glacken, 1985; Nipperdey, 1987). Modern nature thus has become both a quarry of economic resources, open for human exploitation, and a repository of aesthetic and moral values; a haven offering peace and consolation for estranged and alienated romantic individuals (Lepenies, 1969; Bargatzky, 1992a). As such it has been celebrated by poets like William Wordsworth and Joseph von Eichendorff, and by painters like Caspar David Friedrich. Accordingly, the specific content of this modern concept of nature, as well as the concomitant rigid opposition between nature and culture, is not the product of enquiry but rather the condition of enquiry (Horigan, 1988:6). It originated from the singular events of European history leading to the emergence of civil society and its social and cultural repercussions. It would be naive to assume that people with a very different historical background would share with modern Westerners a concept which is not older than 200 years.

Yet the growing anxiety about the state of the earth and the disillusionment with the role science plays in the process of environmental degradation has given rise to a rethinking of our fundamental philosophical concepts and moral attitudes. For example, in a book on the concept of nature and its history which was published posthumously in 1989, the German philosopher George Picht holds that natural science destroys nature and that such a science can not be true (Picht, 1989: 13, 15). To a modern Westerner, reared in the belief of the superiority of science, which is based on its alleged objectivity, such a view may come as a shock. At least readers may raise an eyebrow, not to say a hand of protest. Yet we feel that something is wrong with the state of the world we live in and the role which natural science plays in environmental destruction and its consequences for life on earth. Science alone, however, is not to blame because it grew out of deeper attitudes and beliefs on what is ultimately real and meaningful. Our concern about the preservation of life on earth, therefore, has led to calls for both a new ethics (Altner, 1981; Maurer, 1986) and a reconsideration of ancient concepts of the earth or the cosmos as living beings (Lovelock, 1979; W. Bargatzky, 1980).

In the chapters to follow different ways in which Nature can be conceived today, across the disciplines and in different cultures, will be shown in greater detail. It is obvious that only select aspects of such an extensive and encompassing subject can be broached. Many important issues have to be left out since a small number of specialists can never claim to exhaust a theme of this magnitude; they can only provide single pieces of a mosaic. This introductory chapter intends, therefore, to serve as a foil for these pieces. Two modes of the construction of Nature will be outlined which differ most fundamentally from each other: myth and science. I shall try to show that the two opposites can be reconciled through a view of reality and human action which is based on the ancient Greek concepts of *physis* and *poiesis*. Art, contrary to our traditional opinion, has an objective nature and can serve as a bridge between myth and science. This introduction tries, by this means, to show that the different chapters of this volume, albeit dealing with rather diverse subjects, share with each other some ideas which underlie contemporary thinking about nature.

## II. Nature in myth

The ecological crisis has given rise to a revival of the study of myth, both in the works of philosophers and anthropologists, and in the popular press. There is a tendency, for example, to portray so-called 'primitive' people as the true paragons and saints of ecological salvation. These days, North-American Indians, in particular, are allocated the role of fervent worshippers of Mother Earth, and if we turn to their mythical world-view, it is claimed, all will be well. Thus, our natural environment and our souls will be saved.[1]

In reality, however, there are problems with this view (Voget, this volume).[2] Referring, for example, to the Naskapi-Indians of Labrador, the late Frank G. Speck remarked many years ago, "To arrive at a definite idea of how the manifestations of nature are pictured in the native mind is one of the most

---

[1] For a critique of currently fashionable notions of American Indians as conservationists, see Geertz (1991), Gerber (1988), Bargatzky (1991a), and Schmidt (1988).

[2] For summaries of the problem of tribal impacts on nature, see Bargatzky (1986:56, 139) and Bennett (1976:78, Fn. 11, and chapter 5).

difficult matters" (Speck, 1935:49). What is more, there is a hidden cynicism in our turning to the philosophies of the people whose life styles have been destroyed by our civilization and of expecting these philosophies to give us the recipes for the treatment of the diseases caused by our greed. I want, rather, to deal with the epistemological side of the problem. What we encounter here is the typical 'throwing-the-baby-out-with-the-bath-water' approach: science is identified with rationality and both science and rationality are rejected. Western rationality is represented as the source of everything evil, including environmental destruction. Myth, on the other hand, is said to be 'irrational', and it is this alleged irrationality which attracts many Western intellectuals longing for a spiritual reorientation.

There is, however, a fundamental misunderstanding at the bottom of this opinion. It is true that myth explains the world in a way totally different from scientific explanation. Myth, for example, makes no distinction between subject and object, mind and matter, the part and the whole, the inside and the outside. All these distinctions lie behind the scientific mode of explanation; they follow from Descartes' distinction between *res cogitans* and *res extensa*. It does not follow, however, that myth is irrational. On the contrary, myth is rational. This has been demonstrated most lucidly and convincingly by the philosopher Kurt Hübner in many books and articles (Hübner, 1985a; 1986; 1986/87). Hübner's book on the truth of myth (1985b), in particular, can deservedly be called one of the most important modern treatises on myth. Rationality, as Hübner shows, is a formal criterion for the correctness of an argument and, seen in this manner, myth is indeed rational. The ontology of myth, however, is based on premises of a kind different from the premises of Cartesian ontology. Their content is incompatible with the Cartesian distinction between *res cogitans* and *res extensa*. What is more, the statements of myth cannot be disproved by scientific argument. The ontology of myth lies behind mythical statements in the same way as the Cartesian ontology underlies scientific ones. One cannot disprove the statements based on mythical ontology by confronting them with statements based on Cartesian ontology, since any statement will necessarily be shaped by the ontology in its background. There is no way to decide if the premises of Cartesian ontology are correct or incorrect, but it is also not possible to decide about the correctness of a non-Cartesian, mythical ontology. Hence, a mythical statement about the sacral character of a certain 'thing' in nature - a tree, a stone, etc. - owing to its character as the epiphany of a god, cannot be refuted by a reference to its chemical composition. But within the mythical ontology and based on the *arché*, the mythical tale of its origin, the statement about the sacral character of a tree can be part of a correct, rational argument. Hübner demonstrates, moreover, that the *arché* in myth corresponds to the laws in a scientific explanation.

If Hübner is correct, we can no longer label myth as irrational. In addition, myth cannot serve as a guideline for correct behavior towards nature, since in myth there is no nature, at least no nature in the modern Western sense. To sum up the findings of anthropology (cf. Byers, Faust, Kuschel, O'Brien, Spittler, Voget, this volume), ancient history, and the history of religions (Eliade, 1967; Berner, this volume), we can state with due caution that in myth any so-called 'natural' object is alive and even animated and the potential or actual epiphany of a god. Since many gods active within 'nature' are also active within the human domain, there is no clear-cut distinction between the divine and the human spheres. Take, for example, Hephaistos, the ancient Greek god of metalworking, or the theology of the ancient Hawaiians, as reconstructed by the anthropologists John Charlot (1983) and Valerio Valeri. Valeri (1985:31 and passim) has shown that in Hawaii, natural phenomena, closely linked to a god, signify certain predicates of the human species.

To exemplify my contention that in the ontology of myth there is no clear-cut distinction between what a Westerner would classify as either 'natural' or 'cultural', let me discuss briefly the example of Samoa.

### III. The Samoan example

Samoans do not distinguish between nature and culture. The Samoan word for nature, in the sense of natural environment, is a foreign loanword: natura (Cain, 1986:122). Samoans live in a morally ordered universe which is made up of things Westerners would classify either as natural or cultural. Genealogical metaphor is used to account for the origin of all things, both 'natural' and 'cultural', and the knowledge of this genealogical code has been guarded by the chief members of certain metaphorical families (*'āiga*) which should not be confused with the common Samoan *'āiga*, or cognatic descent groups, since they are not concerned with mundane day-to-day affairs. These metaphorical 'families' serve ceremonial purposes on a supra-local level only; for example they perform certain ritual duties during the life-crisis rites of a traditional Samoan king, a *tama-a-'āiga*.[3] A Samoan king embodies everything considered dignified; it is his privilege not to wield power in the political sense, but to promote the honor system which is strengthened by his moral standing (Ata Ma'ia'i, 1974:147). In other words; a king embodies what a Samoan would designate as Culture. The origin of the first kings, however, is explained through cosmogonic genealogies of a kind which we find among many non-industrial, pre-modern people such as the ancient Greeks (Hübner, 1985b:111) and the Kachins (Gilhodes, 1922:3-45). Material and immaterial things, plants, animals, spiritual beings, and the first humans originate in successive genealogical steps out of some 'primary matter' or 'first principle'. At the end of the Samoan cosmogonic genealogies we find the first kings. Hence, one single principle, procreation, is used to account for the origin of human beings, the first kings, and the entire cosmos. Thus genealogical metaphor is employed as a code to account for the origin of things Westerners of today would classify either as natural or cultural. Strange as this may appear at first sight, it should not be entirely so, since there are similar monistic models in the modern Western philosophical heritage. Johann Gottfried Herder, for example, in his main work, published between 1784 and 1791, has written that the God of History must be the same as the God of Nature. Herder even went so far as to identify the principle underlying nature and history (that is, culture), namely the law of actio and reactio.[4]

To return to the Samoan metaphorical families; these descend from the first kings and their members (*ali'i*, or chiefs) are the guardians of the genealogical knowledge which explains to Samoans the most essential

---

[3] For a detailed ethnographic account on a Samoan metaphoric family, based on fieldwork supported by the *Deutsche Forschungsgemeinschaft* (DFG) 1980-81 and 1985, see my still unpublished Dr. phil. habil. thesis *Die Söhne Tunumafonos* (München, 1987; publication in preparation). Summaries and bibliographies can be found in Bargatzky (1988; 1990; 1991b).

[4] "Gesetze der Wiedervergeltung" in Herder's own words. See Herder (1985:418).

things about the 'natural' and 'cultural' state of their universe. Hence, not only is the cultural order a continuation of the natural order as explained in the cosmogonic genealogies, but humans play an active part in its perpetuation; they are responsible for it. Humans not only have the power of the physical procreation of their kind - as animals do - but, by access to sacral genealogies, some chiefs also have the power to maintain and continue the social and cultural order. The genealogical code guarded by the metaphorical families can therefore justly be called the master-key of spiritual, or mental, procreation of what Westerners would call the cultural order.

What we encounter here is reminiscent of the substitution of the words 'to know' or 'to discern' for 'to beget' in the Old Testament. Both words have a common Hebrew root, $jāda^c$, which means the state of deepest intimacy and familiarity, a state not only characteristic of sexual intercourse, but of knowing as well. Seen from this point of view, we can understand why many pre-modern people have resorted to the code of procreation, as embodied in genealogies, to account for the origin and perpetuation of their most sacred institutions. Those who know - that is, those who possess the necessary genealogical knowledge of the origin of the universe - are also those who know how to perpetuate such institutions as kingship. And these institutions are not, as culture, separate from nature, they are rather the moral part of the universe manifesting itself in human beings.

To end this section on Nature in Myth, we come to the somewhat paradoxical conclusion that it would be futile to look at the example of the so-called 'primitive' people, or 'Naturvölker', as they are called in German, as a source of inspiration in our attempt to save our natural environment. Such 'Naturvölker' do not know nature as we normally understand it because it is an invention of modern Western civilization not older than 200 years. To prevent ecological disaster, we must turn to the moral, philosophical, scientific, and technological means, concepts and values of Western culture. It is here that we have to look for the starting point of global environmental catastrophe and it is here that we can find the categories which may help us to think and act in a meaningful way. Only a culture which 'has' Nature can protect the natural environment (Bargatzky, 1992b; 1992c). But how can this be, since, as has been stated above, natural science destroys nature and therefore cannot be a true science of nature? To answer this question, I must deal with the problem of how nature is conceived in Science. It goes without saying that this can be done here only in a cursory way.

## IV. Nature in science

To begin with the discussion of the way nature is conceived in the natural sciences, it is expedient to take a closer look at the Greek concept of *physis* (Engl. growth, Germ. Wuchs) and its Latin counterpart, the concept of *natura*.[5] The modern concept of nature is derived from *natura*, which is the Latin translation of *physis*. There is a fundamental difference, however, between *physis* and *natura* which can tell us a lot about the modern concept of nature.

According to Picht, *physis* means all that grows, emerges and disappears again. Contrary to modern understanding, growth in this connection does not simply mean 'becoming bigger'; growth is not only a quantitative concept; it also has qualitative connotations. Picht shows that everything which the philosophy of modern times has transferred into the Subject originally belonged to the innermost domain of what the Greeks called *physis*, for example logic and the paramount principles of epistemology (Germ. Erkenntnis). In other words, the very structure of mind and meaning, which Greek philosophy assigned to *physis*, was projected into human consciousness by modern philosophy and interpreted as the structure constitutive of human subjectivity (Picht, 1989:110-113). Next, when *physis* was translated into Latin and became *natura*, it emphasized only one aspect of the movement denoted by *physis*. Natura comes from *nasci*, to be born. Hence, *natura* covers only the aspect of emergence. When Lucretius (96 - 55 BC) translated the title of Empedokles' didactic poem 'peri physeos' as 'De rerum natura', he joined nature with *res*, the thing, or object, something which one can possess. 'De rerum natura' means, therefore, 'on the emergence of that which one can dispose of'.

---

[5] I follow closely the presentation of George Picht (1989:54-57). Cf. Bargatzky (1992a; 1992d).

We hold in our hands, then, the elements of the modern concept of nature and humankind's place in it, such as is epitomized in Descartes' distinction between *res extensa* and *res cogitans*! On the one hand, we have nature as only matter; a 'thing' devoid of meaning and rights, characterized quantitatively as 'extension'. On the other hand, we have the Subject or human consciousness as the container of those qualities which formerly, according to the concept of *physis*, also belonged to the world outside the confines of the Subject. This idea of the absolute epistemological priority of the Subject (the legacy of Descartes and medieval nominalism), however, is only one of the three pillars or principles on which the design of modern natural science is founded. The other two principles are the idea of motionless identity, or Being (the legacy of Parmenides), and the idea of the necessity of logic (the legacy of Aristotle). According to Kant, these three principles are absolute and timeless. However, as Picht claims, they are not. They are a product of European history (Sohn-Rethel, 1990) and if we chose to call them into question, modern science would lose the ground under its feet (Picht, 1989:308-317). And this, he adds, is how it should be because Greek philosophy becomes of immediate interest in the face of today's ecological crisis, which was caused by a science which destroys nature and which is founded on the three principles mentioned above.

It becomes more and more apparent that Greek philosophy has discovered something which modern science has chosen to deny or to forget. Picht thus continues a stream of European philosophy of nature which is represented by thinkers such as Goethe and Schelling, whose philosophy can be interpreted as informed with the gist of the notion of *physis*. As we all know, this tradition has not been the victorious one in the mainstream of European philosophy of nature; it has not been cast into the foundations of the very design on which modern natural science has been based (see, however, Guerci and Torretta, this volume). The victorious tradition derives from Aristotle, then leads via nominalism and Descartes to Kant who, according to Picht, produced a philosophy which still outlines the design of natural science; the results of quantum physics notwithstanding.

Before we proceed, however, let us consider a possible objection to Picht's assertion that natural science destroys nature and can not therefore be true. How can he aver this, since science can undoubtedly produce correct results? For example, who would be ready today to doubt that the earth revolves around the sun, except for some crackpots? Don't we have here a correct scientific statement?

In this case we have to make a distinction between information and design. Picht would on no account claim that science is not in a position to produce correct information. Scientific information, however, is like the several single pieces of a mosaic; any single piece, any information or statement taken by itself, can be correct. The overall view, however, the design or Gestalt it is informed with, the design according to which the single pieces are put together to form the mosaic, can be wrong. In this case, we are left with the single pieces, but we can not put them together into an integrated picture. In this sense only, is natural science not a true science of nature, since the design is wrong, notwithstanding the correctness of single scientific statements and results (Picht, 1989:313). And this design rests precisely on the above-mentioned three fundamental principles: the absolute epistemological priority of the Subject, the idea of motionless identity, and the idea of the necessity of logic.

Summing up, George Picht contrasts the modern concept of nature with the ancient Greek concept of *physis* and claims that Greek philosophy becomes of immediate interest in the face of today's ecological crisis. In addition, I would suggest that *physis* is a term suitable for cross-cultural comparison. Take, for example, *Tirawahat,* the Universe-and-Everything-Inside in Pawnee theology (see O'Brien, this volume), or the Crow Indians' concept of Mother Earth, the source of life (see Voget, this volume). The ideas making up these concepts seem to be akin to those behind *physis*, since they, too, emphasize wholeness, the unity of mind and matter. *Physis* however is, at first sight, a monistic concept. Monism, the doctrine that reality as a whole is made of a sole substance, seems to gain support today among scholars of different disciplines as a way out of the moral and behavioral tangle at the root of environmental destruction. The anthropologist Catherine E. Martin (this volume) criticizes the predominant particularizing North American philosophical perspective which stresses Man's isolation from and power over Nature and which fails to see humans as an integral part of nature. The biologists Antonio Guerci and Oscar Torretta (this volume) also espouse a monistic approach when they refer to the 'inexplicable fantasy of Nature' extending, in a great evolutionary design, principles of biology (e.g., anisotropy, or directedness) to human systems of cultural and social organization. Jörn Greve, on the other hand, takes up the cue given by Guerci and Torretta so that all three envision a unified evolutionary science. However, whereas Guerci and Torretta are rather optimistic about Man as a creative and productive agent within nature, Greve is more pessimistic. He analyses the likely outcome of genetic engineering, a procedure likely to result in a re-invention of the very fabric of organic nature, and forecasts a loss of philosophical alternatives and meaning. Hence, his outlook on the future direction of Man/Nature relations is a rather gloomy one. There are grave philosophical objections to monism, too, which deserve to be mentioned here. Reinhard Löw (1984; 1989) and Robert Spaemann (1987) reject monism and evolutionism on both ethical and theoretical grounds, since they reduce human beings to instruments of superpersonal design, thus denying them the capacity for self-determination.[6]

Yet the concept of *physis* is not a monistic one, since it implies creativity and inventiveness. Creativity means 'capacity for alternative action', a trait characteristic of humans who are beings endowed with an open behavioral program (Freeman, 1981). Hence, the concept of *physis* does not reduce humans to instruments of some superpersonal design. It can, therefore, become a key concept for a unified science open to the objections raised against monism by philosophers like Löw and Spaemann. This will be demonstrated on the following pages.

### V. Art, science and poiesis

In modern times, science alone is believed to be in a position to produce objective knowledge about a nature which is said to be dominated by the law of causality. On the other hand, subjectivity is said to be the domain of

---

[6] The same objection can be raised to the "adaptationist program" which plays an important part in cultural anthropologists' theorizing about the relationship between human sociocultural institutions and the natural environment. The main components of this program are (1) the notion of an all-embracing ecosystem whose evolution is subject to (2) self-regulation that is (3) teleological in character and that selects for (4) the latent functions of the sociocultural institution within the all-embracing ecosystem (see Bargatzky 1984).

freedom. The result of this conception is the modern opposition of nature and history, or culture, where nature is conceived as the realm of necessity and history as the realm of freedom. Hence, while science is believed to be objective, art and religion are subjective; they are, according to this view, not in a position to lead toward objective knowledge. This conception is a legacy of the Renaissance and especially of the age of Enlightenment (cf. Becker, this volume).

As we have seen so far, these familiar modern dichotomies are exploded through the concept of *physis*. Now, if there is truth in the design, or ontology, which lies behind the concept of *physis*, then, Picht (1986:28) asserts, art (poetry, painting, music) is not subjective in character, but art is a medium which reflects in an objective way the world we live in. He goes as far as to stating that true art can not lie. The reason he gives for this claim follows from his investigation into the Greek concept of *poiesis*.

It was F.W.J. von Schelling, in his *Einleitung zu dem Entwurf eines Systems der Naturphilosophie* (1799) who, at the threshold of the era of industrial production, employed a concept of production which is widely separated from everything this concept stands for today. I refer to his distinction between nature as a product (*natura naturata*) and nature as productivity (*natura naturans*).[7] According to Schelling, we can understand nature only if we conceive it as productivity. Picht shows that Schelling's concept of productivity is closely linked to the Greek concept of *poiesis*, which is translated into Latin as *productio*. According to the concept of *physis*, the capacity, or ability, to produce is a predisposition both of what we call 'nature' and of the human species. What is more, the results of human productivity are emulations of nature's products. A human being can produce only because he or she has discovered a tendency inherent in nature. Being part of *physis*, humans share this tendency.

In addition, Picht shows that *poiesis* (*productio*) is essentially what he calls representation ('Darstellung'). The essence of both art and science is representation, but, seen from the perspective of *physis*, they are not

---

[7] After Friedrich Wilhelm Joseph von Schelling, *Sämtliche Werke*, Abtheilung I, Band 3, Seite 284, Stuttgart 1856 ff. The text used here is the reprint, volume I, published by Suhrkamp Verlag, Frankfurt am Main 1985; especially page 352.

representations of but representations within nature. Properly speaking, both are results of the productivity of *physis*. Scientific knowledge, however, is only a very special form of representation, namely, representation through *concepts* and governed by *logos*. By no means may we claim, however, that this special form of representation is the only one capable of telling us something about the world we live in, or that it is superior to representation in art, since art, too, is a product of *physis*. To believe so means one simply follows the beaten path of five hundred years of European thinking about nature.

Following a different path, Thomas Hölscher (this volume) comes to similar conclusions concerning art, science and nature. He also challenges the dichotomy 'natural' vs. 'artificial'. Taking into account, among other things, computer-generated digital pictures on the one hand, and paintings by artists such as Leonardo and Magritte on the other, he points out that the artificiality of images of nature amounts to the artificiality of nature itself. Product of nature and product of Man are artificial or natural, both can be understood as either originals or replicas. Seen from this point of view, it is hard to decide what is 'natural' and what is 'artificial'. Hence, the argument comes full circle, back to the idea presented in different words by Guerci and Torretta.

Does it follow that we have to turn our back on science altogether? By no means. We can not abandon hundreds of years of European tradition - and we need not. Nor does it follow that we should subscribe to 'postmodern' Dadaism, or the 'anything goes' approach currently fashionable in some anthropological circles.[8] Science is a valuable fruit of human inventiveness and resourcefulness and we can not do without it. But we should take it as it is: a useful tool which may help us to make life often easier and which holds some fascinating (and often even correct) information. It is not the only way

---

[8] It should be clear by now that Picht is not a 'postmodernist' in the sense of the anti-science resentments currently popular among a number of mostly North American cultural anthropologists, where the goal of objectivity is replaced through the ideal of biographical honesty or authenticity (see, e.g., Heider (1988), and Shweder and Levine (eds., 1984), or Clifford and Marcus (eds., 1986) for collections of representative articles. For a critical discussion of post-modern anthropology, see, for example, Carrithers (1990) or O'Meara (1990). Picht does not abandon the ideal of objectivity, on the contrary, for him true art is objective in character.

to knowledge, however, no *camino real* or master-key. We must not rely on science alone when we tackle problems such as environmental destruction; a problem that was probably caused by the wrong design of science. On the contrary, we must assign different means of representation, such as art and even - horribile dictu - religion, a complementary role, since they are concerned with design or gestalt, rather than information.

This is not tantamount to a return to myth. We can not become believers in myth by fiat. What is more, myth is always a local phenomenon and it is by no means a safeguard against environmental changes or even destruction. After all, the fundamental transitions from a life based primarily on hunting and gathering to one based primarily on agriculture (the so-called 'neolithic revolution'), and the transition to metalworking, took place during the era of myth. What we need is an adequate picture of Nature and our place in it - I deliberately do not say: 'concept'. This can be gained, as Picht has demonstrated, through a reconsideration of our basic notions, perceptions, concepts, and attitudes, in the light of some fundamentals of Greek culture, enshrined in the concept of *physis*. This concept, hitherto lost to us, deserves to be re-discovered. It not only helps us to link the roots of Western culture to the wisdom of pre-modern, 'primitive' people, thus testifying to the epistemological unity of humankind (Coomaraswamy, 1940:67; Hollis 1982:81), but also entails the notion that humans are both *products* of nature and agents of *productivity within* nature, creating iconic models of the natural world (Byers, this volume) and investing it with meaning (see Santangelo, this volume). Being parts of *physis*, humans share its capacity for productivity, for inventiveness, that is, its 'capacity for alternative action' (Freeman, 1981), for bringing about the new and the unforeseen. This is why the concept of *physis* does not, as monistic concepts would, reduce humans to instruments of some superpersonal design.

*Physis*, as matter to think about and as thinking matter, confronts us with the challenge of overcoming the taken-for-granted limitations of the modern concept of nature and to create a language suited to the cross-cultural comparison of the different ways humans speak about *Tirawahat*, the Universe-and-Everything-Inside. After the invention of Nature in modern times, we must now rediscover the common human legacy that has been lost.

# References

Altner, G. (1981). "Ökologie und die Sozialpflichtigkeit des Fortschritts." In R. Löw, P. Koslowski, and P. Kreuzer (eds.). *Fortschritt ohne Maß? Eine Ortsbestimmung der wissenschaftlich-technischen Zivilisation*. München, Piper, pp. 150-165.

Ata Ma'ia'i (1974). "Western Samoa's general election 1973." *The Journal of Pacific History*, 9:146-152.

Bargatzky, T. (1984). "Culture, environment, and the ills of adaptionism" (with CA comment). *Current Anthropology*, 25:399-415.

Bargatzky, T. (1986). *Einführung in die Kulturökologie. Umwelt, Kultur und Gesellschaft*. Berlin, Dietrich Reimer.

Bargatzky, T. (1988). "Evolution, sequential hierarchy, and areal integration: the case of traditional Samoan society." In J. Gledhill, B. Bender, and M.T. Larsen (eds.). *State and Society. The Emergence and Development of Social Hierarchy and Political Centralization*. London, Unwin Hyman, pp. 43-56.

Bargatzky, T. (1990). "'Only a name'. Family and territory in Samoa." In B. Illius and M. Laubscher (eds.). *Circumpacifica. Festschrift für Thomas S. Barthel*. Frankfurt am Main, Peter Lang pp. 21-37.

Bargatzky, T. (1991a). "Pflug und Erdmutter bei den Hopi-Indianern. Einige kritische Anmerkungen." *Anthropos*, 86:192-198.

Bargatzky, T. (1991b). "Achilles in Samoa. Liturgie, Genealogie und mythische Identität." *Anthropos*, 86:413-425.

Bargatzky, T. (1992a). "Kulturelle Rekonstruktion von Natur: Mythos, Wissenschaft, und der 'Weg der Physis'." In B. Glaeser and P. Teherani-Krönner (eds.). *Humanökologie und Kulturökologie*. Opladen, Westdeutscher Verlag, pp. 71-87.

Bargatzky, T. (1992b). "Ökonomie, Ökologie und die 'Naturvölker'. Anmerkungen zu einer romantizistischen Illusion." *Scheidewege*, 22:151-171.

Bargatzky, T. (1992c). "'Naturvölker' und Umweltschutz - ein modernes Mißverständnis." *Universitas*, 47:876-886.

Bargatzky, T. (1992d). "Die Ethnologie und das Problem der kulturellen Fremdheit." In Theo Sundermeier (ed.). *Den Fremden wahrnehmen* (Studien zum Verstehen fremder Religionen, Band 5). Gütersloh, Gerd Mohn, pp. 13-29.

Bargatzky, W. (1980). *Das Universum lebt* (revised edition, enlarged). München, Wilhelm Heyne.

Bennett, J. W. (1976). *The Ecological Transition. Cultural Anthropology and Human Adaptation*. Oxford, Pergamon Press.

Cain, H. (1986). *A Lexicon of Foreign Loan-Words in the Samoan Language*. Köln, Böhlau.

Carrithers, M. (1990). "Is anthropology art or science?" (with CA comment). *Current Anthropology*, 31:263-282.

Charlot, J. (1983). *Chanting the Universe. Hawaiian Religious Culture*. Honolulu, Emphasis International.

Clifford, J. and G. E. Marcus (eds., 1986). *Writing Culture. The Poetics and Politics of Ethnography*. Berkeley, University of California Press.

Coomaraswamy, A. K. (1940). "The Sun-Kiss." *Journal of the American Oriental Society*, 60:46-67.

Eliade, M. (1967). *Patterns in Comparative Religion*. Cleveland, The World Publishing Company.

Freeman, D. (1981). "The anthropology of choice." *Canberra Anthropology*, 4:82-100.

Geertz, A. W. (1991). "Hopi prophecies revisited. A critique of Rudolf Kaiser." *Anthropos*, 86:199-204.

Gerber, P. R. (1988). "Der Indianer - ein homo oekologicus?" In F. Stolz (ed.). *Religiöse Wahrnehmung der Welt*. Zürich, Theologischer Verlag Zürich, pp. 221-244.

Gilhodes, C. (1922). *The Kachins: Religion and Customs*. Calcutta, Catholic Orphans Press.

Glacken, C. J. (1985). "Culture and environment in Western civilization during the nineteenth century." In K. E. Bailes (ed.). *Environmental History. Critical Issues in Comparative Perspective*, Lanham, University Press of America, pp. 46-57.

Heider, K. G. (1988). "The Rashomon effect: When ethnographers disagree." *American Anthropologists*, 90:73-81.

Herder, J. G. ([1784-1791], 1985). *Ideen zur Philosophie der Geschichte der Menschheit*. Wiesbaden, Fourier.

Hollis, M. (1982). "The social destruction of reality." In M. Hollis and S. Lukes (eds.). *Rationality and Relativism*. Oxford, Basil Blackwell, pp. 67-86.

Horigan, S. (1988). *Nature and Culture in Western Discourses*. London, Routledge.

Hübner, K. (1985a). "Wie irrational sind Mythen und Götter?" In H. P. Duerr (ed.). *Der Wissenschaftler und das Irrationale*, vol. III. Frankfurt am Main, Syndikat, pp. 7-32.

Hübner, K. (1985b). *Die Wahrheit des Mythos*. München, Beck.

Hübner, K. (1986). *Kritik der wissenschaftlichen Vernunft*, (3rd, revised edition). Freiburg, Karl Alber.

Hübner, K. (1986/87). "Die nicht endende Geschichte des Mythischen." *Scheidewege*, 16:16-29.

Lepenies, W. (1969). *Melancholie und Gesellschaft*. Frankfurt am Main, Suhrkamp.

Lévi-Strauss, C. (1969). *The Elementary Structures of Kinship*, (revised edition, edited by Rodney Needham). Boston, Beacon Press.

Löw, R. (1984). "The Metaphysical limits of evolutionary epistemology." In F. M. Wuketits (ed.). *Concepts and Approaches in Evolutionary Epistemology*. Dordrecht, D. Reidel Publishing Co., pp. 209-231.

Löw, R. (1989). "Evolution und die Entstehung des Neuen." *Universitas*, 44:1160-1167.

Lovelock, J. E. (1979). *Gaia: A New Look at Life on Earth*. Oxford, University Press.

MacCormack, C. P. (1980). "Nature, culture and gender: a critique." In C. P. MacCormack and M. Strathern (eds.). *Nature, Culture and Gender*. Cambridge, University Press, pp. 1-24.

Maurer, R. (1986). "Wie wirklich ist die ökologische Krise?" In A. Mohler (ed.). *Wirklichkeit als Tabu*. München, R. Oldenbourg, pp. 117-135.

Nipperdey, T. (1987). "Der Mythos im Zeitalter der Revolution." In D. Borchmeyer (ed.). *Wege des Mythos in der Moderne. Richard Wagner 'Der Ring des Nibelungen'*. München, dtv., pp. 96-109.

O'Meara, J. T. (1990). "Anthropology as anti-science." In H. Caton (ed.). *The Samoa Reader. Anthropologists Take Stock*. Lanham, University Press of America, pp. 68-79.

Picht, G. (1986). *Kunst und Mythos*. Stuttgart, Klett-Cotta.

Picht, G. (1989). *Der Begriff der Natur und seine Geschichte*. Stuttgart, Klett-Cotta.

Schelling, F. W. J. ([1799], 1985). "Einleitung zu dem Entwurf eines Systems der Naturphilosophie." In F. W. J. v. Schelling. *Ausgewählte Schriften*, vol.1. Frankfurt am Main, Suhrkamp, pp. 337-394.

Schmidt, D. (1988). *Indianer als Heilsbringer: ein neues Klischee in der deutschsprachigen Literatur?*, Frankfurt am Main, Brandes & Apsel.

Shweder, R. A. and Levine, R. (eds., 1984). *Culture Theory: Essays on Mind, Self, and Emotion*. Cambridge, Cambridge University Press.

Sohn-Rethel, A. (1990). *Das Geld, die bare Münze des Apriori*. Berlin, Klaus Wagenbach.

Spaemann, R. (1987). *Das Natürliche und das Vernünftige*. München, R. Piper.

Speck, F. G. (1935). *Naskapi. The Savage Hunters of the Labrador Peninsula*. Norman, University of Oklahoma Press.

Valeri, V. (1985). *Kingship and Sacrifice. Ritual and Society in Ancient Hawaii*. Chicago, University of Chicago Press.

# CONCEPTS OF NATURE IN GREEK RELIGION AND PHILOSOPHY

Ulrich Berner

## I. Philosophical Criticism of Western Science and its Concept of Nature

The concept of nature has become an object of philosophical interest again.[1] This recent development is related to the new criticism of modern science. G. Picht in his lectures on the concept of nature takes as his starting point the statement, "daß die Menschheit heute in Gefahr ist, durch ihre Wissenschaft von der Natur die Natur zu zerstören" (Picht 1989: 9). According to Picht a science that destroys nature cannot be a true perception of nature (Picht 1989: 11). He does not doubt the exactness ("Richtigkeit") of science. However, he considers it necessary to develop a new conception of nature. He criticizes the development of science that excludes any question about the essence of nature:

> "Das hätte man so hingehen lassen können, wenn uns nicht heute drastisch vorgeführt würde, daß die Naturwissenschaft genau deshalb, weil sie nach dem Wesen von Natur nicht fragt, die Natur zerstört." (Picht 1989: 5).

Picht believes Greek philosophy to be extremely relevant in this context. For Greek philosophy, in thinking about nature, had perceived something that is repressed and forgotten by modern science (Picht 1989: 8).

Since Greek philosophy in its origin is closely related to Greek religion, its concept of nature is also relevant to the history of religions (Religionswissenschaft). From this point of view, the approach of K. Hübner is perhaps even more interesting. Hübner is also very critical of modern science. But he is more interested in Greek mythology. He is concerned with analysing mythical thinking and comparing it to scientific thinking. In his analysis of mythical thinking he introduces the concepts "mythische Substanz" and "Arché": mythical thinking personalizes the elements of nature and traces back everything to gods (Hübner 1978: 404f; 1979: 76f; 1985: 110-113); it is based on a cyclical conception of time -

---

[1] See for example L. Schäfer (1987): 15f; W.Ch. Zimmerli (1989): 389f.

different from that conception of time upon which the scientific concept of natural law is based (Hübner 1978: 408f; 1979: 86; 1985: 142f).

According to Hübner, the mythical concept of nature differs totally from the scientific concept:

> "Es gibt mythisch keine Natur in unserem heutigen Sinne, die von der Menschenwelt scharf begrifflich zu trennen wäre, sondern beides ist wegen der Einheit von Materiellem und Ideellem unlöslich miteinander verbunden." (Hübner 1985: 114f).

Hübner distinguishes between a mythical and a scientific ontology and does not see any possibility of a rational choice between these two systems of experience (Hübner 1978: 423f; 1979: 90; 1985: 289f; 1988: 29; 1989: 14f). The European development from myth to science is seen as a historical process that does not imply any necessity (Hübner 1978: 425; 1979: 91; 1983: 53f; 1985: 366; 1989: 19f). Such a view had been proposed by W. Nestle in the well-known formula "vom Mythos zum Logos" (Nestle 1975: 20). Hübner states that he does not aim at returning to myth. But he tries to rehabilitate mythical thinking insofar as he wants to demonstrate that its rationality can be compared with that of science (Hübner 1978: 424f; 1981: 13; 1985: 289f).

Regarding these modern discussions about science and its concept of nature, it seems interesting to investigate the concept of nature in Greek religion and philosophy. The following considerations are not concerned with the philosophical question of the rehabilitation of myth but, with the historical question of the origin of the scientific concept of nature in Greek philosophy. In order to define the problem as precisely as possible, it is necessary to ask how the concept of nature and the relationship between science and religion are defined in modern science itself.

## II. The Concept of Nature in Modern Science and Recent Developments

In the 20th century new scientific theories - especially quantum physics - made necessary a new reflection on the concept of nature. W. Heisenberg, deeply involved in the development of quantum physics and interested in its philosophical implications, gave a summary of his reflection on the concept of nature:

"Wenn von einem Naturbild der exakten Naturwissenschaft in unserer Zeit gesprochen werden kann, so handelt es sich also eigentlich nicht mehr um ein Bild der Natur, sondern um ein Bild unserer Beziehungen zur Natur." (Heisenberg 1955: 21).

This view contradicts the common distinction between subject and object (Heisenberg 1955: 18).[2] Theoreticians of the New Age Movement later tried to develop this view and to create a new holistic science. Heisenberg, however, did not draw such a conclusion. On the contrary, he stressed the limits of science, contending that science cannot provide a basis for ethics because scientific theories refer to limited areas of reality only: "Es ist dieser Sachverhalt, der es auch unmöglich macht, Glaubensbekenntnisse, die für die Haltung im Leben verbindlich sein sollen, allein auf wissenschaftliche Erkenntnis zu begründen." (Heisenberg 1955: 20). This statement implies a demarcation between science and religion, without a fundamental criticism of religion. Such a demarcation seems to be characteristic of modern science. Great physicists such as M. Planck and A. Einstein held this view.

M. Planck draws a sharp line of demarcation between the spheres of knowledge and faith. According to Planck, science and religion have different functions: "Die Naturwissenschaft braucht der Mensch zum Erkennen, die Religion aber braucht er zum Handeln." (Planck 1970: 332). This functional differentiation serves as a basis for establishing the compatibility of religion and science: "... sie schließen sich nicht aus, wie manche heutzutage glauben oder fürchten, sondern sie ergänzen und bedingen einander." (Planck 1970: 332). Religion and science have a common task: "Es ist der stetig fortgesetzte, nie erlahmende Kampf gegen Skeptizismus und gegen Dogmatismus, gegen Unglaube und gegen Aberglaube, ..." (Planck 1970: 333). Planck does not see a contradiction between religion and science, but total agreement in all the decisive points.[3]

A. Einstein stresses the connection between science and religion even more than Planck does: "Wissenschaft ohne Religion ist lahm, Religion ohne

---

[2] K. Hübner in his discussion of the ontology of modern physics does not refer to Heisenberg's philosophical reflections (1985: 28-47). G. Picht refers shortly to this process of critical reflection within modern science itself (1989: 5f).

[3] The philosopher A.N. Whitehead had formulated a similar view (1926: 257f).

Wissenschaft blind." (Einstein 1984: 43).[4] Like Planck, however, he distinguishes sharply between the function of science and the function of religion, excluding ethics from science: "Denn die Wissenschaft kann nur feststellen, was ist, nicht aber, was sein soll; Werturteile jeder Art bleiben notwendig außerhalb ihres Bereiches." (Einstein 1984: 42). According to Einstein, it is the function of religion to provide a basis for ethics.

In his autobiography, Heisenberg touches upon the problems involved in this demarcation between science and religion. He reports on a discussion that took place in 1927, during the Solvay Conference at Brussels. Referring on that occasion to Planck's conception, he remembers saying:

> "So erscheinen die beiden Bereiche, die objektive und die subjektive Seite der Welt, bei ihm fein säuberlich getrennt - aber ich muß gestehen, daß mir bei dieser Trennung nicht wohl ist. Ich bezweifle, ob menschliche Gemeinschaften auf die Dauer mit dieser scharfen Spaltung zwischen Wissen und Glauben leben können." (Heisenberg 1984: 102).

His friend W. Pauly also objected to Planck's conception, expressing the hope that things would change in the future. Referring to recent developments in physics, Pauly said:

> "Eine Wissenschaft, die sich auf diese Art des Denkens eingestellt hat, wird nicht nur toleranter gegenüber den verschiedenen Formen der Religion sein, sie wird vielleicht, da sie das Ganze besser überschaut, zu der Welt der Werte mit beitragen können." (Heisenberg 1984: 104).

It is obvious that the demarcation between science and religion was considered problematical by these physicists as early as 1927. According to Heisenberg, W. Pauly already was considering the possibility that this demarcation might be abolished somehow. The decisive step towards a holistic science, however, was taken only recently by theoreticians of the New Age Movement.

F. Capra, who claims to build upon the ideas of Heisenberg, criticizes modern science for demarcating between ethics and science: "Im 17. Jahrhundert trennten Galilei, Descartes und deren Zeitgenossen die Werte von den Fakten." (Capra 1988: 17). He opposes the mechanistic worldview of modern science and demands a shift to a holistic thinking that includes ethics in the realm of science.

---

[4] Cf. B. Gladigow (1986).

Discussions about the New Age Movement have focused on the attempt to establish a relationship between Western science and Eastern religion or mysticism (Lüscher 1988: 25). Such comparisons, however, were established already by some of the great physicists involved in the development of quantum theory. E. Schrödinger, for example, was highly interested in the philosophy of the Upanishads (Schrödinger 1985: 67-72). What is more important is that some New Age theoreticians try to abolish the demarcation between science and religion by including ethics in science.

According to Capra, the new paradigm is not just another theory but a totally new view that does not accept a demarcation between facts and values: "Das neue Paradigma besteht nicht nur aus neuen Denkkonzepten, sondern auch aus einem neuen Wertsystem, ..." (Capra 1986: 142). "Paradigma" means in this context "die Gesamtheit der Gedanken, Wahrnehmungen und Wertvorstellungen, die eine besondere Sicht der Wirklichkeit formen, eine Anschauung, die die Grundlage dafür liefert, wie die Gesellschaft sich selbst organisiert" (Capra 1987: 20). Capra takes up a theory of living systems that leads to a new view of nature - a view that also regulates human behaviour towards nature. Consequently, Capra characterizes the ecological consciousness as a spiritual or religious consciousness (Capra 1988: 12). Referring to a well-known etymology of the Latin term "religio", he describes the aim of holistic science as "Verbundenheit mit dem Kosmos": "Diese religio, dieses Wiederverbinden, ist das tiefste Anliegen des neuen ganzheitlich-ökologischen Denkens." (Capra 1988: 24). When he makes use of the name "Gaia" - an element of Greek mythology - in order to designate the biosphere, the religious character of holistic science becomes even more obvious (Capra 1988: 19).

This overview leads to the conclusion that the fundamental problem is not the contradiction between science and myth, but the demarcation between facts and values, descriptive and prescriptive statements. L. Schäfer distinguishes clearly between two concepts of nature that correspond to the different views of the relationship between facts and values: on the one hand nature is seen "als Domäne, auf die sich menschliches Handeln erstreckt, das sich seiner Handlungsziele und Normen sonstwie versichern muß"; on the other hand "nature" is defined "als ein Begriff ..., der normative Konsequenzen für unser Handeln impliziert" (Schäfer 1987: 17).

The first concept might be called "scientific concept of nature", the second one "religious concept of nature". The philosophical problem as to whether prescriptive statements can be derived from descriptive statements has been discussed as the problem of "naturalism" or "the naturalistic fallacy." Schäfer refers to this concept in his criticism of H. Jonas' new ethics for technological civilization (Schäfer 1987: 23). K. M. Meyer-Abich rejects the very concept of "naturalistic fallacy" and proposes a practical philosophy of nature (Meyer-Abich 1979: 246f).

The following considerations are not concerned with the philosophical question of naturalism, but with the historical question about the origin of the scientific concept of nature. The question is whether the shift from the religious to the scientific concept of nature coincides with the transition from myth to natural philosophy - the process of demythologization in Greek religion. Such a historical investigation could result in new perspectives on myth and its complex relation to religion and to science.

### III. The Origins of Western Science and its Concept of Nature

#### 1. Greek Mythology

The so-called Homeric Hymn to Demeter (HHD) narrates a complicated action among the gods: Hades robs Demeter of her daughter, Persephone; Demeter searches for her daughter and in her anger causes all the vegetation to dry up; Zeus provides a solution to this conflict, resulting in a compromise: Persephone has to stay a part of every year with Hades in the underworld.

This hymn gives a mythical explanation of a fundamental process of nature, the regular dying and coming back of vegetation.[5] This natural process is seen in its regularity and at the same time is related to divine powers that are imagined as persons. The myth explains how an essential part of the human environment came into existence. The supreme god had to solve a conflict among the gods and he established a new order of things that has been stable from that time on:

---

[5] A comparison with the myth of Bacal might be interesting here. See F. Stolz (1982): 95-100. Stolz distinguishes between "Naturmythos" und "kosmologischer Mythos".

> "... and he promised to give her what rights she should choose among the deathless gods and agreed that her daughter should go down for the third part of the circling year to darkness and gloom, but for the two parts should live with her mother and the other deathless gods. Thus he commanded. And the goddess did not disobey the message of Zeus" (HHD, Verse 443-448).

In his analysis of mythical thinking, Hübner often refers to this very myth: "So ist wissenschaftlich der Rhythmus der Jahreszeiten die Folge astrophysikalischer Vorgänge, mythisch aber die Folge eines Urereignisses, das sich beständig wiederholt, wie zum Beispiel die Wiederkehr der Persephone auf die Erde im Frühling und ihre Rückkehr in den Hades im Herbst." (Hübner 1988: 28; cf. Hübner 1985: 138). This "Urereignis" in Hübner's terminology is called "Arché".

An interpretation of this text, however, has to take into consideration also the historical context. It is not difficult to perceive this context as the myth not only narrates an action among the gods, but also refers to Demeter's stay at Eleusis, a well-known place in Greece, and to her encounter with human beings. The hymn itself establishes a relationship between the myth of Demeter and the mystery-cult of Eleusis. The goddess herself is said to have ordered the building of the temple at Eleusis and to have founded the mysteries (HHD, V. 270; 476). So the myth provides a legitimation of a religious institution. The ritual of this mystery cult was meant to provide some kind of salvation for human beings.[6] This aim becomes obvious at the end of the hymn:

> "Happy is he among men upon earth who has seen these mysteries; but he who is uninitiate and who has no part in them, never has lot of like good things once he is dead, down in the darkness and gloom." (HHD, V. 480-482).

The myth of Demeter and Persephone establishes a relationship between processes of nature and the life and destiny of human beings - including even death and the underworld. However, the hope in a good destiny that is promised by the myth is limited to those who are initiated into the mysteries. The myth recommends undergoing a ritual of initiation. Participation in the ritual itself demands keeping to elementary moral norms. So it becomes obvious that the myth contains a normative element. The cognitive function of explaining nature is part of the complex function of providing a framework for a meaningful existence, including norms of

---

[6] Cf. F. Graf (1974): 79f; W. Burkert (1990): 26f.

human behaviour. So the mythical concept of nature proves to be an example of the religious concept of nature as defined in the second section of this paper.

This complex function is to be seen even more clearly in the myth of Prometheus, as narrated by Hesiod. The primal sacrifice made by Prometheus was an act hostile to Zeus. The deceptive action of Prometheus brought about a new order in religious affairs that has been valid from that time on. So the story of Prometheus and his deceiving Zeus explains and legitimates the Greek ritual of sacrifice (Theogony V. 535-560). Saying that the primal sacrifice is repeated eternally would be misleading to some extent.

The total myth of Prometheus - his deeds and his punishment by Zeus - results in the insight that any revolution against Zeus and his divine government will fail definitely (Theogony V. 613-616; cf. Works and Days V. 105). In the context of theogony, the myth of Prometheus describes an irreversible process leading to the final establishment of human environment.

U. Bianchi has discussed the possibility of considering Prometheus as a demiurgic trickster (Bianchi 1959/61: 414f).[7] This comparison makes it even more obvious that the myth of Prometheus can be interpreted without introducing such concepts as "mythische Substanz" or "Arché". Comparing mythical and scientific concepts of nature, one must start with the question as to whether the complex function of myth can be preserved in the transition to natural philosophy - that is, in the process of demythologization.

## 2. Greek Philosophy

Heraclitus is one of the presocratic philosophers who wrote a book "On Nature" (Peri Physeos). According to Diogenes Laertius, Heraclitus left this book, which included also sections on politics and theology, in the temple of Artemis at Ephesus (IX, 5f). So it might be concluded that there is a close relationship between his natural philosophy and religion. Heraclitus,

---

[7] Cf. U. Berner (1983b): 337.

however, is known to be a critic of contemporary religion. He criticized the ritual of sacrifice and the mysteries (Fr. B 5;14) and he polemicized against Homer and Hesiod, thereby objecting to Greek mythical heritage (Fr. B 40;42;57).

Heraclitus perceives a higher unity in the world-process - a coincidence of opposites:

> "And as the same thing there exists in us living and dead and the waking and the sleeping and young and old; for these things having changed round are those, and those having changed round are these." (Fr. B 88; Kirk/Raven/Schofield 1983: 189).

The basic element in this world-process is fire (Fr. B 30f). Heraclitus, however, does not avoid speaking of God (Fr. B 67) or even of Zeus: "One thing, the only truly wise, does not and does consent to be called by the name of Zeus." (B 32; Kirk/Raven/Schofield 1983: 202). So the relationship between Heraclitus' philosophy and Greek religion is not totally abolished. This relationship becomes obvious in the statement that thunderbolt steers all things (Fr. B 64). For the thunderbolt is known as belonging to Zeus. Another and even clearer example is Heraclitus' reference to the bow and the lyre - which are known as belonging to Apollon - in his theory of nature:

> "They do not apprehend how being at variance it agrees with itself (lit. how being brought apart it is brought together with itself): there is a back-stretched connexion, as in the bow and the lyre." (Fr. B 51; Kirk/Raven/Schofield 1983: 192).

The relationship between Heraclitus' natural philosophy and Greek religion can be described as "demythologization". Heraclitus does not give a mythical explanation of nature and, therefore, he is rightly characterized as a philosopher. His concept of nature, however, preserves the complex function of myth. For Heraclitus is concerned not only with a descriptive theory of nature but also with its normative consequences for human existence:

> "Sound thinking (is) a very great virtue, and (practical) wisdom (consists in our) saying what is true and acting in accordance with (the) real constitution (of things), (by) paying heed (to it)." (Fr. B 112; Robinson 1987: 65).[8]

---

[8] The authenticity of this fragment has been questioned (cf. Kirk 1954: 61;229;390). It has been defended by Ch.H. Kahn (1979: 120f) and T.M. Robinson (1987: 153f). On the whole, however, Kirk agrees with Jaeger's interpretation, that Heraclitus

The natural philosophy of Heraclitus seems to include ethics and thereby an essential function of myth is preserved in the process of demythologization - providing orientation, not only knowledge.[9] Heraclitus' concept of nature can be classified as a religious one.

Comparing the natural philosophy of Heraclitus to that of Anaxagoras is perhaps most interesting. For the relationship between philosophy and religion seems to be more strained in the case of Anaxagoras. The fact that Anaxagoras was accused of impiety (Diogenes Laertius II,12) at least could indicate such a tension.

Anaxagoras, in describing the processes of nature, uses the concepts of "composition" (symmigesthai) and "dissolution" (diakrinesthai) (Fr.17). The fundamental concept of his philosophy is "mind" (Nous) (cf. Plutarch: Pericles 4,4). Mind is the power that orders everything in the world (Fr.12; cf. Diogenes Laertius II,6). There is, however, no evidence that Anaxagoras ascribed to this Nous the features of divine providence and care for human beings. His theory, it seems, does not relate natural processes to human life and destiny.

Plutarch narrates a story that is significant in this respect (Pericles 6, 2-4). An abnormal natural phenomenon - a one-horned ram - had been given two different interpretations - one by Lampon, the traditional seer, and another one by Anaxagoras, the philosopher. Lampon considered the phenomenon as a sign having a definite meaning for the life and destiny of Pericles. Anaxagoras, however, by an anatomical demonstration gave a causal explanation of the phenomenon not relating it to human destiny at all. Plutarch does not think these views - that of the seer (mantis) and that of the naturalist (physikos) - exclude each other. Anyway, Anaxagoras himself seems to have considered his view as an alternative to the religious interpretation given by the seer.

---

"connected knowledge of Being with insight into human values and conduct, and made the former include the latter" (1954: 61; cf. W. Jaeger (1964): 132f). K.M. Meyer-Abich, in his reflections on a practical philosophy of nature refers to this very fragment of Heraclitus (1979: 238;243; 1987: 73).

[9] Cf. J. Mittelstraß (1981: 37f; 1987: 49f). Mittelstraß distinguishes between "Orientierungswissen" and "Verfügungswissen".

This story makes it understandable why Anaxagoras was involved in a trial of impiety. Diopeithes, being a seer himself, had a law enforced that banned atheism or teaching theories about the heavens (Plutarch: Pericles 32,1). Anaxogoras, however, according to Diogenes Laertius, "declared the sun to be a mass of red-hot metal and to be larger than the Peloponnesus" (II,8). So the conflict between the natural philosopher and the traditional seer was unavoidable.[10] The decisive point, however, is not that Anaxagoras abandoned traditional myth but that he dissolved any connection between natural processes and human destiny.

If moral norms can be derived neither from myth nor from natural philosophy another possibility has to be explored - for example creating ethics as a rational justification of moral norms. This process is to be seen in socratic and postsocratic philosophy.[11] Aristotle distinguishes clearly between theoretical and practical philosophy, considering natural philosophy as a part of theoretical philosophy (Metaphysics II,1; VI,1). Plato's dialogue "Euthyphro" is perhaps most interesting in this respect.

Euthyphro, being a seer himself, is sure that his moral decision - accusing his own father of murder - is based on religion. He refers explicitly to the myth of Zeus and Kronos (Euthyphro 5E/6A). In the first discourse Socrates demonstrates that it is impossible to derive definite moral assertions from the myths of polytheistic religion. The definition of "holy" as "what is dear to the gods" proves to be useless (Euthyphro 7A/8A). In this context the question is already touched upon as to whether those myths about the gods are to be taken as true (Euthyphro 6B/C). Next, it seems to be necessary to define "holy" more precisely as "what all the gods love" (Euthyphro 9E). Then there arises the question, however, as to whether the holy is holy because it is loved by the gods or whether it is loved by the gods because it is holy (Euthyphro 10A). This reflection finally destroys the naive assumption that morals can be based on myth.[12] In order to provide a basis

---

[10] See also Plutarch: Nicias 23. Cf. R. Schottlaender (1964): 76f.
[11] In this context the report on Archelaus, that is given by Diogenes Laertius (II,16), is interesting: Archelaus, a pupil of Anaxagoras and the teacher of Socrates, "was called the physicist inasmuch as with him natural philosophy came to an end, as soon as Socrates had introduced ethics". Cf. F. Heinimann (1972): 111.
[12] Cf. F.M. Cornford (1987): 233f.

for morals, myth has to be replaced either by rational ethics or by rational theology. That does not, however, prevent Plato from occasionally making use of myths as, for example, he does in the dialogue "Gorgias".[13] Such a recourse to myth, however, occurs at the end of the dialogue and is introduced consciously as a rhetorical argument - the dominating perspective being that of ethical argumentation. At the end of the dialogue "Laws" myth is replaced by rational theology.

Plato takes as his starting point the statement that "No one who believes, as the laws prescribe, in the existence of the gods has ever yet done an impious deed voluntarily, ..." (Laws 885B). However, Plato is not concerned with a belief that is based on the mythical heritage but with the belief that "the gods exist and that they are good and honour justice more than do men" (Laws 887B). The belief in God which Plato is interested in is defined as the belief "that the gods exist, and that they are careful, and that they are wholly incapable of being seduced to transgress justice" (Laws 907B). The opposite of this belief is not just atheism but also two concepts of God - firstly that the gods don't care for human beings; secondly that the gods can be influenced by offers and prayers (Laws 885B/888C). In justifying the belief in God - in order to provide a final basis for legislation - Plato does not take up traditional myth, because its content is incompatible with his concept of God to some extent. He consciously ignores the mythical heritage in this context (Laws 886 C/D). Myth is replaced by a rational proof for the existence of God (Laws 893B-899D). The decisive point, however, is not the contradiction between mythical and scientific thinking, myth and rationality, but the distinction between wrong and right concepts of God. This is also obvious from his objections to atheistic natural philosophy. The view that everything is caused either by nature and chance or by art results in relativity of morals - the righteous being based not on nature but on convention only (Laws 889E/890A).[14] Plato's criticism does not concern the tendency of demythologization, for he objects as well to the

---

[13] Cf. K. Rudolph (1988): 373f. Rudolph takes up C. Colpe's term "Mythos mit Logos ohne mythische Valenz".

[14] The report on Archelaus is interesting in this context again: according to Diogenes Laertius (II,16), Archelaus, a pupil of Anaxagoras, also treated of ethics, contending that "what is just and what is base depends not upon nature but upon convention". Cf. D. Mannsperger (1969): 264-272.

mythical conception of gods who behave arbitrarily. He opposes the scientific view of nature not because of its destroying myth, but because of its denying divine providence.

According to Plato, what is decisive is not the demarcation between myth and natural philosophy, but the distinction between right and wrong concepts of God. This view is even more obvious with Plutarch who, in his treatise on superstition (169F), contends that superstition - a wrong conception of God - is worse than atheism. The central aspect of Plato's concept of God - God's goodness and incorruptibility - can be preserved in the transition from myth to natural philosophy. This development is perhaps to be seen with Euripides, in Hecuba's prayer to Zeus:

"O Earth's Upbearer, thou whose throne is Earth,
Whoe'er thou be, O past our finding out,
Zeus, be thou Nature's Law, or Mind of Man,
Thee I invoke; for, treading soundless paths,
To Justice' goal thou bring'st all mortal things".
(The Daughters of Troy, V. 884-888)

This development is clearly to be seen with the stoic philosopher Cleanthes, in his hymn to Zeus.[15] There are only a few elements of traditional myth preserved in this hymn, for example the reference to Zeus' thunderbolt (V. 10). On the whole, Zeus is described in philosophical language as Lord of nature, governing everything according to his law - rational human beings will obey and praise this just law and their obedience will result in a good life. Eventually the name of a god can be replaced by the concept of nature itself, as, for example, in an orphic hymn to Physis. This hymn contains a religious concept of nature - the decisive point being, however, not the fact that Physis is called a goddess, but the reference to justice (Dike), fate (Aisa) and providence (Pronoia) (V. 13;26;27). These concepts establish a meaningful relationship between the processes of nature and the destiny of human beings.

### IV. Summary and Discussion

The origin of science and its concept of nature does not coincide with the transition from myth to natural philosophy - the process of

---

[15] Cf. H. and M. Simon (1956): 56; B. Effe (1985): 156f.

demythologization in Greek religion. The comparison of Heraclitus and Anaxagoras has shown that natural philosophy is compatible with a religious concept of nature as well as with a scientific one. The decisive point is whether natural philosophy claims to establish a meaningful relationship between natural processes and human life and to derive normative consequences from its perception of nature. Compared to science, myth has a more complex function. This complex function, however, can be preserved in the process of demythologization: in natural philosophy of a special kind - a demythologized system of thought that is based on a religious concept of nature - as well as in natural theology - a combination of natural philosophy and a religious tradition that is based on the concept of revelation.

Comparing myth and science as two different theoretical systems or ontologies might be misleading if the functional difference is not taken into consideration. Apart from Hübner's work, the most interesting comparison of myth and science is R. Horton's essay "African Traditional Thought and Western Science".[16]

In the first part of his paper, Horton argues at great length "that important continuities link the religious thinking of traditional Africa and the theoretical thinking of the modern West" (Horton 1967: 155). One of the points he makes is, for example, that the gods of traditional religion might be compared to the theoretical entities of modern science: "Like atoms, molecules, and waves, then, the gods serve to introduce unity into diversity, simplicity into complexity, order into disorder, regularity into anomaly." (Horton 1967: 52; 1970: 134). In order to show this basic continuity - the immanent rationality of traditional thought - he plays down the difference between non-personal and personal theory - a difference between myth and science that is most often considered as being the fundamental one (Horton 1967: 69f; 1970: 152f).

In the second part of his paper, Horton analyses the differences that he does not want to ignore. What he takes to be the key difference is "that in traditional cultures there is no developed awareness of alternatives to the

---

[16] Cf. H.H. Penner (1986): 654-667. Penner has summarized Horton's arguments in great length.

established body of theoretical tenets" (Horton 1967: 155; 1970: 153). This key difference is called by Horton "the 'closed' and 'open' predicaments" (Horton 1967: 155).

Horton's comparison, which is based on the African material, provides an interesting alternative to Hübner's approach which is based on the Greek material. Horton is right in not taking the difference between personal and non-personal theory as the basis for his comparison. However, Horton's approach also does not take into consideration the functional difference - the fact that myth has a more complex function than science and that the shift from a religious to a scientific concept of nature means reducing the complexity of its function.

Different aspects of this complex function have been stressed by different theoretical approaches. The functionalist approach has stressed the non-cognitive, normative function of myth (Malinowski 1983: 79-93); the structuralist approach has stressed the cognitive function (Lévi-Strauss 1980: 27-37). Both theories are based on a one-sided view, stressing only one part of the complex function of myth. It is just the transition from descriptive to prescriptive statements that is provided by myth - as by any other form of religious language.[17] The question about the rationality of myth or traditional thought might be misleading if the complexity of its function is neglected and the comparison focuses on the cognitive aspect only.[18] Anyway, in an age of religious pluralism, myth could not fulfil its function completely. So, the question about its rehabilitation loses something of its fascination.

The more fundamental problem concerns the relationship between science and religion: whether it is sufficient to establish the compatibility of both - following a physicist like M. Planck or a philosopher like A. N. Whitehead - or whether the scientific concept of nature has to be replaced by a new concept, for example a religious one - following a holistic approach or

---

[17] Cf. P.S. Cohen (1969): 351f. Cohen considers prophecy and history or pseudo-history as possible substitutes for myth. Cf. also U. Berner (1983a): 104f.

[18] Cf. H. Poser (1986): 131. Poser, discussing Hübner's approach, also stresses that myth has several functions.

establishing a practical philosophy of nature.[19] These philosophical questions, however, cannot be answered within the history of religions.

## References

Diogenes Laertius: *Lives of Eminent Philosophers,* with an English Translation by R.D. Hicks, Cambridge, Mass./London 1979/80 (First Printed 1925) (The Loeb Classical Library).

*Euripides,* with an English Translation by A.S. Way, Vol. I, Cambridge, Mass./London 1978 (First Printed 1912) (The Loeb Classical Library).

Hesiod. *The Homeric Hymns and Homerica,* with an English Translation by H.G. Evelyn-White, Cambridge, Mass./London 1982 (First Printed 1914) (The Loeb Classical Library.)

Plato: *Euthyphro. Apology. Crito. Phaedo. Phaedrus,* with an English Translation by H.N. Fowler, Cambridge, Mass./London 1982 (First Printed 1914) (The Loeb Classical Library).

Plato: *Laws.* Vol. II, Books VII-XII, with an English Translation by R.G. Bury, London/Cambridge, Mass. 1968 (First Printed 1926) (The Loeb Classical Library).

*Plutarch's Lives,* with an English Translation by B. Perrin, Vol. III, London/Cambridge, Mass. 1967 (First Published 1916) (The Loeb Classical Library).

*The Orphic Hymns.* Text, Translation and Notes by A.N. Athanassakis, Missoula, Montana 1977 (Society of Biblical Literature. Texts and Translations 12. Graeco-Roman Religion Series 4).

*********

Berner, U. (1983a). "Gegenstand und Aufgabe der Religionswissenschaft". *Zeitschrift für Religions- und Geistesgeschichte,* 35: 97-116.

Berner, U. (1983b). "Das Prometheus-Motiv in antiker und moderner Literatur". *Saeculum,* 34: 334-343.

Bianchi, U. (1959/61). "Prometheus, der titanische Trickster". *Paideuma,* 7: 414-437.

Burkert, W. (1990). *Antike Mysterien. Funktionen und Gehalt.* München, Beck.

Capra, F. (1986). "Die neue Sicht der Wirklichkeit. Zur Synthese östlicher Weisheit und westlicher Wissenschaft". In S. Grof (ed.), *Alte Weisheit und modernes Denken.* München, Kösel, pp. 131-144.

Capra, F. (1987). *Das Neue Denken.* Bern/München/Wien. Scherz.

Capra, F. (1988). "Die neue Sicht der Dinge". In H. Bürkle (ed.), *New Age. Kritische Anfragen an eine verlockende Bewegung.* Düsseldorf, Patmos, pp. 11-24.

Cohen, P.S. (1969). "Theories of Myth". *Man. The Journal of the Royal Anthropological Institute* 4: 337-353.

---

[19] See for example A. Gierer (1990: 71) and K.M. Meyer-Abich (1979: 253). Gierer tries to show that modern science is consistent with different religious ideas; Meyer-Abich reflects on a normative concept of nature, referring to pre-socratic philosophy of nature.

Cornford, F.M. (1987). "Plato's Euthyphro or How to Read a Socratic Dialogue". In A.C. Bowen (ed.). *Selected Papers of F.M. Cornford*. (Greek and Roman Philosophy 10). New York/London, Garland, pp. 221-238.

Effe, B. (Ed.). (1985). *Hellenismus* (Die griechische Literatur in Text und Darstellung Band 4). Stuttgart, Reclam.

Einstein, A. (1984). *Aus meinen späten Jahren*. Frankfurt/Berlin/Wien, Deutsche Verlags-Anstalt.

Gierer, A. (1990). "Physics, Life and Mind: The scope and limitations of science". In J. Fennema/I.Paul (eds.). *Science and Religion. One World. Changing Perspectives on Reality*. Dordrecht/Boston/London, Kluwer Academic Publishers, pp. 61-72.

Gladigow, B. (1986). "'Wir gläubigen Physiker'. Zur Religionsgeschichte physikalischer Entwicklungen". In H. Zinser (ed.). *Der Untergang von Religionen*. Berlin, Dietrich Reimer, pp. 321-336.

Heinimann, F. (1972 [1945]). *Nomos und Physis. Herkunft und Bedeutung einer Antithese im griechischen Denken des 5. Jahrhunderts*. Darmstadt, Wissenschaftliche Buchgesellschaft.

Heisenberg, W. (1955). *Das Naturbild der heutigen Physik*. Hamburg, Rowohlt.

Heisenberg, W. (1984). *Der Teil und das Ganze. Gespräche im Umkreis der Atomphysik* (8th edition). München, Deutscher Taschenbuch Verlag.

Horton, R. (1967). "African Traditional Thought and Western Science". *Africa* 37 (1967), 50-71; 155-187.

Horton, R. (1970). "African Traditional Thought and Western Science". In B.R. Wilson (ed.). *Rationality*. Oxford, Basil Blackwell, pp. 131-171.

Hübner, K. (1978). *Kritik der wissenschaftlichen Vernunft*. Freiburg/München, Karl Alber.

Hübner, K. (1979). "Mythische und wissenschaftliche Denkformen". In H. Poser (ed.). *Philosophie und Mythos. Ein Kolloquium*. Berlin/New York, de Gruyter, pp. 75-92.

Hübner, K. (1983). "Wissenschaftliche und nichtwissenschaftliche Naturerfahrung". In G. Großklaus/E. Oldemeyer (eds.). *Natur als Gegenwelt. Beiträge zur Kulturgeschichte der Natur*. Karlsruhe, von Loeper Verlag, pp. 43-57.

Hübner, K. (1985). *Die Wahrheit des Mythos*. München, Beck.

Hübner, K. (1988). "Der Mythos, der Logos und das spezifisch Religiöse. Drei Elemente des christlichen Glaubens". In H.H. Schmid (ed.). *Mythos und Rationalität*. Gütersloh, Gerd Mohn, pp. 27-41.

Hübner, K. (1989). "Die moderne Mythos-Forschung - eine noch nicht erkannte Revolution". In: *Berliner Theologische Zeitschrift* 6: 8-21.

Jaeger, W. (1964). *Die Theologie der frühen griechischen Denker*. Stuttgart, Kohlhammer.

Kahn, Ch.H. (1979). *The art and thought of Heraclitus. An edition of the fragments with translation and commentary*. Cambridge, Cambridge University Press.

Kirk, G.S. (1954). *Heraclitus. The Cosmic Fragments, edited with an Introduction and Commentary*. Cambridge, Cambridge University Press.

Kirk, G.S./Raven J.E./Schofield M. (1983). *The Presocratic Philosophers. A Critical History with a Selection of Texts*. (2nd edition). Cambridge, Cambridge University Press.

Lévi-Strauss, C. (1980). *Mythos und Bedeutung. Fünf Radiovorträge. Gespräche mit Claude Lévi-Strauss.* A. Reif (ed.). Frankfurt/M., Suhrkamp.

Lüscher, E. (1988). "Physik und Wirklichkeit". In H. Bürkle (ed.). *New Age. Kritische Anfragen an eine verlockende Bewegung.* Düsseldorf, Patmos, pp. 25-41.

Malinowski, B. (1983). *Magie, Wissenschaft und Religion. Und andere Schriften.* Frankfurt/M., Fischer.

Mannsperger, D. (1969). *Physis bei Platon.* Berlin, de Gruyter.

Meyer-Abich, K.M. (1979). "Zum Begriff einer Praktischen Philosophie der Natur". In K.M. Meyer-Abich (ed.). *Frieden mit der Natur.* Freiburg, Herder, pp. 237-261.

Meyer-Abich, K.M. (1987). "Naturphilosophie auf neuen Wegen". In O. Schwemmer (ed.). *Über Natur. Philosophische Beiträge zum Naturverständnis.* Frankfurt/M., Vittorio Klostermann, pp. 63-73.

Mittelstraß, J. (1981). "Das Wirken der Natur. Materialien zur Geschichte des Naturbegriffs". In F. Rapp (ed.). *Naturverständnis und Naturbeherrschung. Philosophiegeschichtliche Entwicklung und gegenwärtiger Kontext.* München, Fink, pp. 36-69.

Mittelstraß, J. (1987). "Leben mit der Natur. Über die Geschichte der Natur in der Geschichte der Philosophie und über die Verantwortung des Menschen gegenüber der Natur". In O. Schwemmer (ed.). *Über Natur. Philosophische Beiträge zum Naturverständnis.* Frankfurt/M., Vittorio Klostermann, pp. 37-62.

Nestle, W. (1975). *Vom Mythos zum Logos. Die Selbstentfaltung des griechischen Denkens von Homer bis auf die Sophistik und Sokrates.* (Reprint of 2nd edition 1941). Stuttgart, Kröner.

Penner, H.H. (1986). "Rationality and Religion: Problems in the Comparison of Modes of Thought". *Journal of the American Academy of Religion*, 54: 645-671.

Picht, G. (1989). *Der Begriff der Natur und seine Geschichte.* Stuttgart, Klett-Cotta.

Planck, M. (1970). "Religion und Naturwissenschaft". In M. Planck, *Vorträge und Erinnerungen.* Darmstadt, Wissenschaftliche Buchgesellschaft, pp. 318-333.

Poser, H. (1986). "Die Rationalität der Mythologie". In H. Lenk (ed.). *Zur Kritik der wissenschaftlichen Rationalität.* Freiburg/München, Karl Alber, pp. 121-132.

Robinson, T.M. (1987). *Heraclitus, Fragments. A Text and Translation with a Commentary.* (The Phoenix Pre-Socratics 2). Toronto/Buffalo/London, University of Toronto Press.

Rudolph, K. (1988). "Mythos - Mythologie - Entmythologisierung". In H.H. Schmid (ed.). *Mythos und Rationalität.* Gütersloh, Gerd Mohn, pp. 368-381.

Schäfer, L. (1987). "Selbstbestimmung und Naturverhältnis des Menschen". In O. Schwemmer (ed.). *Über Natur. Philosophische Beiträge zum Naturverständnis.* Frankfurt/M., Vittorio Klostermann, pp. 15-35.

Schottlaender, R. (1964). *Früheste Grundsätze der Wissenschaft bei den Griechen.* (Deutsche Akademie der Wissenschaften zu Berlin. Schriften der Sektion für Altertumswissenschaft 43). Berlin, Akademie-Verlag.

Schrödinger, E. (1985). *Mein Leben, meine Weltansicht.* Wien/Hamburg, Paul Zsolnay.

Simon, H.; and M. Simon. (1956). *Die alte Stoa und ihr Naturbegriff. Ein Beitrag zur Philosophiegeschichte des Hellenismus.* Berlin, Aufbau-Verlag.

Stolz, F. (1982). "Funktionen und Bedeutungsbereiche des ugaritischen Bacalsmythos". In J. Assmann/W. Burkert/F. Stolz (eds.). *Funktionen und Leistungen des Mythos. Drei altorientalische Beispiele.* (Orbis Biblicus et Orientalis 48).Freiburg Schweiz/Göttingen, Universitätsverlag/ Vandenhoeck u. Ruprecht, pp. 83-118.

Whitehead, A.N. (1926). *Science and the Modern World.* Cambridge, Cambridge University Press.

Zimmerli, W.Ch. (1989). "Technik als Natur des westlichen Geistes". In H.P. Dürr/W.Ch. Zimmerli (eds.). *Geist und Natur. Über den Widerspruch zwischen naturwissenschaftlicher und philosophischer Welterfahrung.* Bern/München/Wien, Scherz, pp. 389-409.

# THE DIVINIZATION OF NATURE IN EARLY MODERN THOUGHT

Gerhold K. Becker

## I. The elusiveness of nature

The 17th and 18th centuries are usually catalogued as the era in which reason made its most dramatic appearance. Dispelling the clouds which shrouded previous ages, reason is seen to irresistibly enlighten the world and disperse the darkness over things, human and divine, natural and supernatural. It was hoped that the introduction of the scientific method into all departments of knowledge would lead to the definitive understanding of nature and of man's place in it. Neither God's revelation in the Bible nor the teachings of the Church would remain unchallenged. "Nullius in Verba" (nothing by mere authority) was the motto of the Royal Society. The Book of Revelation should gradually be replaced by the Book of Nature.

Reason and nature together, therefore, dominate the age and become the focus of the emerging modern world-view. They "represent a co-equal center of force and a co-equal target" (Crocker, 1959:XVI). It has even been argued that if one were to assess their individual contribution to the shaping of modernity, the prize had to be given to nature since, "no conception played a more significant part than that of Nature" (Willey, 1950:1). The "unprejudiced openness to the phenomena of nature" is therefore rightly seen as the key-formula to any interpretation of the age (Sühnel, 1978:17).

Yet, whereas the concept of reason seemed to provide the reliable foundation for the optimism of the Enlightenment and should therefore remain unchallenged throughout, the concept of nature soon displayed its rather enigmatic character. The more people appealed to nature in order to settle their ideological disputes and the greater the triumphs of the sciences of nature were, the less plausible became the concept itself. It is now apparent that the early success of the natural sciences was overshadowed by the crisis of its fundamental concept, the concept of nature.

For the sceptic there has always been a nagging suspicion that nature was not so much discovered as invented. "J'ai grand peur que cette nature ne soit elle-même qu'une premiere coutume, comme la coutume est une seconde nature" (Pascal, 1972:no. 93). In our times, this suspicion has gained momentum in the various and conflicting approaches to nature ranging from the hard natural sciences all the way down to eco-philosophy, both deep and shallow (cf. Taylor, 1986; Rolston, 1988; Brennan, 1988). Quite a few people therefore would not hesitate to agree with Garret Harding that "nature is a fiction" (Harding, 1976:16).

Usually, eighteenth-century philosophers did not go that far. Instead, they clearly noted the vagueness and ambiguity of the term[1] and tried to rid it of its obscurities. Yet, the realization of this goal proved extraordinarily complicated by the lack of a common frame of reference within which the concept of nature could be investigated. In his *Free Inquiry into the Vulgarly Received Notion of Nature* Robert Boyle (1686) lists eight different significations comprising all levels of being from the finite to the infinite.[2] Concluding that they are "either not intelligbile, or not proper, or not true" (Boyle, 1772:167), Boyle took pains to avoid the term altogether by introducing clearly defined substitutions for its various connotations. However, the more he got entangled with the concept of nature the greater was his bewilderment. Before he cautiously outlined his own definition of nature, he confessed that sometimes he was no longer sure, "*whether nature be a thing or a name* - I mean, whether it be a *real* existent being, or a *notional* entity, somewhat of kin to those fictitious terms that men have devised that they might compendiously express several things together by one name" (Stewart, 1991:183).

In his list, Boyle includes three usages of the term which fall within the scope of this article and are of particular interest: nature denoting the corporeal universe, the concept of 'natura naturans' and, finally, nature as (semi-)deity. Obviously, each of these terms refers to nature as a whole, to

---

[1] David Hume's remark that "none (is) more ambiguous and equivocal" than the "word nature", (Hume, 1980:474; see also Condorcet, 1847-9:507) echoes earlier complaints which can be traced back to J. Chr. Sturmius, 1689:359: "Nullum fere per universam philosophiam naturalem occurrit vocabulum magis ambiguum et aequivocum eo ipso, quod isti nomen dedit." See also Bayle, 1706:713.

[2] Excerpts can now be found in M. A. Stewart's excellent edition (Stewart, 1991).

nature in the most comprehensive sense. Yet, just because of that a tension in the concept itself became noticeable which made Boyle doubt its viability. It also revealed far-reaching consequences in that it eventually led to the demise of the once generally recognized Christian world view.

On the one hand, each of these concepts expresses a holistic view of nature by relating it to and distinguishing it from nothing less than God Himself. This provides the term nature with its unique semantic extension which comprises everything but God. Nature is everything that is not God. On the other hand, within the confines of the Christian theology of creation, nature and God, although distinct, cannot fall completely apart. On the contrary, they are thought to be most intimately related to each other, since God is not just a one-time Creator but also the constant Preserver of His creation and therefore everywhere present 'in' nature. That is to say, nature acquires its holistic signification through its precarious relation to God. God is both counterpart and co-operator; is the wholly-other and nature's most intimate principle. Since outside this onto-theological context the term nature loses its plausibility, God becomes an intrinsic part of the definition of nature.

As long as this Christian frame of reference was left intact and was also fully understood in its implications for any theology of creation, nature's relation to and distinction from God was well defined. When, however, this framework began to crumble, the multiplicity of meanings attached to nature made it easy and common to slip more or less insensibly from one connotation to another (Lovejoy, 1978:69). Once the carefully balanced relationship between nature and God was blurred, a speculative tendency was set free which almost inevitably led to the fusion of the two concepts. The holistic perspective within which this process evolved provided basically only two options: to dissolve either nature into God, or God into nature. For the speculative minds this would either lead to forms of pantheism or of metaphysical materialism. For them God's dominance over nature and with it the substance of the Christian world view seemed preserved in both cases: For pantheism, there was nothing outside God, and God was all-in-all. For materialism of d'Holbach's provenance, nature (matter) was not less divine since it had absorbed all of God's attributes; nature (matter) was just a more intelligible signification of God. For the pious, however, the result in both cases was invariably the same: atheism.

Against this background it may become less difficult to understand how at the height of the ages of Reason and Enlightenment nature could be elevated to divine status and in thinly veiled metaphorical language addressed as 'semi-deity' or 'goddess' (Boyle, 1772:177, 180). In the following, some of the major stages of the development towards the divinization of nature will be explored as they represent an important albeit largely forgotten aspect of the *'Invention of Nature'*. In the face of the recent debate on environmental ethics it seems worthwhile remembering that one of the many names by which nature once was called is that of a goddess.

## II. Shifting horizons

There are mainly two major philosophical and theological roots in the early modern history of thought which made the divinization of nature conceptually possible by providing the framework within which it could unfold. The first is found in the metaphysical problems raised by Cartesianism which overshadowed the development of philosophy down to the 18th century stimulating as well as predetermining most of the answers. The second is the theological controversy on the relationship between nature and grace, the impact of which on the divinization of nature can hardly be overestimated. That the identification of nature with God became a conceptual possibility is mainly due to a new type of the theology of grace which brought an unprecedented absolute opposition into nature's relationship to the realm of the divine. The more the supernatural, however, became subjected to doubt the more nature could step in to take over its vacant functions.

### 1. Cartesianism and the divinization of nature

The divinization of nature in early modern thought can be seen as evolving in direct opposition to the Cartesian philosophy. In this philosophy the dualism between the material body which is subject to mechanical causal laws and the mind existing independently from them stripped nature of any teleology or inherent principle of motion and denied it any significance for the mind.

However, Descartes' depriving nature of all substantial properties apart from mere extension brought an ambiguity into his system which could be exploited in various ways, all of which finally amounted to two types of answers diametrically opposed to each other.

Both developed out of attempts to resolve Descartes' major problem of how to account for the fact that mind and matter could interact if they were thought to be metaphysically distinct substances in the strict sense, i.e. in Descartes' terminology, "a thing which exists in such a way that it needs no other thing in order to exist" (Descartes, no. 51). This was one of the points of departure for Spinoza who drew out the full consequences in his more precise definition of substance using 'Occam's razor' as a principle of economy according to which, "entia non sunt multiplicanda praeter necessitatem" all one had to do was either to show that matter is of no use and somewhat redundant since all knowledge attainable from it is anyway innate to the mind, or to extend the essential attribute of matter to the mind. The most radical solution based on the first option is Berkeley's immaterialism which is in direct response to the form of Cartesianism reformulated by Malebranche. The second option was to be realized in the development which led to the form of metaphysical materialism this paper is investigating as an epicentre of the divinization of nature.

On the other hand, however, one could argue in quite the opposite way. The metaphysical devaluation of matter which was thought to secure the superiority of the mind seemed to imply some sort of autonomy insofar as matter could solve its mechanistic task without resorting to its antagonist. Descartes himself had contributed to this kind of solution through his theory of animals as soul- and senseless little machines. Since then the various attempts to bridge the gulf which separated the animals from man by explaining both through the same laws of nature, struck at the heart of Descartes' metaphysical system. The more successful this attack was, the more the concept of matter could be expanded at the expense of that of mind. Ironically, the materialist answer had been helped on its way by Cambridge Platonists like More and Cudworth who never intended to do anything else but refute what they regarded as the atheistic implications of Cartesianism together with all the other forms of atheistic materialism. Regarding the dichotomy between mechanism and spiritualism as absolute,

Cartesian mechanism characterized by the complete absence of mind was nothing but nihilism to them, and they tried to fight it by introducing a new concept of mind making it the only all encompassing substance.

However, since More tried to resolve the problem by applying the very attribute of matter - extension - to the mind, in principle the door was open to a fully fledged materialist theory of the mind. And when Cudworth resorted to the notion of 'plastic nature' to avoid the mechanical explanation of life below the level of soul, he not only re-introduced teleology into nature but also related this activity of nature most intimately to God as its principle of motion.[3]

Both approaches to nature show, firstly, that the Cartesian system could in fact foster the monistic systems of spiritualism and pantheism as well as of materialism and thus provide the structural frame of reference within which ideas could develop which were to lead to the divinization of nature. In this perspective, Descartes' rejection of any attempt to transform nature into "quelque Déesse, ou quelque autre sorte de puissance imaginaire" does not seem entirely successful. The old stoic image of the world soul which shines through Cudworth's plastic nature endowed nature with all the characteristics of life. The tranfer of the attribute of extension to the mind made it possible in principle for thinking to develop out of matter. Within the traditional framework this could easily be taken to mean that matter and nature could operate autonomously and develop into all life forms without recourse to God. All one had to do was to absorbe into nature those qualities which were thought to be essential to mind alone and, as Descartes himself had feared, nature in fact was made into a Deity.

Secondly, since the opposition to Cartesian dualism provided the means to reformulate the idea of nature it also predetermined the answers which could be developed within its boundaries. And since these answers are relative to the questions for which they were sought they also have to be

---

[3] Although placed as intermediary between God and nature, the notion of plastic nature is a step closer to the animation of nature in the stoic tradition. The task of plastic nature is to, "Drudgingly Execute that Part of his (God's) Providence, which consists in the Regular and Orderly Motion of Matter." "And by this means the Wisdom of God...will display it self abroad, and print its Stamp and Signatures everywhere throughout the World" (Cudworth, 1678).

evaluated within that perspective and cannot easily be transplanted into a different conceptual setting. This may account for the intellectual distance felt by those who no longer share the metaphysical assumptions held in an age which apparently had little difficulty in attributing divine qualities to nature.

## 2. Nature in theological perspective

In classical philosophy the meaning of nature was usually derived from its polarity to human practice and custom designating that which was not made by man.[4] Human practice is dependent on nature in a twofold way: nature is always prior to it, and nature ultimately determines what is possible and how man can achieve it. This double aspect of nature was taken up once again when I. Kant distinguished "the formal signification" as the "primal, internal principle of everything that belongs to the existence of a thing" from the "material signification" which denotes "the sum total of all things insofar as they can be objects of our senses and hence also objects of experience" (Kant, 1786:3). Yet, since human practice is itself grounded in nature this distinction is never absolute but always related to its complementary concept. This applies to the famous sophistic distinction between physis and nomos as well as to the Aristotelian distinction between nature and man or the Ciceronian one between natura and voluntas.

Things changed considerably when Christian theologians tried to clarify the significance of salvation through Christ with the help of the classical concept of nature. In the course of this discussion nature was no longer contrasting the counterparts derived from human practice but was brought in an absolute opposition of God himself. Now, the distinction is no longer between nature and human practice but between the natural and the supernatural. In that way the theological concept of nature absorbed everything that had previously been distinguished as its counterpart, and a most disturbing tension was built into nature since it was measured by its relation to that which is absolutely beyond it. "Knowledge of 'nature' is synonymous with knowledge of creation. It is knowledge so far as it is accessible to a finite, created, dependent being, and it includes no other

---

[4] In the following I draw on the outstanding contributions by Robert Spaemann to the analysis of this relationship (Spaemann, 1983).

content than the finite objects of sense... To nature belongs everything in the sphere of 'natural light', everything whose understanding and confirmation require no other aid than the natural forces of knowledge. The 'realm of nature' is thus opposed to the 'realm of grace'" (Cassirer, 1957:41-42).

Nature was defined through its opposition to the supernatural, and to secure the gratuity of grace legal terms were introduced into the theological discourse which prevented salvation being turned into a legal entitlement.

However, it gradually became clear that this concept rested upon precarious fundamentals and could work in a contrary way to that for which it was invented - to the metaphysical autonomy of nature. This has first been realized in Renaissance thought which could even be defined through its opposition to the traditional theological concept of nature and man. Instead of seeking the true essence in the realm of the created (natura naturata) this philosophy focused on the creative all-pervading forces of nature (natura naturans) in which it recognized the original divine power. Nature thus was set on its way to become divine since God was no longer seen as a force external to it but operating from within. Girodano Bruno's pantheism is the clearest indication of this new conceptualization of nature, "God is not an external intelligence rolling around and leading around; it is more worthy for him to be the internal principle of motion, which is his own nature, his own appearance, his own soul than that as many entities as live in His bosom should have motion" (Cassirer, 1957:41).

Subsequently, under the strictures of the modern 'freethinkers' and liberal theologians the once carefully balanced tension between the natural and the supernatural finally collapsed and attention shifted from grace to nature. Yet, as soon as the realm of the supernatural had become implausible and finally disappeared altogether nature had no longer any counterpart at all against which it could be measured. The consequence was that nature became now synonymous with the totality of being and was turned into that substance which Spinoza could call "deus sive natura". - The scene was set for an interpretation of nature vacillating between pantheism and materialism, both of which bore the stamp of their theological heritage quite visibly even in their terminology.

## III. Stages in the Process of Divinizing Nature

### 1. The Ambiguity of Physicotheology

Physicotheology is rightly seen as the answer which pious philosophers of nature gave to the widespread nihilism of the baroque period.[5] Resulting from the insight into man's precarious state within a vast universe which suddenly had lost its centre, this nihilism is being challenged with the very means by which it had been brought about, - the new natural sciences and their methodology. Rather than being frightened by the silence of infinite space which seemed to preclude any access to God through nature, the physicotheologians saw God's presence in nature amply documented. They tried to prove that, contrary to face value, world and nature are not the chaotic mass of corpuscular atoms moving around in the void but show the signs of order, regularity and purpose. And instead of nourishing theological pessimism which could see in nature nothing but, "the image or picture of a great Ruine" with all the marks "of a World lying in its rubbish." (Burnet, 1681-9:125) they approached nature in a different, optimistic temper, contemplating its beauty with an eye unimpaired by doctrinal prejudices. Scrutinizing all areas of nature they found ample support for the idea that the most minute parts as well as the biggest bodies in the universe undoubtedly bear the stamp of a designer God continuously supporting their being and making them work.

The significance of physico-theology for the re-evaluation of the concept of nature is mainly due to its new approach to and the ontological perspective into which nature was placed in relationship to God. It is more than just coincidental that in this context the ancient metaphor of nature being God's other book besides the revelation in the Bible is being revived.[6] As a

---

[5] See: John Ray, *Wisdom of God in the Creation* (1691), for whom the study of nature was the "true preparative to Divinity", and William Derham, *Physico-theology, or a Demonstration of the Being and Attributes of God from his Works of Creation* (1713). - For the whole movement, see the classical study by Wolfgang Philipp (Philipp, 1957).

[6] The tradition dates back to Clement of Alexandria, Origen, Augustine and other Church fathers, and has been revived in the 15th century by Raymond of Sabonde's *Theologia Naturalis* (1436) (tr. by Michel de Montaigne into French): "Libri duo dati sunt a deo scilicet liber naturae et liber sacrae scripturae." For the history of this metaphor see Blumenberg (1986).

source of knowledge about the divine they placed nature not below the Scriptures but besides them. They looked at it neither through the theories of Aristotelian philosophy nor through the teachings of the Church but in the confidence of laymen-experts in natural sciences seeking to reconcile the new worldview with the theological heritage. The copper plate of Julius Bernhard von Rohr's *Compendieuse Physikalische Bibliothek*, Leipzig 1724-28, is quite characteristic: The protestant canon is seated in front of a huge wall of books. But in lightening and rainbow Nature herself forces her way through the books and unveils in the shape of a many breasted magna mater her mysteries to the admiring scholar (Philipp, 1957:15).

Although physico-theologians attempted to clearly draw the line between nature as God's creation and the transcendent God himself, they seem to have played into the hands of those promoting nature's divinization. In their eagerness to prove God's presence everywhere in nature the proponents of physico-theology did not pay equal attention to the metaphysical implications. From hindsight I. Kant seems therefore justified in observing that physico-theologians in fact were heading towards pantheism: Those, "who wished to be theologians as well as physicists" interpreted "the unity of a number of purposively combined substances" ... "to be the unity of beings *in* one substance". This, "considered on the side of the inherent world beings, becomes pantheism, (later), on the side of the subject subsisting by itself as original Being, becomes Spinozism" (Kant, 1974:290).

This interpretation had been foreshadowed by D. Hume. In his radical criticism of the traditional proofs from design he outlined very clearly the ambiguity of this way of thinking by claiming that the same arguments could be used to prove nature itself as the ultimate cause of everything (Hume, 1980:162), thus bestowing on it the most essential attribute of God in traditional Christian thought.

## 2. Implications of deism

The other undercurrent in 18th century religious thought which contributed widely to the divinization of nature is deism (Stephen, 1962:131). As R. Stromberg put it, "Eagerly the physico-theologians had proved the existence of God by pointing to his masterly works; the deists now inquired why it was then necessary to go any farther" (Stromberg, 1954:57). Deism sees the culmination of a typically modern approach to religion which derives its force from the idea that God had enclosed all knowledge necessary for the salvation of man in nature, making thus any special revelation redundant. Even when the influence of deism had weakened, the concept of natural religion did not lose its fascination. Thomas Jefferson still struck the right note when he asked, "Why should I go in search of Moses to find out what God has said to Jean Jacques Rousseau?" (Becker, 1966:37).

Yet, the concept of natural religion reverses traditional thinking about nature and bestows on it a new dignity which will eventually blur the difference between nature and God. This reformulation of the concept of God proved to be problematic as it stripped God of his traditional attributes and transformed him into an impersonal (and psychologically abstract) principle which either lost all religious significance or could be more and more identified with the principle of nature itself. As a result, the Christian God himself is less needed and gradually removed.

The ambiguity of this revised concept of nature comes through in the philosophy of Lord Shaftesbury who has traditionally been counted among the deists. Renowned historians of philsophy such as Leslie Stephen (Stephen, 1962, vol. II:17) and B. Willey (Willey, 1950:62) find "the divinization of nature" very obvious in Shaftesbury. Nature is sometimes even directly addressed as personified creator-being ('creatress') bearing all the attributes of divinity.

The same ambivalence is characteristic for the writings of Charles Blount, John Toland (Sullivan, 1982:20; O'Higgins, 1971:484)[7] and Anthony Collins (Berman, 1988:78-82). Although not intending to develop a pantheistic theory, Collins nevertheless maintained, "that all the perfections visible in the world must be attributes of the eternal being, from whence all particular

---

[7] Instead of the philosophy of Spinoza, however, Toland preferred the pantheistic immanentism of Giordano Bruno, whose life he wrote and whose *Dialogues* he translated according to his own list of *"Manuscripts of mine abroad"*, now in the British Museum.

perfections that exist in time proceed" and thought that God's perfections are univocal with ours (Collins, 1710:3).

When deism nevertheless continued referring to God in traditional terms, for many it seemed to do so just to avoid persecution. This was at least Richard Bentley's conviction when he charged the deists with covering, "the most arrant Atheism under the mask and shadow of a Deity; by which they understand no more than some inanimate Matter, some universal Nature and soul of the world" (Bentley, 1692:10).

Despite all counterclaims by the deists themselves, it seems safe to say that they in fact greatly contributed to nature's taking over the place vacated by God and acquiring the divine predicates for herself. As Carl L. Becker observed, "The Eigteenth century ... did not cease to bow down and worship; it only gave another form and a new name to the object of worship: it deified Nature and denatured God" (Becker, 1966:51).

### 3. Transfer of divine attributes

Against this intellectual background it is no surprise that many attributes which previously had an intrinsic relationship to the realm of the divine should gradually be transferred to nature. Foremonst among them were the attributes of *infinity, eternity* and *self-motion* which in the classical tradition could only be ascribed to God. Nature was no longer thought of in terms of ontologically finite and inactive (inert) matter set in motion by God but as the independent centre of infinite energy. For John Toland it was obvious that motion is inherent in matter and belongs essentially to its definition so that all other qualities can be reduced to relations of motion. The essence of matter is an active force, not just something which could be expressed in terms of physical qualities. Nature thus was animated and became the self-sustaining great organism from which everything, even feeling and thinking, could be deduced without recourse to God. In his *Pantheisticon* Toland attributed to matter a life creating spontaneity, 'panspermia', which can account for all forms of natural life. This clearly proves that by 'God' he did not mean the transcendent cause of the animated world, but nature. 'God' has become simply a way of referring to the universe or the sum-total of reality: the idea of God as a personal spirit has been given up as one of the untenable 'mysteries' (Nicholl, 1965:64).

The full implications of interpretations such as these became apparent only later when the pantheistic view turned into its materialistic opposite. In his *Systeme de la Nature* Baron d'Holbach (1770) did not hesitate in the least to show (very similarly as L. Feuerbach later argued) that all divine attributes either rightly belong to nature from which a superstitious mind had projected them onto God or had to be dismissed as utterly meaningless. He discussed at length for that purpose S. Clarke's celebrated argument a priori for God's existence. Although he rejected as superstitious the idea of a world-soul and interpreted nature as causally determined mechanistic system, nature in fact acquired divine status. Nature represents the complete mechanism of material reality beyond which nothing else can exist. All physical, biological and social events as well as the cognitive, emotional, aesthetic and moral acts of man are explained as the necessary consequences of the forces and laws of nature. He specifically excluded all personifying language from nature, but due to the inherited structural theological framework and nature being turned into the ultimate cause, he himself could not help talking of nature in personal terms. Man was not yet prepared to subscribe to an anonymous, blind force which accounted for everything.

D'Holbach ended his book with what Peter Gay has called "the hymn to nature": "O Nature, sovereign of all beings... it is to you that belong the praises and the homage of the earth. Shew us then, O Nature, that which man ought to do in order to obtain the happiness which thou makest him desire" (Gay, 1973:372, 381).

It appears that Ralph Cudworth had been on the right track when he denounced the atheists worshipping matter "as the only numen" as fanatics of the "Goddess of Nature" (Shaftesbury, 1900:196-7). And when Boyle observed that philosophers, "ascribe so much to nature, that they think it needless to have recourse to a deity for the giving an account of the phaenomena of the universe" he in fact and unwittingly described a development he had worked hard to prevent (Boyle, 1772: 158).

## References

Bayle, P. (1703). *Résponse aux question d'un provincial. Oeuvres Diverses.* Vol. III. La Haye (1727-31). Reprint, Hildesheim, G. Olms (1964-68).

Becker, C. (1966). *The Declaration of Independence.* New York, Alfred Knopf.

Bentley, R. ([1692] 1976). *The Folly of Atheism, And (what is now called) Deism.* Being the First of the Lectures Founded by the Honourable Robert Boyle. London, T. Parkhurst. Reprint: New York, Garland Publ.

Berman, D. (1988). *A History of Atheism in Britain.* London, Croom Helm.

Blumenberg, H. (1986). *Die Lesbarkeit der Welt.* Frankfurt, Suhrkamp.

Boyle, R. (1772). *Free Inquiry into the Vulgarly Received Notion of Nature.* Works V. London, J. and F. Rivington.

Brennan, A. (1988). *Thinking about Nature. An Investigation of Nature, Value and Ecology.* London/New York, Routledge.

Burnet, Th. ([1681-9] 1965). *Telluris Theoria Sacra. Sacred Theory of the Earth.* Carbondale, Southern Illinois University Press.

Cassirer, E. (1957). *The Philosophy of the Enlightenment.* Princeton, Princeton University Press.

Collins, A. (1710). *A Vindication of the Divine Attributes, in Some Remarks on His Grace the Archbishop of Dublin's Sermon Intituled Divine predestination...* London.

Condorcet, M. S. A. (1847-9). *Eloge de M. Tronchin.* Oeuvres II, publiées par A. Condorcet, O'Connor, M. Arago, Paris.

Crocker, L. (1959). *An Age of Crisis. Man and World in Eighteenth Century French Thought.* Baltimore, Johns Hopkins Press.

Cudworth, R. ([1678] 1978). *The True Intellectual System of the Universe.* Vol.I. London, R. Royston. Reprint: New York, Garland Publ.

Derham, W. ([1644] 1977). *Physico-theology, or A Demonstration of the Being and Attributes of God from his Works of Creation.* London, W. Innys. Reprint: New York, Arno Press.

Descartes, R. ([1644], 1984). *Principles of Philosophy.* Tr. by Miller, V.R. and Miller, R. P. Dordrecht, D. Reidel Publ.

Gay, P. (1973). *The Enlightenment. A Comprehensive Anthology.* New York, Simon and Schuster.

Harding, G. (1976). "The Rational Foundations of Conservation". *North American Review*, 259:14-17.

Holbach, P. H. T, Baron d' ([1770] 1970). *Systeme de la Nature. The System of Nature, or Laws of d'Holbach.* New York, Burt Franklin.

Hume, D. ([1739-40], 1978). *A Treatise of Human Nature.* Ed. by Selby-Bigge/P. H. Nidditch. Oxford, Clarendon Press.

Hume, D. ([1779] 1980). *Dialogues Concerning Natural Religion.* Ed. by N. Kemp Smith, Indianapolis, Bobbs-Merrill Co.

Kant, I, (1786). *Metaphysical Foundations of Natural Science.* Tr. by J. Ellington. Indianapolis, Bobbs-Merrill Co.

Kant, I. ([1790] 1974). *Critique of Judgment*. Tr. by J. J. Bernard. New York, Hafner Press.

Lovejoy, A. O. (1978). "Nature as Aesthetic Norm". In A. O. Lovejoy, *Essays in the History of Ideas*. Westport, Greenwood Press, pp. 69-77.

Nicholl, H. E. (1965). "John Toland: religion without mystery". *Hermathena*, 100:54-65.

O'Higgins, J. (1971). "Hume and the Deists". *Journal of Theological Studies* NS, 22:478-501.

Pascal, B. ([1670] 1972). *Pensées*. Ed. by Léon Brunschvicg. Paris, Librairie Générale Française.

Philipp, W. (1957). *Das Werden der Aufklärung in theologiegeschichtlicher Sicht*. Göttingen, Vandenhoeck and Rupprecht.

Ray, J. ([1691] 1977). *The Wisdom of God Manifested in the Works of Creation*. London, W. Innys, 1771. Reprint: New York, Arno Press.

Rolston III, H. (1988). *Environmental Ethics. Duties to and Values in the Natural World*. Philadelphia, Temple University Press.

Shaftesbury, ([1711] 1900). *Characteristics of Men, Manners, Opinions, Times*. Ed. John M. Robertson, 2 vols. London, Grant Richards.

Spaemann, R. (1980). "Zur Vorgeschichte von Rousseaus Naturbegriff". In R. Spaemann. *Rousseau - Bürger ohne Vaterland*. München, Piper, pp. 57-77.

Spaemann, R. (1983). "Natur". In R. Spaemann. *Philosophische Essays*. Stuttgart, Reclam Verlag, pp. 19-40.

Stephen, L. ([1876] 1962). *History of English Thought in the Eigteenth Century*. Vol I and II. New York, Harcourt, Brace and World.

Stewart, M. A. (1991). *Selected Philosophical Papers of Robert Boyle*. Indianapolis, Hackett.

Stromberg, R. (1954). *Religious Liberalism in Eigteenth-Century England*. London, Oxford University Press.

Sturmius, J. Chr. (1689). *Philosophia Eclectica*, vol. 2, Altdorf.

Sühnel, R. (1978). "Augusteischer Klassizismus. Das Zeitalter der Aufklärung in England". In B. Fabian/W. Schmidt-Biggemann (Hrsg.). *Das Achtzehnte Jahrhundert als Epoche*. Nendeln, KTO Press, pp. 11-24.

Sullivan, R. (1982). *John Toland and the Deist Controversy*. Cambridge, Harvard University Press.

Taylor, P. (1986). *Respect for Nature. A Theory of Environmental Ethics*. Princeton, Princeton University Press.

Willey, B. (1950). *The Eighteenth Century Background. Studies on the Idea of Nature in the Thought of the Period*. London, Chatto and Windus.

# ECOLOGY, DUALISM, AND UTILITARIANISM: ATTITUDES TOWARD NATURE IN AMERICAN SOCIETY

Catherine E. Martin

Threats of a greenhouse effect combined with heat and fires of recent summers, unprecedented oil spills, and superfluous garbage have frightened some Americans in the United States, as well as other nature 'imperialists', into attempts at political manipulation of governments and industries to reduce actions immediately threatening to environmental ecosystems. But concerns over the degradation of the environment have not profoundly modified the dualistic notion setting man apart from and as controller of his environment. Philosophically, the perspective remains the same; in order to rectify the problems, we are seen as merely needing more information and better technology. Here the relationship of this view to our Darwinian heritage and to sociobiological arguments is explored.

## I. Preserving our environment

The messages that those living in the United States receive from the environmentally concerned societies are standard: help protect the environment, or some portion of it; save endangered or threatened species; manage nature through our wildlife refuges, on our rangeland, or in our national parks; conserve our natural resources from unchecked development. The dualism of the view of nature in relation to oneself is readily apparent even here. When something is seen as an integral part of oneself, an equal in an interacting system of multiple feedback loops, terms such as 'manage,' 'save,' or 'conserve' are not used in referring to it. If applied to human beings, these terms are again dualistic and denigrating. Band and tribal cultures are preserved for posterity; unruly crowds, dissidents, prisoners, and deviants are managed; the homeless, the poor, the aged, the suffering, orphans, refugees, the abused, and the misunderstood are saved. In their compassion, Americans reach out to those in need, but from a paternalistic and dominant stance. We refer to ourselves as threatening, attacking, and destroying nature.

This dualism has a long history in western society (Passmore, 1980) and is still basic to the thinking and actions of many Americans living in the United States today. Paul Taylor, in *Respect for Nature* (1986), distinguishes between an anthropocentric view of nature, resulting in our constant evaluation of the status of natural phenomena and beings in relation to our own needs and convenience, in contrast to what he terms the life-centered or biocentric view: "When a life-centered view is taken, the obligations and responsibilities we have with respect to the wild animals and plants of the Earth are seen to arise from certain moral relations holding between ourselves and the natural world itself. The natural world is not there simply as an object to be exploited by us, nor are its living creatures to be regarded as nothing more than resources for our use and consumption" (1986:12-13).

A discussion of the metaphysics of Charles Hartshorne (Dombrowski, 1988) disputes the misuse and even eating of other animals, and exhorts us to recognize our own animality. Much emphasis today is placed on preserving tropical rain forests. Mention is made of climatic regulation, unknown species, and biodiversity. But environmental defense is heavily based on economic incentives: the potentials of resources for medicinal or food use if managed properly. "[The World Wildlife Fund] has signed Ecuador's largest debt-for-nature deal agreeing to purchase approximately 5.4 million dollars of Ecuador's outstanding commercial debt at greatly discounted rates to support conservation efforts in that country" (*Focus* 11(3):1, May/June 1989).

In another mailing (August 1990), the Fund asks, "Why should you care about the fate of these [rain] forests thousands of miles away?" The response is, "Because not only do they provide food and shelter to at least half the world's species of wildlife, these tropical forests are also the world's largest 'pharmaceutical factory'... A letter from the Sierra Club reiterates the practical advantage of nature preservation: So much of what Big Timber is doing, with the cooperation of the U.S. Forest Service, makes good business sense for the lumber companies, but it's contrary to common sense. And it's bad business for the U.S.

Increasingly, tourism has been seen as a means of saving national parks and endangered ecosystems, but presents its own sets of problems. Public fear of disease, warfare, and natural disasters have also plagued some areas. In 'Global Interconnections' Boersma (1989:9) points out the less obvious effects of human intervention on natural ecosystems:

"The intrinsic value of natural land should be calculated before the land use is changed. Private owners will object. Their freedom to do with the land as they please has been unlawfully curtailed, but on the other hand, the right of individuals and governments to damage, pillage, and destroy natural ecosystems cannot be tolerated by society."

Those who argue against the idea of moral obligation are also articulate in this decade. Psychiatrist Willard Gaylin's *Adam and Eve and Pinocchio* argues that humans are more than mere animals and must, for their own sense of self-esteem, recognize their special features. While we have a moral obligation, in his view, it is not the same toward all animals and clearly distinguishes our own interests from theirs. Increasing emphasis on natural variation in climate and ecosystems relieves us of responsibility for the greenhouse effect and for habitat destruction. The recent environmental conference in Rio was in many respects a mere palliative, and the United States was criticized for lack of commitment to environmental conservation. The island biogeography model of conservation so popular with scientists in the United States - setting up small islands for native faunal and floral reserves with narrow corridors connecting them - has yielded disappointing results as many animals will not use these corridors. Any conservation efforts under way before the recent economic recession have had to defend themselves against those arguing that any reduction at all in our business competitiveness or job possibilities yields untold suffering of today's American population. Free-trade agreements with Mexico and Canada are cloaked not in ideological ideas of justice and opportunity for all, but the supposed economic advantages.

Appeals for conservation by environmental societies are sometimes made to our sense of tradition - our desire to have our grandchildren see the forests and animals of our current world. Thus Cousteau argues, "Let us make personal commitments to live and work in such a manner that we pass on values that focus on quality of life rather than quantity of profits" (Cousteau, 1992:3). With more Americans conscious of the problems of disease, the Audubon Society claims, "The destructive processes man has set in motion resemble a cancer" (Beyea in 1992 mailing).

Increasingly, opposition is felt between industry and the ecologically-minded (see lead article in *USA Today*, Sept. 9, 1992). Emphasizing the preservation of certain natural resources for human posterity leads quickly to Ronald Reagan's, "If you've seen one redwood, you've seen 'em all" philosophy (quoted by the Sierra Club in its Spring 1989 mailings). Just a thin screen of forest is enough, populated by a few highly visible bears, coyotes, and mountain lions - as long as they are kept safely away from even the most adventuresome tourists tempted to handle or feed them. But backpacking to see these wild beings has diminished significantly in recent years (Roderick, 1989), so easy accessibility to these creatures is essential. One false move and they become a 'management' problem.

It is assumed even by the educated public that with all the technical knowledge of environments and genetics, surely scientists can make this microcosm work! It is necessary merely to control inputs and outputs into this 'display' diorama. Theoretically, scientists can manipulate reproduction of small gene pools, such as the leopard, with the aid of biotechnology and sperm banks. If a small habitat cannot sustain sufficient nutrient production, it is simple to intervene by adding or substituting nutrients. Deficiencies are the result of a lack of money or knowledge, and can be remedied. In a laudable attempt at animal conservation, education, and display, the National Zoo's BioPark in Washington, D.C. is an example of the artificial creation of wetlands and other 'natural' habitats (see Page, 1989).

In his *Philosophy of Biology Today*, Ruse (1988) points out that Americans fail to see themselves as an integral part of nature, and nature as a complex system, in part due to the difference between the predominant North American philosophical perspective on biology and adaptation (traced to Britain) when compared to that of a more holistic general European outlook, associated by Ruse with a Marxist philosophy. "Europeans have stressed ... structure, form, *Bauplane* [sic], hierarchies, and holism," according to Ruse (1988:38), who also cites Reif (1983) and Riedl (1983) on this issue. In keeping with Ruse's interpretation, one junior high school history teacher was recently heard lamenting that relativism and holism were impossible to impart to his students given the orientations of current American youth. A symposium held at the Los Angeles Zoo on teaching about tropical forests (1987) reiterated the difficulties of educating students to view nature in an ecosystemic, holistic perspective; the American Museum of Natural History in New York City held a forum on biodiversity in 1990.

## II. Views of nature in The United States today

Over the past eight years, research has been conducted by the author in a variety of groups and a number of settings in Los Angeles, California. Based on analysis of the media, responses to essay questions concerning natural ecosystems, interviews, and questionnaires, it would appear that the concept of progress - with its manipulation, control, replacement, and even destruction of 'nature' - is viewed as inimical to the preservation of natural ecosystems by children, adolescents, and adults living in the Los Angeles area. The essays, questionnaires, and interviews have been conducted in schools, universities, churches, and youth groups. Although sympathy for the 'underdog' is shown, it is thought that if we save a few grey whales, preserve large but isolated California oaks, and accelerate the pace of our technological mastery of the environment, we can create good replacements for habitats lost, much as animated cartoon characters were created in the film *Who Framed Roger Rabbit*.

When undergraduate classes recently were asked about the future of the human species, the responses were surprising. Students saw technological capabilities of mastery as unlimited, for manipulation of both environments and genetic types, but sociopolitical power and greed were seen as the main factors which would determine which individuals would be enhanced in genome, power, or wealth; while others, those currently less influential in these respects, would become the losers and even the prey of the chosen few! Clearly the much publicized concern over the prevalence of cheating, complicity, and lack of ethics in the United States today has been noted. Since greed and lust for power are taken for granted, it hardly surprised students to learn, for instance, that Lake George in the Adirondacks of Upstate New York is endangered by developers building hotels along the shores. While many reacted negatively to the Exxon Valdez oil spill, most interviewed felt it was typical of the selfishness, greed, and lack of concern for others characteristic of today. Sociobiological discussions of selfish genes, cheaters, and adulterers, and recent political exposés of malfeasance and fraud in government and the economy merely conform to current views of how the world operates and, rightly or wrongly, who wins.

In a mailing of The Wilderness Society (1989), several relevant points are reiterated. These concern the short memory we all have after an ecological disaster; our willingness to be manipulated by public relations specialists serving corporate interests; and our general belief that human interference puts merely a localized and temporary damper on the growth of natural ecosystems. The optimism generated by the regrowth of Yellowstone National Park confirms this laissez-faire attitude. The decision by the Federal Government not to attempt to control the fire in its initial stages has since come under much criticism, but in defense of this position it has been pointed out that nature achieves its own balance, and that there is far more instability in nature than American scientists had formerly believed. James Lovelock's Gaia, the earth as a huge interacting system where all life participates in the healing and formation of the biosphere, merely adds to the view that in nature everything takes care of itself. Even after the eruption of Mount Saint Helens, plant and animal populations rebounded, sometimes to the advantage of large and 'weedy' species by clearing the deadwood.

Among environmentalists, education is often stressed as a preventive for destruction of natural habitats, but it is not easy to communicate a sense of respect or understanding for the tremendous complexity of ecosystems. Particularizing the message by showing pictures of cute, fuzzy animals that are losing their 'home' is indeed a better strategy at present, but reinforces atomism and the replacement concept of habitats. One student, when discussing ecosystem preservation, felt that in the United States conservation efforts serve as rationalizations for further destruction rather than solutions to real problems. Killing baboons to transplant their liver into human patients is only one more indication that other animals are seen as merely utilitarian objects.

Views of nature of many interviewed in the Los Angeles area are reflected in the popular media in the United States today and involve a number of underlying themes:

A. **Dualism**: 'man' (usually male) and 'nature' are seen as separate and unequal entities, with women partaking more of the 'natural' than the more masculine and controlled cultural aspect (cf. Midgley, 1978; Merchant, 1983).

B. **Domination**: 'man' controls 'nature,' fabricating or replacing it to suit his needs.

C. **Utilitarianism**: 'nature' is for man's benefit; it is man's duty, as well as his privilege, to use nature for his own needs (cf. Taylor, 1986). Animals are "sugar in the black coffee of life", an "advanced toy" (expressions used by undergraduate students in essays).

D. **Fragmentation**: nature is infinitely divisible into organisms and their parts (including genes), each of which can be individually tampered with, reconstructed, altered, and put back in place. Reporting on the destruction of some of the only remaining virgin forest of the Pacific Northwest for logging, *ABC Morning News* (April 26, 1989) mentioned that we have no law allowing the protection of endangered ecosystems, but only species. Therefore, preservation of the forest took on the mascot of the endangered spotted owl (an endearing creature).

E. **Mechanism**: all parts of nature function as a big clock, intricately but with predictability and precision requiring monitoring and fixing by man (see Cartmill, 1983:66 on nature as a "gorgeous windup toy").

F. **Materialism**: nature is simply there, a 'natural resource' to be used by man for his relaxation, enjoyment, and economic utility. The extent to which various parts of nature can be destroyed, injured, or exploited varies, however, with some creatures gaining some additional rights by virtue of their favor with man. Behavioral and biochemical studies have shown the close relationship of the chimpanzee to ourselves, but even The Animal Welfare Act (1966, 1970, 1976, 1985) administered by the U.S. Department of Agriculture's Animal and Plant Health Inspection Service protects some laboratory animals but not others (see The Human Society's *HSUS* News, Winter 1989, 34(1):19). Included are dogs, cats, guinea pigs, hamsters, rabbits, and other warm-blooded animals; but not rats, mice, birds, or cold blooded-animals.

G. **Fixability**: 'nature' can be fixed up by humans, with substitutions, replacements, and artificial inputs.

H. **Isolability**: 'nature' is not a part of daily life and doesn't - if 'managed' properly - intrude upon it, but can be entered voluntarily and carefully (to avoid dangers) for recreational purposes. Since fewer people are willing to adventure into backlands, most want nature as a backdrop of serenity, more suggestive and symbolic than real.

I. **Irreality** and Symbolic Capacity: 'nature' is romanticized, simplified, and symbolized, but the true complexity is not understood (see Lopez, 1978 for a contrast of Inuit and western views of animals; also Nelson, 1983). People choose animals as symbols, usually to convey power: cougars, mustangs, tigers, or eagles. Negatively, humans can be bats, pigs, dogs, rabbits, worms, toads, or cows (see Leach, 1964). Doves, in fact aggressive birds, are construed as symbols of peace; wolves, socially cooperative and predictable animals, as cunning and evil. Animals and plants are decorative and symbolic of beauty, power, majesty, evil, or ferocity. Christmas catalogues from the large art museums in the United States are replete with especially animals, and to a lesser extent, plant motifs; children's gifts almost all show animal designs.

J. **Abstraction**: the totality of natural ecosystems cannot be comprehended. Particularization is necessary, as in campaigns to save beleaguered whales in the American Delta, surrounded by icebergs in Alaska, or in Adopt-a-Whale programs.

K. **Substitutability**: one animal or plant is as good as another of the same species and breeding. In "Our National Parks: The Case for Burning",

Peter Matthiessen (1988) echoes the idea that burning is beneficial in providing more vegetation and herbivores for the large carnivores, even if many organisms are destroyed, as in the Yellowstone fire.

L. **Ranking**: some animals or plants are preferable to others. Thus pedigreed dogs are not euthanized as soon as mongrels, and large, warm-blooded animals are protected over smaller rodents, reptiles, and birds. Rules for research at Cambridge exclude "reptiles, amphibians, mice, rats and rabbits" (*The New York Times*, June 28, 1989, p. A21).

M. **Atomism**: a single leopard as a pet is as impressive as a leopard as part of a natural ecosystem, if not more so by contrast with its surroundings; saving a large oak tree in one's front yard shows commitment to conservation, even though no seedlings are allowed to grow (talk by Bruce Pavlik, 1992).

When we interfere with someone's treatment of a pet, development of lands, or landscaping of the yard, we are seen as violating an important principle of personal liberty. The illusion persists that these are objects, albeit natural ones, and that there are still plenty of them out there. Thus: (1) organisms and ecosystems are not generally seen as endowed with natural rights - although animal rights activists, as well as animal sacrifice cults - both appear to have increased their activities and membership in recent years; and (2) education of people for better treatment of natural ecosystems is, indeed, not an easy matter, as holistic thinking flies in the face of so many dictums.

### III. Dualism, social structure, and metaphor

The biotic component of ecosystems to which humans most closely relate is other animals, but this relationship varies greatly with culture. The American view toward other animals is dualistic, utilitarian, and metaphorical. Animals are good, bad, or ugly; good if they are useful and/or friendly; bad if they are pests or unfriendly; ugly if they are seen as ferocious and behave in ways inimical to human values: e.g., carrion eaters; mythical monsters and not so mythical rats, bats, rhinoceri, and gorillas. Of course, even monsters can turn out to have feelings and souls - King Kong liked Fay Raye. Animals are sources of amusement in American society, from circuses to animal shows to television comics, as in David Letterman's Stupid Pet Tricks. But we do not have the same notion of the dignity of an animal and its right to respect and reverence held by many gathering/hunting people, where hunters make special ritual provisions to ensure that they are not offending an animal's spirit when killing it. While discussing the Eskimo view of nature, Barry Holstun Lopez states, "It is not hard for Western minds to miss the seriousness of this ritual: the link between hunter and hunted (symbolized in the meal) lies at the very foundation of every hunting society" (1978:90).

The difference in our view toward animals and that of the Naskapi and other Native American groups is discussed by Lopez with reference to the wolf. Wolves stir our imagination, but our view is overly simplistic and too cut and dried. To the Eskimo, the wolf is a more variable creature, a part of nature that remains unknown and unknowable. We Westerners, "do not know very much about animals. We cannot understand them except in terms of our own needs and experiences." And to approach them solely in terms of the Western imagination is "really, to deny the animal" (1978:86).

Another example of the difference in views of ourselves in relation to animals and nature is found in a recent article on the Navajo Nation Zoological Park near Window Rock, Arizona (Hillinger, 1990:E4), entitled "Indian and Animal Worlds Converge at the Navajo Zoo." According to curator Loline Hathaway, "Traditional relationships between Navajos and animals and birds are vastly different than those of non-Indian cultures." Eagle feathers which fall from the birds are coveted for conveying strength, for instance, and shamans are consulted concerning treatment of animals and their parts.

In all societies, animals play an important role (see Wilson, 1984). They motivate children to learn, and serve a metaphoric capacity in reinforcing or satirizing human behavior. In ritual systems, animals often mediate between humans and the gods, and are seen somehow as a link between ourselves and the power and harmony of the natural/supernatural worlds. Urton asks, "What similarities and differences do humans see between themselves and animals? Why do people commonly make metaphorical comparisons between human beings or social groups and animals? And to what degree are people's attitudes and beliefs about animals parallel to or contingent upon their attitudes and beliefs about human beings and human society?" (1985:3).

According to a discussion in Mary Douglas' *In the Active Voice*, societies contrast nature in general with nurture or culture, but how this contrast is made depends on the experience of society. If society is seen as potentially good, contrast with nature may lose sharp definition; but if evil, then nature by contrast is seen as good. This contrast is, of course, much more complicated (1982:209), but social divisions into social heroes and villains, ingroups and outgroups, may follow natural divisions into lambs and wolves. Cosmology and social context are related to social structure and environment.

In a provocative section of her work, Douglas relates a society's views of nature to its social environment. She divides social environments into four types based on two dimensions: (1) the strength of the social group; and (2) the degree of individualization and autonomy. This yields four types: (A) those with weak social cohesion of the group but little individual freedom because of the constraint of strong social classification; (B) social environments characterized by weak social pressure but a strong sense of individualism, with high emphasis on competition for power; (C) societies marked by strong group cohesion, with marked separation of roles and social complexity, interdependence, and constraint; and (D) those with a strong definition of the social group as distinguished from outsiders, but with little specialization and interdependence among individuals within the group.

In each type of social environment, the contrast between nature and culture differs. Thus, where the group and individual are both weak (A), there is little theoretical elaboration of the concept of nature; the concept of nature is more fragmentary and the most adaptive response is passivity (1982:211). In social environments characterized by high individual autonomy (B), the individual identifies with nature against the fetters of society. American views of nature today appear to be derived from a frontier attitude of the second type, shifting toward a weaker, more passive view as individual autonomy has less chance for expression in a more conservative and stratified society. By contrast, in a society in which the strong group is held together by interdependence of its parts (C), "an ideal undivided nature is part of the encircling ambience of culture with God sustaining both" (*Ibid.*:210). Here we find, "an intellectual effort to elaborate a transcendental metaphysics which seeks to make an explicit match between civilization and the purposes of God and nature." Ritual processes, including divine sacrifice for maintaining the harmony of nature and culture, are expected in these societies, such as the ancient Maya. For the strong group held together with reference to outside threat (D), nature has both a positive and a negative aspect, divided according to, "the vulnerable 'us' and predatory 'them.'" Scapegoating and witchcraft in African societies discussed by Douglas are examples of this type of social environment.

While attempting to include all animals ever documented in our scientific classification, many Americans nonetheless have a highly simplified view of nature. Animals are good if they are friendly and loyal; bad if they bite, attack, or show too much independence. Animals can switch rapidly from good to bad: witness the wolf as portrayed in early European folklore and the very different wolf of movies like *The Journey of Natty Gann* and *Never Cry Wolf*.

With the attack of a child by a cougar in an Orange County park, cougars swung in one incident from good to bad. Both views are simplistic and romanticized; in neither do wolves or cougars have the depth and special relationship to us that is described for other cultures.

The western European view of animals was once heavily stereotypic, based on imputed characteristics of metaphor, not science. With the emergence of scientific studies of nature, more detailed and accurate pictures of animals emerged, but they lack empathy and soul, and have not generally filtered into public consciousness. Although not everyone accepts the possibility of organic evolution, there is still some agreement as to which animals are 'higher,' which 'lower.' The ordering would be rats, dogs, monkeys, apes, humans, for example. More people (nearly 9 out of 10) had no objection to using rats in laboratory experiments, whereas only 55% approved of using dogs (*The New York Times, Science Times*, Oct. 29, 1985:C-4).

The study of the view of animals in the United States is based in part on interviews of children from several elementary schools and Cub Scout groups representing a wide range of socioeconomic, ethnic, and educational backgrounds in the greater Los Angeles area; interviews of and questionnaires completed by college students; studies of local gallery art and that of local children on animals and nature; numerous trips to museums and zoological gardens to observe exhibits and people's reactions to them; statistical analyses of animal motifs in catalog gift collections and corporate advertisements; and, for comparison, trips to Mayan sites in the Yucatan. The results, while only preliminary, do demonstrate the comparative simplicity of our world view concerning animals and nature.

Part of the lack of complexity of how many Americans view most animals, and the lack of diversity reflected in the choice of animal motifs in gifts and for emblems or symbols, has to do with the paucity of immediate knowledge of these creatures, given our urban ecological circumstances. But as commented by Hunn (1977), complexity of animal usage and classification does not reflect mere ecology or practical utility; it also reflects our perspective on our social environment. There are good or bad people and groups, but not much complexity of interaction, interdependence, or character. In a society claiming relativism of values, tolerance, and equality, anyone has access to a cougar, lion, or tiger as a personal or even corporate symbol; this right is not tied to a person's social rank.

## IV. Dualism as an historical concept

How did Americans arrive at this conception of ourselves as isolated from and dominant over nature? In his "Four Legs Good, Two Legs Bad: Man's Place (If Any) in Nature", Matt Cartmill claims, "In our speech and thought today we tend to separate man from nature by definition. For us, the word *nature* by itself normally means something like the earth's surface and the plants and animals that live on it - as they exist *without human interference*" (1983:66).

In his discussion of three general western schools of thought, which Cartmill calls Christian, mechanistic, and Romantic, he sees Darwinism and modern views of nature as traceable to a combination of these. For traditional

Christians, man and nature were both sick, with man rising above nature in his supernatural aspects. The bestial in man, as well as nature itself, was ignored or subdued. The later mechanistic view saw nature, rather, as an intricate example of God's laws and man as a part of the design. In the late 18th Century, Romanticism changed this view as the universe became "animated by something like a human soul" (p. 66), with man at the top of the hierarchy. Darwinism took an essentially Romantic vision of the world as a great upward struggle and reduced it to Newtonian mechanism. Some traditional Christian ideas - man's supremacy over nature, and the adaptive 'design' in living things... also got women into the Darwinian synthesis. (*Ibid.*:67)

A Panglossian view of the world results, with the struggle for existence merely a mechanical means of insuring the supremacy of the best. The illusion of plenty persists; there seem to be many redwoods, tropical forests as far as the eye can see, too many elephants, a dangerous resurgence of the great white shark in California coastal waters, and dolphins, seals, and sea otters interfere with fishing there. In a world advocating selfishness as a moral imperative, it is hard to mobilize concern for these animals or the ecosystems of which they (and we) form a part.

### V. Sociobiology, dualism, and morality

Rifkin's "desacralization of nature" (see also Passmore, 1980) is also appropriate here. The Darwinian framework views organisms as the result of naturalistic, mechanistic, materialistic processes involved in organic evolution. With the emergence of sociobiology, biosocial anthropology, and bioanthropology in recent decades, humans have been added to the naturalistic, desacralized realm. The extent to which this attempt to place humans in the same naturalistic framework as other life forms has brought about reaction from not only the lay public, but from students in the biological and behavioral sciences, cannot be overemphasized. For many, this desacralization has proceeded too far, leading to a rejection of desacralization and a return to mysticism. Yet, despite its highly controversial beginnings and the stature of the original opposition to sociobiology, the paradigm has become basic to much research in primatology, including human behavior - focusing especially on mate selection, mating systems, fertility, parental investment, and competition for power, resources, and mates. The explanatory paradigm still has its critics, from without and within, but has been seen as increasingly useful both as a stimulant to research and an explanatory device in realms heretofore relatively ignored or inexplicable in more traditional social science and ecological frameworks.

Why should this expansion of the use of this paradigm occur, when it 'desacralizes' man as well as nature and interferes, in some ways, with his spiritual ascendancy? This is especially true when considering sociobiological approaches to ethics and morality, returning these to the realm of survival strategies or epiphenomena. With Ruse (1988:2), "It really does matter to the traditional problems of epistemology. . . and ethics. . . that we are modified monkeys, not the special creations of an all-loving God some six thousand years ago."

In *The Structure of Biological Theories* (1989), Paul Thompson describes the tendency for scientists to prefer a syntactic to a semantic conception of biological science. A syntactic conception is more akin to Michael Ruse's North American outlook, with a set of logical, deductively derived and empirically-based axioms and correspondence rules. A semantic conception is less satisfying for most: hierarchical, complex, with a number of different bodies of theory involved and an internally-consistent but non-empirically derived set of axioms for each body. In North America in general, biological scientists aim toward a more syntactic conception. Is it any wonder, then, that educated laymen find the complex set of theories, hierarchies, and feedback loops of an ecosystemic approach less satisfying than conceptions set forth in linear, more simply causal fashion? Complexity and indeterminacy are not the cornerstones of the atomistic, action-oriented approach to predicting events and their outcome.

By adopting a syntactic view based on certain aspects of a sociobiological paradigm - stressing competition for power, resources, and social status in relation to sexual selection and inclusive fitness - human systems of ethics and morality, as well as human emotions and behaviors, can be explained and predicted in a manner that is seemingly deterministic, straight forward, and empirically relevant. Hope, for instance, has been viewed by Tiger (1978) as a human quality with survival value. In *The Tangled Wing* biological anthropologist Melvin Konner discusses a Darwinian perspective on rage, lust, grief, and love. Many people, however, including college students, are upset by biological/evolutionary explanations of morality and ethics. While intrigued by the explanatory power of sociobiology in a domain normally relegated to ethical philosophers and religion, they feel this approach goes one step too far in mechanizing humans. As Ruse points out, "Turning now to ethics, for all its distinguished advocates, we find that the position which would base moral justification on the evolutionary process continues to find little favor - even with those generally disposed towards a biological approach to morality...." (1988:77).

While 'nature' may be governed by these materialistic laws - although not everyone would see nature, either, as a product of Darwinian evolutionary forces - 'man' is not. To place humans in the same paradigm as the apes and other creatures of nature is to threaten the dualistic dissociation of man and nature, to reduce the superiority of man by lowering him to a position among the beasts, and to threaten the notion of control man has over his own destiny, both on an individual and group level. What remains appealing about this paradigm, however, and accounts for its resilience and spread, is its simplicity and empirical reference, as well as the smoothness of fit with current ideas of selfishness and cheating as more conducive to individual survival and success than altruism and group effort.

In a world where science, philosophy, and economy are linked, theory structure and action are inseparable from one another and the total context of which they are a part. Should we desire a Kuhnian 'revolution' (Kuhn, 1970) to a more holistic, systemic theoretical conception, more than a scientific change is needed. A number of new scientific approaches, however, do attempt to introduce a more integrative viewpoint. Among these are Lovelock's *Gaia* (1979) and ecofeminism, repudiating a linear view with man as dominant. Additionally, chaos theory has clear implications for a syntactic conception because of the emergent properties of materials, resulting in physical behavior or events not predictable from the laws governing the operation of these materials under other conditions.

If we are, indeed, adaptive organisms competing for inclusive fitness by utilizing environmental resources in a better manner than our competitors, perhaps our ethics, morality, and conception of the world will change as we enter a new, different, and more threatening adaptive situation. The United States and the Soviet Union formed a joint Committee on Global Ecology Concerns in December, 1988. In the summer of 1989, twenty-two of the forty points resulting from the recent Economic Summit focused on the environment. Spring 1992 saw the Earth Summit in Brazil, with many participants and some tentative agreements. Yet, the current level of fear produced by the 'greenhouse' effect is insufficient to effect major changes in attitude and action, especially given the disagreement concerning the importance and immanence of this effect and its relationship to other climatic factors in the droughts and heat waves of recent years (as is evidenced by the continuing barrage of articles in *Science*). While environmental concerns have become better integrated in the rhetoric of modern politics on both the national and international level, what is needed is a better grasp of ecosystem complexity and functioning, requiring both greater knowledge and a holistic perspective. With a greater interpenetration of ecological and sociobiological theory, the limits of human adaptability may better be understood. For Thompson (1989:117), "What I have called the 'new' evolutionary epistemology differs from these analogical approaches in that it emphasizes that human knowledge is *literally* a product of Darwinian evolution: that is, human knowledge is a function, in important respects, of our biology. And, since our biology is a product of evolution, the nature of our knowledge must also be a product of evolution."

Ruse (1988:70) claims that, "Good science demands a holistic, hierarchical approach", and this requirement applies as much to human nature as it does to the fossil record. In our present economic circumstances, however, sensitivity to the needs of our environment and other creatures and reorientation of our conceptual framework are obscured by concerns for daily living. It is even more important now than ever to find ways to coexist in our earthly world, but the challenge of doing so is greater than ever.

# References

Boersma, P. D. (1988). "Global interconnections." *Women in Natural Resources*, 10(2):8-9, 12.

Cartmill, M. (1983). "'Four legs good, two legs bad': man's place (if any) in nature." *Natural History*, 97(11):65-79.

Cousteau, J. (1992). "Caring for the Future." *Calypso Log*, 19:3.

Dombrowski, D. A. (1988). *Hartshorne and the Metaphysics of Animals Rights*. Albany, N.Y., State University of New York Press.

Douglas, M. (1982). *In the Active Voice*. London, Routledge and Kegan Paul.

Ehrlich, P. R. and Ehrlich A. H. (1981). *The Causes and Consequences of the Disappearance of Species*. New York, Random House.

Gaylin, W. (1990). *Adam and Eve and Pinocchio: On Being and Becoming Human*. New York, Viking.

Hillinger, C. (1990). "Indian and animal worlds converge at the Navajo zoo." *The Los Angeles Times*, July 22, p. E4.

Hunn, E. S. (1977). *Tzeltal Folk Zoology: The Classification of Discontinuities in Nature*. New York, Academic Press.

Konner, M. (1983). *The Tangled Wing: Biological Constraints on the Human Spirit*. New York, Harper and Row.

Kuhn, T. S. (1970). *The Structure of Scientific Revolutions*. 2nd ed. Chicago, University of Chicago.

Leach, E. (1964) "Anthropological aspects of language: animals categories and verbal abuse." In E. H. Lenneberg (ed.). *New Directions in the Study of Language*. Cambridge, MIT Press, pp. 23-63.

Lopez, B. H. (1978). *Of Wolves and Men*. New York, Charles Scribner's Sons.

Lovelock, J. (1979). *Gaia: A New Look at Life on Earth*. New York, Oxford University Press.

Lumsden, C. and Wilson, E. O. (1981). *Genes, Mind, and Culture*. Cambridge, Mass, Harvard University.

Manes, C. (1990). *Green Rage: Radical Environmentalism and the Unmaking of Civilization*. Boston, Little, Brown and Company.

Matthiessen, P. (1988). "Our national parks: the case for burning." *The New York Times Magazine*, December 11, Sec. 6.

Merchant, C. (1983). *Death of Nature: Women, Ecology, and the Scientific Revolution*. New York, Harper and Row.

Midgley, M. (1978). *Beast and Man: The Roots of Human Nature*. New York, Meridian.

Mowat, F. (1985). *Never Cry Wolf*. Toronto, Seal Books.

Nelson, R. K. (1983). *Make Prayers to the Raven: A Koyukon View of the Northern Forest*. Chicago/London, University of Chicago.

Page, J. (1989). "Toward a new window on Smithsonian's world." *Smithsonian*, 20(1):26-35.

Passmore, J. (1980). *Man's Responsibility for Nature*. 2nd ed. London, Duckworth.

Pavlik, B. (1992). "Oaks of California. Presentation on his book of the same name." *Southwest Museum*, July 26.

Reif, W. E. (1983). "Evolutionary theory in German paleontology." In M. Greene (ed.). *Dimensions of Darwinism*. Cambridge, Cambridge University Press, pp. 173-204.

Riedl, R. (1983). "The role of morphology in the theory of evolution. "In M. Greene (ed.). *Dimensions of Darwinism*. Cambridge, Cambridge University Press, pp. 205-238.

Rifkin, J. (1984). *Algeny: A New Word - A New World*. New York, Penguin.

Roderick, K. (1989). "Roughing it less: call of wild fades for babyboom." *Los Angeles Times*, May 31, pp. 1, 17.

Ruse, M. (1988). *Philosophy of Biology Today*. Albany, N.Y., State University of New York.

Taylor, Paul W. (1986). *Respect for Nature: A Theory of Environmental Ethics*. Princeton, N.J., Princeton University.

Thompson, P. (1989). *The Structure of Biological Theories*. Albany, N.Y., State University of New York.

Tiger, L. (1978). *Optimism: The Biology of Hope*. New York, Simon and Schuster.

Urton, G. (1985). *Animal Myths and Metaphors in South America*. Salt Lake City, University of Utah Press.

Wilson, E. O. (1984). *Biophilia: The Human Bond to Other Species*. Cambridge, Mass., Harvard University Press.

# THE BELLONESE ATTITUDE TOWARD NATURE

Rolf Kuschel

> HE SAW A FINE GEOMETRICAL STRUCTURE,
> ORDER MASQUERADING AS RANDOMNESS.
> (JAMES GLEICK, 1988:22)

## I. Introduction

A prerequisite in understanding one's world, or even part of it, is the ability to combine and differentiate among the almost indefinite number of sensorial stimuli in one's surroundings. To discern between what in a specific historic period and situation is significant and what is not, is the beginning of creating order out of chaos. The way we in our minds cut up and classify the world and combine and intertwine these entities varies from culture to culture, from subculture to subculture and changes to a certain extent over time. The way in which a society has compartmentalized the world, influences its organization as well as it forms the building blocks on the basis of which the individual behaves and understands his world. In order to understand another culture and its members one should start uncovering these categories and unravel the way in which they are mutually intertwined.[1]

The study of a totally foreign culture can, in its initial phase, remind one of putting together a jigsaw puzzle with an unknown number of pieces. What in the beginning looks like a seemingly well-defined Gestalt can later prove to be part of a much more complicated whole. Something which at a certain point is perceived as a figure can, just as we know from studies in the psychology of perception, suddenly appear as 'ground' (Rubin, 1921).

One of the difficulties facing any professional observer of an unknown society is how to develop an ability to effectively push aside the culture visor through which he normally sees his world, in order to perceive and

---

[1] For a discussion of problem solving as an adaptive strategy among living beings and its relation to play behavior see Petersen (1988). For an anthropological discussion of man's search for giving a 'shapeless or undifferentiated world' a stable form, see Radin (1957:248ff).

understand the world as the people he is studying do. This step of going from a kind of aspect-blindness to becoming aspect sighted, to use Wittgentein's (1968:213-214) terminology, can probably never be fully realized. Such an attempt can rarely be more than a qualified asymptotic approach.

## II. Physical environment

In the present paper I shall deal with the pre-contact attitude toward nature on Bellona Island, a Polynesian Outlier in the Solomon Islands of only 22 square kilometers whose population before 1938 when Christianity was introduced, probably never exceeded 500 - 600 individuals at a time. What makes Bellona an interesting object of study apart from its small size and population, is its long period of isolation. Before the introduction of Christianity in 1938, contacts with the outside world were scarce, both in terms of interaction with other South Sea Islanders and with Europeans and Americans. Ships which called on the island before 1938 only stayed for a few hours or days and their visits did not have any measurable impact on the islanders' traditions or patterns of behavior (Kuschel, 1988c).

Before we enter into a discussion of the Bellonese attitude toward nature let me say a few words about 'the Bellonese' as term. When we speak of 'the Bellonese' attitude toward nature, it sounds as if everybody on the island shared the world view we are about to describe. This is not the case. Though there were no formal restrictions concerning the sharing of knowledge, great differences appeared. Women had very little knowledge about religious matters as did children and neither of them were allowed to participate in temple rituals. Many men lacked depth, solidity and comprehensiveness in their understanding of the surrounding world. They were either not interested or did not have the ability to grasp the intrinsic complexities of the topic.[2] Those who were the real carriers of knowledge, especially the religious wisdom, were the religious leaders, the priest-chiefs. So, when we talk about the Bellonese attitude toward nature, we refer to

---

[2] For a discussion of the distribution of the sociology of knowledge in non-industrialized societies see Keesing (1987).

those men who were the carriers and inventors of the sociology of knowledge.

On sailing toward the island, the ellipse-shaped, uplifted atoll of Bellona looks almost like a large turtle that has risen to the surface of the sea. The steep and densely overgrown limestone cliffs that rim the island are in some places up to 60 meters high. However, seen from inside the island where the two parallel cliff formations along the coast can be seen, the island is suggestive of the hull of a canoe. Though the Bellonese lived on a coral atoll with cultivable soil having a 'carrying capacity' almost twice as large as the size of the population (Christiansen, 1975), and though they were surrounded by the Coral Sea supplying them with an abundance of fish, life was not always easy. They were surrounded by strong forces including:

- Atmospheric turbulence creating cyclones, spreading death and destruction in their dwellings and gardens.
- Sudden gales arising, beating the waters and forcing canoes and their crews into a tarantella.
- Changes in water temperature keeping the fish away from the fishermen's hooks and nets.
- Inexplicable diseases, throwing the population into a state of wild alarm.

Such phenomena represented what Gleick (1988:3) has termed, "the irregular side of nature." They appeared a-periodically, and were thus unpredictable. Such situations created feelings of distress and helplessness.

In addition to such natural events other phenomena also called for explanations like the origins of islands, celestial bodies, trees, plants, fish, birth and death, as well as the origin of particular parts of the human body. On the social level answers were sought to the provenance of certain human values, deviant behavior, etcetera.

How then did the Bellonese attack these 'grand questions', and what kind of cognitive architecture did they develop in answer to these issues? As in many other societies, religion seems to form the cognitive frame of reference for an understanding and a partial protection against the various unknown forces which influence the lives and activities of human beings.

## III. Religion

The Bellonese themselves made a clear semantic distinction between human beings and supernaturals, a conceptual distinction to be employed in the following. In the traditional religion, there were seven different categories of supernaturals: culture heroes, the island's aboriginal population called *hiti*, sky gods, district deities, unworshipped gods, worshipped ancestors, and unworshipped ancestors. An active and lively interaction existed between humans and the supernatural world. Humans could communicate by way of ritual offerings and prayers with the sky gods, the district deities and the worshipped ancestors. The gods were regarded as "anthropomorphic, anthroposocial and anthropopsychic" (Monberg, 1966:36), thus enabling human beings to communicate and socially and psychologically cope with them.[3] Due to the very sacredness of the sky gods man usually, but not always, directed his requests to this group of supernaturals through his ancestors. None of the other supernaturals were the object of rituals - besides some minor ones to please the aboriginal inhabitants, the *hiti*. The success of a worshipper's approach to the heavenly abode would show in his prosperity, fertility and protection against major diseases, homicides and major catastrophes.

If people fulfilled their duties toward the gods by performing rituals, making offerings and, on the whole, by not breaking too many taboos, in return they expected success in their diverse activities. In some cases an unpleased god would let his viewpoint be known to the Bellonese through a medium. If the gods and ancestors lived up to man's expectations, rituals were performed and songs were composed in their honor something the gods valued highly. Likewise, if the gods did not comply with the wishes of their worshippers in a satisfactory way, they were made the objects of verbal attacks in which the people proclaimed their dissatisfaction. One of my informants, a respected leader of rituals, once scolded one of the gods for

---

[3] Santangelo (1989) believes that man ascribes anthropomorphic features to gods, because man spontaneously could conceive of it.

being weak and unimportant, because the god had not provided him with a son. He even stopped performing rituals to this god for a time and only resumed after urgent requests from his kinsmen. In another case a man humiliated his god by flinging a terrifying curse at him, "Shit! Lie with your ancestor!" (*Poi! Ta'o ou sa'amaatu'a!*). An example of a god being rejected forever can be found in Elbert and Monberg (1965:T 155), where a man became so outraged by the conduct of a goddess that he began to worship her brother instead. Ancestors were also dependent upon their worshippers. In case they proved to be too weak to fulfill the wishes of their worshippers, they would fall into oblivion among their equals.

Communication between the sacred and the profane world took place during shorter or longer rituals and food offerings presented by ritual leaders (see Monberg, 1991). An important link in the interaction between the world of gods and mortals were the ancestors. At death the 'spiritual selves' (souls) were believed to travel to the heavenly abodes where they were welcomed by the gods. But they did not stay permanently with the gods. They traveled between the homesteads of the gods and their graves on Bellona, acting as messengers between gods and mortals. "In rituals", says Monberg (1966:98) "they were asked to convey to the gods the wishes of living man for health, fertility, and good fortune." The religion of the Bellonese was marked by a lively interaction between the secular and the sacred world, where people, worshipped ancestors, and gods were mutually - though asymmetrically - dependent on each other. Though human beings were unable to control their gods, they were at liberty to protest and even revolt against them in situations they felt humiliating.

*Creation of the world*

To the Bellonese their own island had been in existence from time immemorial. According to local oral tradition, the island was formed when a Nerita shell, covered with soil and inhabited by animals, rose out of the sea. Later the Polynesian arrowroot started growing on the island, but there was not enough room for it, as the sky stretched low and heavy across the island. Then, two culture heroes stepped in. The first one, Tangangoa, lifted the sky on to his head and pushed it up on his arms. He stood on tiptoe to push the sky even further, but that did not suffice. The other culture hero, push the sky even further, but that did not suffice. The other culture hero, Tongangengeba, was taller, and he came to the rescue. He stood on tiptoe and lifted the sky by stretching his arms above his head, but he needed a priest-chief's sacred staff to push the sky sufficiently high to provide enough air and light for the plants (Elbert and Monberg, 1965:T 10).

The neighboring Rennell Island, situated 22,5 km south-east of Bellona, was also created by a culture hero, Mautikitiki. According to the oral traditions Mautikitiki and his two younger brothers went fishing and got an island on their hook. They pulled it up and it became Mungaba, or Rennell Island (Kuschel, 1975:A 8). Though the Bellonese were knowledgeable about other islands in the Pacific, including their supposed homelands 'Ubeangango and 'Ubeamatangi, probably Ouvea in the Loyalty Islands and 'Uvea or Wallis Islands, the stories about Bellona and Rennell are the only two tales in the traditional folklore concerned with the creation of land. Nobody knows when Bellona and Rennell Island originated. When the Bellonese and Rennellese arrived on the scene, their islands had already been there for a long time and were inhabited by a people called the *hiti*.

Bellona and Rennell were the center of the world to the indigenous people. It was surrounded by the firmament in which were the stars. The Bellonese believed the stars were fixed in the sky, some of them being former culture heroes (Elbert and Monberg, 1965:T 62). The natives found their bearings for planting, fishing, and sailing in the stars. It is uncertain whether other celestial bodies like the sun and the moon also were former culture heroes, but since - according to oral tradition - they cheated each other while climbing up a hibiscus tree, one finally reaching the sky and the other falling down into the sea, one would assume they once were regarded as having been culture heroes.

Unlike other Polynesian societies the Bellonese had no oral tradition about the origin of animals. A few stories concern the transformation of land animals into sea creatures: a snake turned into a black and white banded sea snake; the skipjack and the green turtle, which originally were believed to be land animals, changed their habitat and lived in the ocean (Kuschel, 1975). In all cases the transfers of habitat is from land to sea, it never goes in the opposite direction.

A greater variety exists about the etiology of certain animals' specific behavior, their colors, and their taste. Species specific behavior is mostly related to the interference of culture heroes. The flounder is said to be flat with many bones because Mautikitiki and the flounder had a fight during which the culture hero stamped on the fish and threw his bundle of spears into its body. Other etiological stories explain why the hermit crab carries its turban shell all the time, why the needlefish skips along the surface, why the fruit bat flits to and fro, why the marsh crab has a furrow in the center of its carapace, and why the skink approaches instead of trying to escape fire. In a very few cases gods were made responsible for a characteristic behavior as when a god embodied himself in the small swiftlet. He was too heavy for the small bird and that is why the bird flutters around (Kuschel, 1975).

Culture heroes are also made responsible for the conspicuous colors of birds, like the reddish breast of the fruit dove, the different colored feathers of the graybird and the song parrot, the red color of the honey eater, the black feathers on the tufted back of the white ibis, just to mention a few examples. The bitter taste of a few fish like the parrot fish, the rock cod and the sea perch, is ascribed to the eating of a very poisonous mythical fish. Special attention is given the bad smell and taste of the shark: The culture hero Mautikitiki urinated on it (Kuschel, 1975:A 3).

Comparing Christiansen's list of important animals on Bellona (Christiansen, 1975:Appendix B-4), and Wolff's list of birds (Wolff, 1973) with the oral tradition on animal characteristics (Kuschel, 1975:Table 3) only a small part of the local fauna seems to have been a topic for explanation. The discrepancy is even more noticeable in the area of local flora. The general idea that people always try to account for the traits which are most conspicuous or different does not hold for the Bellonese. In their tradition certain, but far from all traits, are accounted for. No stories for example exist to explain the anatomy of the hammerhead shark, the ray, or the voraciousness of the sea perch, nor do the Bellonese have any oral traditions explaining why the lizard sheds its tail or the flying fox soars in the sky at night. A reason could be that these etiological tales have been forgotten. However, another more culturally relevant reason may be that the Bellonese - unlike Westerners - feel no need to explain everything. They are content with the notion, that humans are ignorant about a series of matters.

*The appearance of human beings*

The Bellonese have no tales about the creation of man, nor do they seem to miss it. They even appear surprised when asked for any such tales. Their knowledge about the human body, its functioning and malfunctioning is equally pale. Besides being the architects of certain parts of the universe the culture heroes left a few marks on human beings, like man's flexible joints, or the creation of the vagina and clitoris. The origin of death and the emergence of certain forms of behavior such as the killing of agnates and close relatives were also invented by the culture heroes (for details see Elbert and Monberg, 1965:chapter 5).

It thus appears that a systematic understanding of the origin of the universe and the creation of humankind held little interest for the native population. Whatever was explained was the result of the intervention of culture heroes, beyond reach of memory. Neither the sky gods nor the district deities were involved in the creational process of the universe and humans. This probably has to do with the Bellonese emigration. When they arrived at their new home after a long and dangerous sea journey, they found an entire island full of trees, plants, vines, fish, birds, and other animals. The arriving gods thus had no need to bother about creation.

### IV. Major natural events

Major natural events, like conspicuous natural phenomena and disasters, mental diseases, and exceptionally cruel actions were attributed to the sky gods, controllers and benefactors of nature. Since the sky gods were related to nature, offerings to them consisted of raw, uncooked food. They were in possession of great sacred strength (*tapu*), were violent by nature and sometimes unpredictable even toward their own worshippers whom they would kill out of jealousy (Kuschel, 1988b:R 40). Any contact with the power of the sky gods, whatever the reason, was fatal if it did not occur through the established formal channels, the rites. But they were not just cruel and truculent, they were also believed to be benevolent. The sky gods cruel and truculent, they were also believed to be benevolent. The sky gods provided the Bellonese with garden products, large fish catches, and guests in castaway canoes from overseas.

Cyclones and gales were the most severe natural catastrophes for which the sky gods were made liable. The island was afflicted by cyclones approximately every seven to eight years. Most of these caused only minor damages with temporary food shortages, but in a few extreme cases, as when the cyclone named after the priest-chief 'Oso'eha ravaged the island in 1911, the situation immediately after was catastrophic. Christiansen (1981:4) writes about the strength and devastation of this storm, "The extremely high winds lasted for a whole night and reached unbelievable force. No trees were left standing, and no houses. Severe droughts prevailed for 2-3 years after the catastrophe. One had an unobscured sight from the one end of the former heavily wooded island to the other, and a lot of people had to sail to neighboring Rennell to survive." For the first six months after the cyclone the nutritional situation was so severe that several people died. Most of them were older people. People with access to the beach collected mollusks, whereas others literally stripped the bush for anything edible. Such cyclones have been recorded both earlier and later than the one described by Christiansen. The Bellonese had no explanation as to why the sky god would send such cyclones. Earth-quakes were also said to be caused by the sky god Tehainga'atua, who ordered one of the minor gods to make the island tremble from the underworld by shaking the aerial roots of a banyan tree (Elbert and Monberg, 1965:T 21; Kuschel 1988b:R 22). According to oral tradition, the earthquakes hardly ever got enough strength and duration to demolish the island, because a famous district deity, the protector of homesteads, intervened and broke the minor god's arms.

Most conspicuous natural phenomena were attributed to the sky gods, such as thunderstorms, considered to be the sign of gods approaching the island, and a firmament clothed in scarlet as a sign of the coming death of an important man. The endless killings which have marred the island for generations, as well as any horrendous and exceptional accident taking place during an attack, were also related to the sky gods. Before an attack a raiding group performed special rituals (*kuba*), in which they requested that the sky gods weaken the victim and reduce his suspiciousness, enabling them to come within close range and kill him. As one of the last rituals before the attack, the raiders dedicated their weapons to the sky gods. In this ritual, the gods were requested to 'enter' the weapon and aim a lethal blow at the chosen victim. Without the assistance of the sky gods any attack would be unsuccessful. The Bellonese had no clear-cut conception of how their allies from the sacred world 'entered' the weapons, and it appears that they have never occupied their minds with what seems to them a trivial problem.

If unusual and, for society, horrendous behavior was displayed during an attack, for example like the killing of a brother-in-law (Kuschel, 1988b:R 145), signs were sought as an indication that the person had been temporarily possessed by a sky god. When a man during an attack gouged out his enemy's eyes from their sockets it was said that one of the sky gods had been on a killing spree and, arriving on Bellona, had heard the attacker call for assistance. Immediately, the god threw down his own weapons, took the attacker's hands and buried them deep in the victim's eye sockets. One by one, the attacker could then rip out the victim's eyes with his bare hands and throw them on the ground (Kuschel, 1988b:R 106).

Physical deviance like getting twins, having a club foot, or goiter, as well as aberrant appearances like being troubled with many abscesses, small breasts, having red or thin hair, no beard, and other such characteristics were believed to be the results of taboo breaches committed by the mother during pregnancy. Her children then had to suffer from her earlier behavior due to the punishment from the sky god. Human beings who for a lengthy period of time exhibited deviant behavior (Kuschel, 1988b:R 79), like a women shouting invectives at her brother toward whom she was supposed to show decorum in her behavior, were believed to be possessed by one of the sky gods. The same explanation was given for people running around naked or roaming about with their clubs, spears, machete or axes threatening to kill somebody. The usual treatment of mentally sick people was to place them inside a huge wooden fence, ignite a fire outside the wooden posts, while hoping to scare off the gods so that they would leave the diseased. Sometimes, such a treatment could go on for several weeks.

Whatever went right or wrong in the ecological sphere of nature, the sky gods were made accountable. They represented everything contrary to social order, they were married to their own sisters, reversed the social status of gender (the goddess being more ferocious and powerful), ate raw food, and roamed about noisily. The sky gods represented the 'powers controlling the forces of nature' and were thus made responsible for the larger, unpredictable, a-periodical natural events as well as extraordinarily hideous and terrifying human behavior.

## V. Minor casualties

Injuries, minor casualties and misadventures like falling from trees, tripping over a stone, loosing one's canoe, even plant diseases were not just something which happened by sheer accident, it needed an explanation. If no other reason could be encountered the Bellonese held unworshipped gods called *'apai* responsible. They lived mainly in the impenetrable virgin forest, at the coast, or in graves and in contrast to ancestors could not be worshipped. They were the essence of evil and were made responsible for everything which could not rationally be attributed to the anger or displeasure of the worshipped gods or ancestors. From a Western point of view the *'apai* were made the scapegoats for minor casualties that could not otherwise be explained.

## VI. Annoyances in everyday life

The many annoyances and inexplicable events which life is so full of needed an explanation. Especially bad luck in hunting coconut crabs or flying foxes and ill-luck in fishing was supposedly caused by the original inhabitants of the island, the *hiti*. *Hiti* is the name of a historical-mythical population said to have inhabited the island before the Bellonese arrived. In addition to creating irritation the *hiti* were said to have taught the first immigrants how to catch flying fish, to climb with climbers, and how to eat certain roots and fruits. When met by human beings the *hiti* turned into stones. One way of succeeding in fishing and hunting was to outsmart the *hiti* by performing small rituals at the stones believed to be the embodiment of a *hiti*, or to place a puzzle made out of interlaced leaves on the path leading to the fishing ground or hunting place. The *hiti*, who were believed to be very curious, would then spend a lot of time with the puzzle, trying to separate the leaves instead of bothering the hunter or fisherman (see Kuschel, 1988a:Fig. 13).

## VII. Procreation

For many societies the process of procreation has been a puzzle which needed a rational explanation. Where do children come from and how are they implanted in women. In a society like the Bellonese, with no mammals except for whales, bats, flying foxes and the Pacific rat, and no pets which could have provided them with some clues to the relationship between intercourse and pregnancy, this was a serious problem. They nevertheless developed an ingenious idea which could explain not only how children were born within a marriage, but also why some unmarried women got pregnant and why some couples were barren. According to the traditional belief the 'spiritual selves' of unborn children were kept in a store house belonging to the district deity. A man who wanted a child asked his ancestor to intercede with the district deity for the latter to grant offspring to his worshipper. If the wish was granted, the district deity gave a child or two to the ancestor who then planted it in the womb of the woman. The specifics of the 'planting' process were of no interest to the Bellonese. A district god who was very pleased with his worshipper would sometimes also impregnate the worshipper's daughter. Barrenness, on the other hand, was explained as the result of a district god's displeasure with his worshipper's offerings or behavior. Another explanation was that an enemy of the worshipper had performed a ritual to the district deity asking him not to provide the former with a child. In such situations the district deity was confused since one of his worshippers asked for a child while another asked him not to fulfill the wish. A district deity caught in such a dilemma was described as turning his head from one side to the other (*hekeukeu'aki*), unable to make a decision. Since the Bellonese had no idea about the relationship between sexual intercourse and pregnancy (Monberg, 1975), the procreation process was solely explained with reference to the decision of the district gods.

## VIII. Protection against natural forces

Living in a world of total instability is inhuman. Humans cannot live in a world while being totally subjugated to uncontrollable forces. Some cognitive means of control must be created, and the Bellonese consequently incorporated in their religious system a group of supernaturals who could protect them against the forces of nature. These were the district deities, descendants of the sky gods. They were called district deities because each clan and subclan, living in specific areas of the island, had their own district god. An interesting correspondence between the number of district gods and the Bellonese level of strain has been noted. According to local tradition, during the 15th and 16th generation, a dramatic increase in conflicts and homicides appeared. At the same time the different agnatic groups on Bellona supplemented and annexed more and more district gods. With an increasing escalation of hostilities among the different groups, earlier group coherence deteriorated and thus created the need for more protection. This is a beautiful example of what Monberg (1966:73) has called "a correlation between the changing world of the district gods and the changes taking place within the social system."

The district gods protected the homes and families of their worshippers. They protected a settlement and its inhabitants against attacks, and their worshippers from diseases, misfortunes, and the failure of crops. A man of importance who always kept his part of the interaction with the heavenly abode, i.e. performed his rituals and presented plenty of food in his rituals, expected to be well protected by his district deity.

In addition to the district deities, ancestors were also important in protecting the settlement and its inhabitants. But in contrast to the district gods, the ancestors' interests were highly connected with their agnatic kin in order to ensure the continual existence of the lineage. If the protection failed for some unknown reason or because of a breach of a taboo, extraordinary offerings and rituals were believed to appease the deity or the ancestor. In more severe cases, as when a man was not blessed with children or only had daughters (who were less appreciated than sons), he stopped his offerings to the deity deemed responsible for his misfortune and threatened to exchange him with a more powerful one. If, on the other hand, an ancestor did not fulfill his duties, he would immediately be deprived of further offerings and another more powerful ancestor would be approached instead. Such a replacement could have fatal consequences for the deposed ancestor, because without offerings, he fell into disgrace in the heavenly abode and was literally 'wiped out'. His 'life principle' was crushed on a stone in the underworld and erased. Thus both parties, the ancestors and his kin, were mutually dependent on each other.

Curiously enough, there was one serious exception to the Bellonese expectation for protection of the settlement and its inhabitants. If a homestead was attacked and its male members killed by enemies, the Bellonese did not blame or make the district deity responsible for neglecting his duty, in spite of the fact that they were believed to protect the homestead. The Bellonese themselves had no plausible explanation of such failure on behalf of a district deity.

### IX. Features of Bellonese world view

What then characterized the Bellonese attitude toward nature? First of all it seems that not everything needed an explanation, and that the principle of continuation was momentous. The Bellonese, like some other small-scale tribal societies as the Eskimo (see Hoebel, 1974:69), did not try to explain all the mysteries of nature. "Every plant or star need not be named, not every god needed a father and a mother. Some aspects of life and culture, the circulation of blood, the nature of gravity, or grammar, did not need any explanation at all", as Monberg (1966:118) phrased it. The Bellonese explanation of the creation of the Universe, and the creation of human beings, were fragmentary and lacked coherence. Even vital questions like why district gods did not protect their worshippers in a more effective way during attacks, did not occupy their minds. Thus many aspects of life were left unexplained. Whether this lack of interest was part of their ancient traditional world view or whether some knowledge was lost in earlier generations, cannot be ascertained today. However, the lack of completeness of certain parts of their orientation toward nature, did not disturb the Bellonese as much as it bothered the researcher. Sometimes the Bellonese thought my search for coherence and the lengthy questioning connected with it was more than irksome. A not unusual comment to my endless questioning of what to me seemed important questions, were brushed aside with the counter-question, "Who knows?"

As stated earlier, the creation of the world did not have any great significance in Bellonese cognition. What mattered was the continuation from the past via the present to the future. Continuity in life was not merely related to the individual but was important to the whole lineage and clan. The mortals of the present had to ensure that the persistence of their agnatic kinsmen would continue in the future. If the patrilineage, subclan or clan was annihilated, the result would be catastrophic, because in the world of light, nobody would be left to relate the deeds of this agnatic group. Likewise nobody could make offerings to and worship the ancestors who in the underworld would be forgotten and finally 'wiped out'. This ever present occupation with continuity appears for example in the Bellonese classification of homicides where distinctions were made between gradual extermination and substantial extermination (Kuschel, 1988a:Fig.39). The principle of continuity is perpetuated by oral tradition. Attitudes toward nature are confirmed and reinforced by consulting the ancient tales.

It seems as if Bellonese society in general was fairly conservative. Major deviances from and changes of the accepted values did not occur. On the other hand the Bellonese society accepted a certain degree of individualism, leaving room for private opinions and interpretations of behavioral norms. The Bellonese had great respect and veneration for the knowledge inherited from their forefathers and thus were reluctant to make major changes in their beliefs about the forces of nature. However, not all men did totally surrender themselves to the supernaturals controlling the world. Some of the more powerful men experienced a form of individual freedom to challenge some of these forces if they worked contrary to their own interest. There are several examples where mortal men purposely violated religious or social taboos, cursed the gods, or even abandoned them, i.e. stopped presenting offerings to them. These actions, as dangerous as they might be to human beings, nevertheless clearly show the great emphasis placed by the Bellonese on individual freedom. The Bellonese' power to create, his demand for fairness, and his defense of honor are strong forces working against the so-called principle of immutability.

Raymond Firth formulated this principle in an excellent way. "Every human society," he said, "seems to be at once unified by the centripetal force of the common interests of its members and riven by the centrifugal force of their individual and sectional interests" (Firth, 1970:108).

The question is, however, how much deviation from the basic beliefs a society can and will tolerate. For a man's actions may not only be dangerous to himself but may endanger his whole family, lineage or clan, and sometimes even jeopardize the whole society. No examples have been collected where a transgression of a severe religious taboo has been punished by the islanders. Wisely, they left the castigation to the gods.

## X. Conclusion

In the present chapter I have tried to unravel the Bellonese society's attitude toward nature comprehended as the cognitive map which they developed in order to find meaning in their world, and in the light of which they interacted with their surroundings. The explicit hypothesis was that people need to create order and secure coherence in a seemingly chaotic world, i.e. to transform randomness into patterns of assumed stability. In summary we can say that by developing a system of supernaturals, each being responsible for certain events, the Bellonese had created a frame of reference for understanding and coping with the apparent instabilities of nature. Through religion they created a coherence in their universe. Furthermore, by developing a structure in which supernaturals and mortals were enmeshed in mutually dependent economic transactions (supernaturals were dependent upon offerings and rituals in order to keep their status in the heavenly abodes, and human beings were dependent on the gods' and deities' favorable considerations for their survival) the Bellonese had developed a bilateral - though asymmetrical - strategy of interaction with the controllers of life and death.

Where many scientists in the Western world have searched to find the secrets of Nature by way of hypothesizing the existence of so-called 'laws of nature', the Bellonese in their quest for understanding their environment developed a frame of reference, religion, in order to grasp the workings of the universe. As long as their belief was workable, it did not invite major revisions. Like Western scientists, or even more than these, they realized the existence of instabilities. But instead of regarding them as monstrosities the Bellonese acquired a tolerance toward 'the irregular side of nature', because they did not need to understand everything in detail.

As noted earlier, the understanding of nature was not the same for men and women, old and young. There were few men, the priest-chiefs, who were the carrier of the deeper knowledge of the ultimate meaning of reality. They were the experts and sometimes important mediums, too. Since knowledge "is a key to power as well as to meaning," as Keesing says (1987), "those who command knowledge use it to control as well as to communicate." It is not surprising then, that the priest-chiefs, who also were high-status men, were the most influential in maintaining, explaining and changing the world. Through intuition - or as the Bellonese would say through the divine messages received while in trance - they had the key to suggest changes in behavior and belief.

Though religion was crucial in the explanation of the force of nature, religion was also the ultimate source for understanding the social reality of life. It was through religion women were excluded from major rituals. They were not thought to be suitable to interact with the religious world, because the gods, it was said, would feel nauseated if a woman tried to address them (Kuschel, 1992). Women were thus regarded as inferior to men. They could not own land, and in the practice of avoidance behavior, it was their duty to keep out of a man's, and especially a brother's way. Thus, all religious, economic, and social decisions were reached by men who had more status and power than women. Religion, then, provided the foundation which consigned women to obey men and restrained them from participating in the ritual and political activities. Beside being explanatory of nature, religion regarded as 'cosmically ordained', also legitimated the schism between the sexes, between the powerful and the powerless. Since the structure of the Bellonese world view was created many centuries ago, we do not know who the human entrepreneurs were but their gender, nonetheless, seems incontestable.

# References

Christiansen, S. (1975). *Subsistence on Bellona Island (Mungiki). A Study of the Cultural Ecology of a Polynesian Outlier in the British Solomon Islands Protectorate.* Copenhagen, C.A. Reitzels Forlag.

Christiansen, S. (1981). "Subsistence System under Stress. Effects of the Hurricane 'Kerry' on Bellona Island (Mungiki), Solomon Islands." Copenhagen, (mimeographed).

Elbert, S.H., and Monberg, T. (1965). *From the Two Canoes. Oral Traditions of Rennell and Bellona Islands.* Language and Culture of Rennell and Bellona Islands, Vol. 1. Honolulu and Copenhagen, The Danish National Museum in Cooperation with the University of Hawaii Press.

Firth, R. (1970). *Human Types.* London, Sphere Books Ltd.

Gleick, J. (1988). *Chaos. Making a New Science.* London, Cardinal.

Hoebel, E.A. ([1954] 1974). *The Law of Primitive Man. A Study in Comparative Legal Dynamics.* New York, Atheneum.

Keesing, R. (1987). "Anthropology as Interpretive Quest." *Current Anthropology,* Vol. 28(2):161-169.

Kuschel, R. (1975). *Animal Stories from Bellona Island (Mungiki).* Language and Culture of Rennell and Bellona Islands, Vol. IV. Copenhagen, The National Museum of Denmark.

Kuschel, R. (1988a). *Vengeance is Their Reply: Blood Feuds and Homicides on Bellona Island.* Part 1: Conditions Underlying Generations of Bloodshed. Language and Culture of Rennell and Bellona Islands, Vol. VII. Copenhagen, Dansk psykologisk Forlag.

Kuschel, R. (1988b). *Vengeance is Their Reply: Blood Feuds and Homicides on Bellona Island.* Part 2: Oral Traditions. Language and Culture of Rennell and Bellona Islands, Vol. VII. Copenhagen, Dansk psykologisk Forlag.

Kuschel, R. (1988c). "A Historical Note on the Early Contacts with the Outside World of Bellona and Rennell Islands (Solomon Islands)", *The Journal of Pacific History,* 23(2):191-200.

Kuschel, R. (1992) "'Women are Women and Men are Men': How Bellonese Women Get Even." In Bjørkvist, K. et al. (eds.) *Mice and Women.* Festschrift for Kersti Lagerspetz. San Diego, Academic Press.

Monberg, T. (1966). *The Religion of Bellona Island. A Study of the Place of Beliefs and Rites in the Social Life of Pre-Christian Bellona.* Part 1: The Concepts of Supernaturals. Language and Culture of Rennell and Bellona Islands, Vol. 2, Part 1. Copenhagen, The Danish National Museum Press.

Monberg, T. (1975). "Fathers were not Genitors." *Man,* 84(2):218-224.

Monberg, T. (1991). *Bellona Beliefs and Ritual Practices.* Honolulu, University of Hawaii Press.

Petersen, A.F. (1988). *Why Children and Young Animals Play. A New Theory of Play and Its Role in Problem Solving.* Historisk-filosofiske Meddelelser 54. Copenhagen, Munksgaard.

Radin, P. ([1927] 1957). *Primitive Man as Philosopher.* New York, Dover Publication.

Rubin, E. (1921). *Visuell Wahrgenommene Figuren.* København, Gyldendals Boghandel.

Santangelo, A. (1989). "Culture as 'a world of meanings'." In Antonio Santangelo. *L'Uomo: eredità e promozione culturale*. Milano, La Pietra.

Wittgenstein, L. (1968). *Philosophische Untersuchungen*. Oxford, Basil Blackwell.

Wolff, T. (ed. 1973). "Notes on Birds from Rennell and Bellona Islands." In T. Wolff (ed.) *The Natural History of Rennell Island, British Solomon Islands. Scientific Results of the Noona Dan Expedition (Rennell Section, 1962) and The Danish Rennell Expedition 1965*. Copenhagen, Danish Science Press, Vol. 7.

# THE DESERT, THE WILD, AND CIVILIZATION
- AS SEEN BY THE KEL EWEY

Gerd Spittler

## I. Introduction

The development of mankind, from savage to barbarian to civilized human being, was the central theme of evolutionary ethnology in the 19th century. The number of stages could vary, as could the criteria used to define the individual phases. But one thing remained constant: development was not simply a change but an upward progression, and the highest level was European society in the 19th century. Ethnologists of this century have challenged this view of evolution, but have had little impact on every-day opinion. The following definition is taken from Grimms' dictionary, which continued to uphold 19th century tradition even in 1956: civilization means, "in today's language the sum total of material and socio-ethical values, the possession of which raise the way of life of the civilized world ('Kulturvölker') above the level of barbarity" (Grimm, 1956, XV:1730).

In this chapter I am concerned neither with the propagation of this evolutionary perspective, nor with an ideological discussion of it, but rather with the more productive ethnological question of how 'the savages' themselves view this division. I shall start from the premise that, although this division between the wild and civilization is recognized and accepted by them, the so-called savages regularly perceive themselves as belonging to civilization.

I do not here intend to offer a world-wide overview of this topic; my goal is much more modest. I shall investigate how one society, the Kel Ewey Tuareg in Niger, perceive the desert, the wild and civilization. Nomads are the barbarians par excellence in the evolutionary tradition. It could therefore be of particular interest to investigate how a nomadic society views the boundary between the wild and civilization. In the case of the Kel Ewey, they are not completely, but semi-nomadic. They are nomads in so far as they keep herds of camels and goats and travel great distances in caravans from the Aïr mountains in the southern central Sahara to Nigeria. But most of them still have a fixed abode in one of the Aïr oases - the most important is Timia - where they grow grain and vegetables or at least own a few date palms.

The first Europeans to meet the Kel Ewey were the travellers Richardson, Barth, and Overweg in 1850. Henry Barth gives us a detailed and interesting portrayal, which, although it relies heavily on the evolutionary thinking of the 19th century, also strikes a note which is critical of civilization. The following passage in which Barth portrays the setting-out of a Kel Ewey caravan takes us right into the world of the savages, "The general start of the united 'aïri', or caravan, took place with great spirit; and a wild, enthusiastic cry, raised over the whole extent of the encampment, answered to the beating of the drums. For though the Kél-owi are greatly civilized by the influence of the black population, nevertheless they are still 'half demons', while the thoroughbred and freeborn Amoshagh (whatever name he may bear, whether Tárki, ba-Asbenchi, Kindin, or Chapáto) is regarded by all the neighboring tribes, Arabs as well as Africans, as a real demon (*'jin'*)" (Barth, 1890, Vol.I:222).

The wild cries, which Barth mentions frequently elsewhere, indicate the affinity of the Kel Ewey with dumb animals. Compared with the other Tuareg, however, the Kel Ewey are only semi-demons. But Barth does not only limit himself to this evolutionary ranking, he also pays attention to how the Kel Ewey see him and other Europeans. He notes and accepts the fact that as a Christian he is not welcome. After his first meeting with Annur, the chief of the Kel Ewey, he notes, "We saw the old chief on the day following our arrival. He received us in a straightforward and kindly manner, observing very simply that even, if as Christians, we had come to his country stained with guilt, the many dangers and difficulties we had gone through would have sufficed to wash us clean, and that we had nothing now to fear but the climate and the thieves... Some days afterwards he sent us the simple and unmistakable message, that if we wished to proceed to Sudán at our own risk, we might go in company with the caravan, and he would place no obstacle in our way; but if we wanted him to go with us and to protect us, we ought to pay him a considerable sum. In stating these plain terms he made use of a very expressive simile, saying that as the *leffa* (or snake) killed everything that she touched, so his word, when it had once escaped his lips, had terminated the matter in question - there was nothing more to be said" (Barth, 1890, Vol.I:158).

Even here the tag of barbarian and the animal-like reference are still present - Annur compares himself to a snake - but Barth, nevertheless, feels warmly towards the openness of Annur. The more time he spends with him, the more intense are their conversations in which they talk about civilization and barbarity. Each is prepared to learn from the other, as can be seen in the following passage where Barth praises Annur, "He was, in short, so pleased with our manners and our whole demeanor that one day, after he had been reposing in my tent and chatting with me, he sent for Yusuf, and told him plainly that he apprehended that our religion was better than theirs.... He was a man of business, who desired to maintain some sort of order in a country where everything naturally inclines to turbulence and disorder. In other respects he allowed every man to do as he liked; and notwithstanding his practical severity, he was rather of a mild disposition, for he thought Europeans dreadful barbarians for slaughtering without pity such numbers of people in their battles, using big guns instead of spears and swords, which were, as he thought, the only manly and becoming weapons" (Barth, 1890, Vol.I:217).

After 1900 the Kel Ewey were part of the French colony of Niger, since 1960 they have belonged to the independent state of Niger. Since then, they have been unable to decide whether they prefer their previous form of 'anarchy' as a higher level of civilization to the modern state with its warfare which has been thrust upon them. But in other areas they have been able to maintain their old way of life, and there is still the question of the wild versus civilization.

## II. Solitude and sociability

For the Kel Ewey *asuf* means the uncultivated land outside of the permanent settlements. This includes mountains, valleys and plains. Part of this land is covered with grass, bush and trees (savannah), the mountains are partly free of vegetation. At first we might translate the word *asuf* as 'bush.' Bush is the standard term for the wild African savannah in contrast to the wilderness of the tropical rain forests, which are referred to as jungle or primeval forest. *Asuf* is used in contrast to settlement (*akal*) or town (*aghrem*). Of course, caution must be exercised with the word 'bush.' One should be aware that 'bush', just like 'Busch' or 'brousse' are all words that were in use during the colonial period in particular. Their use expresses above all the European colonial rulers' view of the African wild.

If we wish to understand what the Kel Ewey understand by the wild, then we must look more closely at their use of language. The original meaning of *asuf* is solitude, so it is not so much a geographical as a sociological concept. The antonyms are not bush and settlement, but isolation and communication, solitude and sociability.

If the word *asuf* is also used for bush, then this is due to the fact that solitude is far more apparent there. In the bush there are no permanent settlements but only camps in which few people live. They are far apart from one another and are frequently moved. Only on the rare occasions where a camp consists of solely one person, does absolute solitude occur. Herding itself, however, is almost always a lonesome activity. A woman who looks after a herd of goats is alone with them from sun-rise to sun-set. She has no-one to talk to, she can only sing songs and this she does for much of the time that she is out with the herd. A camelherd spends less time looking after his camels, but even he usually sets off alone to look for them. The work of herdsmen and women is therefore marked by a degree of solitude scarcely found in any other job.

If we wish to understand the concept *asuf* in its spatial dimension, then the term 'Einöde' would seem to be the most appropriate translation in German. 'Einöde' (wilderness) denotes a lonely, desolate, empty region. This is just what a Kel Ewey has in mind when he compares *asuf* with a settlement where many people come into daily contact with one another.

"Who have you seen ?" is a standard greeting when a Tuareg meets a friend. "No-one, only solitude (*asuf*)" is the reply if the person in question has no guest at the time. This response is both possible in the bush as well as in the oasis of Timia. *Asuf* as solitude is not bound to any one particular place, but can be observed everywhere. If my neighbor, colleague and friend Aghali in

Timia is away for a day, then my female neighbors commiserate with me, "Today you are all alone (*asuf*), your friend has gone away!"

The opposite of solitude is sociability. Whoever meets another person, chats and exchanges news. Conversation (*edawanne*) is particularly important for the Kel Ewey. The word *edawanne* in Tamajegh means much more than conversation; it means not only the words themselves but also a free and easy way of passing the time. Anyone who knows how to relate new and interesting events (*isalan*) is a much sought-after interlocutor. These events include not only news about friends and relatives but also world news. The most valued interlocutor is the guest (*amagar*) since he has the most to relate. The guest from elsewhere - in Tamajegh the word *amagar* means both stranger and guest - is the surest guarantee for entertainment until the early hours of the morning. Solitude and boredom do not arise as long as he is there. On the day when the guest leaves the camp he is usually paid the following compliment, "Now solitude is returning here."

Sociability, which I am comparing here with solitude, makes no particularly high demands on conversation or the social integration of individuals. Naturally, news is of great value for the listener when he asks, for example, about relatives or what grazing conditions are like elsewhere. But many conversations are simply gossip or exciting news from near and far; they satisfy curiosity and allow the listener to be a part of a larger world without the events having to have any direct significance for him. Sociability as described here is the most elementary form of social integration, people talk with one another without necessarily having a close relationship. But this simple social integration is so fundamental that it marks the first boundary between wilderness and civilization. In the wild one is alone, solitary. Civilization begins when people talk together.

### III. Animal and man

The fact that a human being feels alone in the bush is not as self-evident as might first appear to be the case. The wilderness is indeed desolate, but it is anything but empty space; this space is divided up into mountains, valleys and plains. In most places the land is covered in vegetation (trees, bushes, grasses). Demons live in the mountains and trees and occasionally meet people. There is abundant animal life: numerous birds, predators (hyenas and jackals), monkeys, big game (ostriches, barbary sheeps, antelopes and gazelles), small game (hares, bustards and guinea fowls). At ground level there are snakes and scorpions and mice, beetles and ants live underground. Last but not least there are also the goats and camels.

The herdsmen and women are continuously involved with their animals. The female goatherd spends the entire day with her herd and at night the goats sleep beside her. She has to protect the goats from the jackals. In camp she has to put up with birds, mice and ants, which eat her provisions. Animals are present everywhere, even at night she can feel mosquitoes, ants and beetles on her skin.

If one feels alone in such a situation, then it is not so much a physical, but rather a sociological observation. Mountains and valleys, trees and grasses, demons and animals obviously do not provide sociable company for a human being; sociability is only established through the presence of other human beings. A human being is radically different from the rest of nature and if he is not among others of his kind, then he feels lonely and abandoned. Here again, spoken communication plays an important role, "In Timia I can talk with a lot of people, here I only have stones and trees" - with these words a herdsman poignantly marks the difference between town and bush.

The demarcation between humans and animals is rather more highly charged than that between humans and stones and trees; animals are similar to humans. If a Kel Ewey describes the behavior of his camels or goats, then he frequently uses expressions which describe human behavior. These expressions indicate a similarity but still do not conceal fundamental differences - even from the point of view of the Kel Ewey. The social organization of herd animals is only apparently similar to that of humans, in reality they are essentially different. While each animal is concerned only with feeding itself, humans share their food. Relations are by no means as long-lasting as is the case with human beings and disappear after a short time. Furthermore, animals lack the essential elements of human civilization in the sense of a material culture. They do not cook their food, but eat it raw; they wear no clothes, but go naked; they have no home, but sleep in the open. They lack not only spoken communication but also any sense of shame (*takarakit*) as expression of a moral order.

Of course, in the fairy tales the female goatherds tell one another around the camp fire at night, animals can also talk and humans and animals are not different from one another. Fairy tales are only told for entertainment, the goatherds are well aware that they do not reflect reality today. However, once upon a time animals and humans could talk to one another - in the days when Mohammed - in fairy tales the jackal has the name of the prophet! - was not the goatherds' most feared enemy, but looked after the goats with them. These days are long gone but it is evident that folklore is not considered a mere tissue of lies by the precautions that are taken when telling these tales. They may only be told at night and the animals are given different names - otherwise one would not know how they might react.

If animals were once like human beings - and not the other way round - then today they are part of a different world; that of the animals is a lower, wild, uncivilized world. These worlds are separate, but human civilization is precarious and there is always the danger that humans might sink to the level of animals and behave like animals. This is particularly true in times of crisis. In times of famine, "children forget their parents, just like dogs", people eat wild berries like animals, no longer share their food but "pasture like ostriches", i.e. each person is concerned only with feeding himself. In times of war they are no longer sociable, "they flee into the mountains like barbary sheeps and keep an eye on the enemy from behind a stone." In war, even the dignity of human death can be foregone, "the people were slaughtered like goats." They are not buried, but "lie by the roadside like the bodies of animals." Furthermore, in times of crisis a human being can change into an animal and become a werewolf (*kumbultu*). He changes into a wolf or hyena and steals the goats from the goatherds.

This animalistic regression is particularly threatening in times of crisis and is a continuous latent form of danger for the Kel Ewey. In daily life comparisons with animals are mostly used to make fun of others, particularly between cousins who enjoy a joking relationship. "She's as afraid of people as a gazelle", "He has ears like a dog", "He walks like an ostrich", "She has the mouth of a jackal", "He has teeth like a donkey."

These and similar comments can be heard daily. Comparisons with animals are nearly always negative for humans. Even if one says that someone can spend days in the bush without water, just like a camel, then this not only expresses admiration, but also contempt. Anyone who would rather live in the bush than in town is often described as a fox or a jackal. Anyone who lives in the bush where the animals are at home is at the very least in danger of behaving like one himself. It is maintained that herdsmen who always live at the grazing grounds develop a fear of humans just like the animals. If they come to Timia, they do not leave their families' homes because they are afraid of people. Moreover, their manners are coarse. Like animals, they lack any sense of shame (*takarakit*), one of the most important civilized virtues. Only sociability, social contact, can prevent this brutalization.

## IV. Chaos and order

Wilderness means not only solitude and the animal, but also disorder in the form of danger, the unknown and disorientation. How dangerous is life in the bush for the Kel Ewey? Fifty years ago there were still lions and wolves in Aïr. They could pose a threat not only for humans, but, above all, for domestic animals. Nowadays there are no predators which threaten the safety of the camels and donkeys. They can graze freely both night and day. Hyenas, jackals, lynxes and leopards are a threat for the goats, which therefore have to be guarded. Only hyenas can be a danger for humans. Men who travel by night always carry a sword. Women do not leave the settlements and camps at night. Hyenas are rare today in Aïr. Poisonous snakes represent the greatest danger. Every year people from Timia die from snake bites.

Demons, described as *aljennan* or *kel asuf* (literally people of the wild), pose another threat.[1] They inhabit rocks, trees and abandoned ruins. One can meet them by day, but more frequently at night. They are not usually seen, but can be heard whispering. In appearance they are ugly and look more like wild animals than human beings. They are dangerous both for people and domestic animals in that they can enter their bodies and make them

---

[1] The *aljennan* are none other than the *djin*, whom Barth mentions by their Arabic name in the above quotation.

insane. Men nearly always claim that they are not afraid of them and that they cannot do them any harm. Women are more cautious in what they say. But many female goatherds maintain that they are not afraid of demons.

None of the Kel Ewey deny the existence of demons, but all agree that there are fewer of them about nowadays than there used to be. The higher density of population but above all modern technology have driven them away. For some time now the sound of vehicles has been heard more frequently in Aïr. Government officials, various experts and tourists cross the bush in vehicles with four-wheel drive, even where there are no proper roads. Demons cannot stand the noise and exhaust fumes and have therefore retreated to completely empty areas - into the real wilderness.

The wilderness was formerly a place where bandits who attacked and dragged off people and animals were to be reckoned with. In precolonial times raids by the Tubu, Arabs and various Tuareg groups were common. Since the twenties there have been no more raids in Aïr. Even thefts are not a common occurrence, so the area is considered perfectly safe. It is different in Hausaland; there, camel thefts are frequent and the herdsmen must be both armed and vigilant.

The most threatening thing about the wilderness lies perhaps not first and foremost in any open danger but rather in the strange and unknown, in contrast to the familiar and trusted. The Kel Ewey make a distinction between a 'foreign' marriage (literally wild marriage, *teduwat n-asuf*) and a 'home' marriage (*teduwat n-aghiwan*). In the second case, marriage is to a close relation, e.g. a cousin, in the first to an unrelated woman. The criterion is, therefore, social rather than spatial. Those who are outside the family constitute the wild, those who are related the home, civilization.

The boundary between civilization and wilderness is here particularly strictly interpreted. It runs between the home as social unit and everything else. But because most people in Timia are in some way related, the difference is, to a great extent, connected to the boundary between settlement and bush. The word *aghiwan*, house, must be considered in both its meanings of spatial and social unit. Therefore, instead of the word *asuf*, the wild is often simply referred to as *atakas*, outside, in contrast to *aghiwan*, inside the home. Whatever is a part of the house is inside, and whatever does not belong is outside.

This notion of belonging may also be interpreted as a relation of ownership. The land on which the house stands belongs to the family, or rather the women, who, in the matrilocal system of the Kel Ewey, determine the place of residence. Even a garden has an unequivocal affiliation and indicates an owner. The word *afarag*, garden, originally meant the fence around the garden, protecting it from strangers and animals. In contrast, the bush, the wild is owned by no one individual. It is accessible to all, but, on the other hand, it belongs to no-one and no territorial claims can be made. All this has a considerable effect on its use, since no-one feels personally responsible for the wild as they do for their own property. In precolonial times this was not the case. Each tribe had his own territory with clearly marked boundaries. The numerous small walls which one comes across in Aïr bear eloquent testimony to this fact. In this respect, the bush today is far wilder than in precolonial times; in contrast to former days it is a wild country where anyone can go without question.

The wilderness also means a place where people cannot find their way around. For European tourists travelling through Aïr, this is certainly the most powerful impression. They find themselves in a landscape with neither roads nor sign posts, they do not know the names of the mountains and valleys, the vegetation is unfamiliar. Moreover, the latter is neither cultivated nor ordered, but simply grows wild. They see no settlement, at the most a female goatherd with whom they cannot communicate. They feel that they are really in the wild and would be totally lost if they did not have the guide so wisely prescribed by the tourist office in Agadez.

Nothing could be more wrong than if the tourist were to ascribe his own feelings to the Tuareg. They know this landscape in every detail and in this sense it is therefore not the wild. They know the name of every mountain and every small valley. They have been here many times before and will hardly ever get lost. They know the scattered water holes in Aïr and can get water from them. They are familiar with every tree and almost all the grasses and also know what properties they possess. Therefore, the vegetation of the bush does not seem chaotic but well organized. Even when they fail to come across any people or animals, they can tell by the tracks who was here when and in which direction they went. The landscape is alive for them even when there is no living thing in sight.

For a Kel Ewey, the wild, in the sense of unfamiliar country, is only somewhere far distant. Possibly, when looking for a lost camel, he may find himself in an area where he has never been before, where he lacks orientation and does not know where the camps and water holes are to be found. Here, the landscape, even for him, will become the wild. The wild is, therefore, a relative concept, which according to the dimension involved can constitute quite different areas. In one instance, *asuf* may start just outside Timia, if not simply outside the home; in another, the whole of Aïr may be a space in which a person feels quite at home.

The Kel Ewey hardly ever get lost in the bush, even without roads and signposts. The word *anakaw*, to get lost, to lose one's way, has however, a far-reaching meaning which is important for my line of enquiry. Above all, *anakaw* expresses a social distance or division. If I had not visited a friend for some time, he would greet me with the expression "you were lost." Herdsmen and women who live at distant grazing grounds year in, year out, caravans, who graze their camels 1,000 km from Timia in Nigeria, do not so much run the risk of getting physically lost, but rather of becoming socially lost and thus becoming *kel asuf*, or people of the wild. The fact that this scarcely ever happens is proof of the triumph of civilization over the wild. Neither the goat nor the camelherd is lost to their relatives. The female goatherd is regularly sent provisions from Timia and she, in turn, supplies them with cheese. Many of the herdsmen and women admittedly only come to Timia for a few days once or twice a year. But these are festive occasions, important Islamic feasts, weddings, baptisms where they meet all their friends and relatives.

The never-ending stream of news from, to and between the herdswomen plays an important role. A herdswoman who has just come from Timia will tell all the others at the well about their relatives, just as in Timia she previously supplied these same relatives with news and information about the herdswomen. This oral communication maintains the network of relationships. The importance thereof is well demonstrated by the comment passed by a female goatherd on my telling her that some nomads live lives of complete isolation in the desert. She was horrified, "we would get lost if we had no news of whether our parents were alive or dead."

If people do get lost today, then it is not the herdsmen and women in the bush, but those who have been to school and move to the towns, or those who go to Nigeria, Algeria or Libya to look for work. They do not live in the wilderness, but among many other people and they could make use of modern means of communication to maintain contact with their families. But the phenomenon of *anakaw*, to get lost manifests itself earliest in their case. They break off contact with home for months, years, sometimes for ever. In their eyes they have chosen civilization over the wild. But in the eyes of their parents, it is just the opposite; anyone who fails to keep in touch with his relatives loses himself and gives up the basis of civilization. One of the few camelherds who attended an intermediate school in Arlit was of the same opinion. When I asked him what the difference was between town (*aghrem*) and bush (*asuf*), he replied, "in the town there was solitude (*asuf*), I had no friends or relations as I do here." This is an extreme position, which few would agree with and yet, paradoxically, it illustrates the primary meaning of *asuf* as solitude. I asked him about the difference between town and *asuf* (wilderness, bush) and he replied that there was only *asuf* (solitude) in the town.

### V. Privation and abundance

The contrasts between the wild and civilization which I have described above are concerned with elementary forms of human social integration. The opposition between animal and man emphasizes the uniqueness of man in the universe. The opposition between solitude and sociability highlights man as a social being. The third opposition focuses on the order and security of human society. If we in Europe talk about civilization, then this includes these elementary forms of human social integration, but frequently much more is meant. As the above-mentioned quotation from Grimms' dictionary shows, 'high culture' is primarily thought of. In this evolutionary tradition nomads represent a classic example of the opposite of civilization - barbarity. They may well have gone beyond the stage of mere savages, but they lack a highly developed material, spiritual and ethical culture.

I am not interested here in the Europeans' judgement of other peoples, but rather in the question as to whether the Kel Ewey themselves recognize material and moral development and how they rate themselves in this respect. Let us begin with the material side, with needs that have developed and with a differentiated supply of goods. For the Kel Ewey the word *tenafliy* signifies an abundance of material goods. A rich meal prepared with a number of different ingredients, a piece of clothing made from fine materials, a house built of stone or clay: all these are a part of *tenafliy* in the sense of luxury and abundance. Abundance is only to be found in the town, life in the bush, on the other hand, is characterized by privation for both rich and poor alike. Frequently there is a shortage of tea, millet, even water, let alone any delicacies. The direct confrontation with the elements without the usual material equipment which separates man from nature is also typical. Herdsmen and women have almost no protection against the forces of nature: they bear the direct brunt of sun, rain, cold, wind and sandstorms. They stumble over wood and stones in the trackless bush.

In the camps there is a great deal of variety in the degree of protection and comfort. The more mobile the herdsmen or caravans, the more simple the life. The camp of a caravan consists of a campfire and piled-up camel load to act as a windbreak. If they settle on a farmer's land in Hausaland for any length of time, he provides them with a mat as windbreak. But even so, during the rainy season they are still completely exposed to the down pour. The camp of camel herdsmen in Aïr consists of a campfire and a tree where the water bags and provisions are hung. In comparison the camps of female goatherds, who stay for a longer time in one place are rather more comfortable. In winter they build a hut of tree bark which gives at least some protection against the cold and wind. Only married herdswomen have a primitive mat tent, which not only affords protection against sun, rain, wind, sand, cold and animals but also conceals the couple from the others.

The herdsmen and women lack comfort not only in their housing but also in their sleeping arrangements. In Timia most adults sleep on a bed made of palm branches on which a mat is spread. Most herdsmen and women wrap themselves up for the night in a thin cotton cloth and only a few have an extra woollen blanket in winter.

The privations described here are considered to be such not only by a spoilt European, but also by the Kel Ewey themselves. The herdsmen and women do not usually complain about conditions, but they are, nevertheless, clearly aware of them, "I've got used to the shady house" a herdswoman explained to me when I asked her in Timia when she was going to return to her goats in the bush. Here she was referring to the significance of habit. In fact, this plays an extremely important part in putting up with privation. Anyone who grows up in Timia and becomes accustomed to the convenience of oasis life will hardly at some later date be in a position to tolerate the hardship of life in the bush. Therefore, boys as young as seven are sent to camel camps in order to get used to life there. The ability to tolerate hardship is made easier by the cyclical nature of privation and comfort. When the caravan returns from an arduous expedition, the men remain in the oasis for weeks or months. When the herdsmen and women come to Timia on festive occasions, they enjoy good food, nice clothes and the comforts of home. This tension between privation and comfort determines not only their tolerance of hardship but also their sense of life. Moreover, the hard life of a herdsman is usually only a phase and not a life-time occupation. When the children are old enough to look after the camels and goats by themselves, the parents usual return to Timia and limit themselves to 'trips' into the bush to visit the children and check up on their work.

Adaptation, on the one hand and fluctuation between hardship and comfort on the other provide only a partial explanation. The specific esteem of a simple way of life also plays a part. This is not to be equated with a savage, uncivilized life. The distinction between man and animal is maintained even in the most primitive camps. The herdsmen always wear clothing, however torn or dirty it may be. The campfire and food are to be found in every camp and distinguish it from the life of the animals. Wherever these minimal, civilizing accoutrements are lacking, then this is always seen as being an instance of particular hardship. A herdswoman who has to spend the night away from camp with her goats because she has been cut off by a flood points out how close this situation is to that of the animals, "you can't cook anything, but have to eat wild berries like the jackal. Instead of chatting with the others you have to answer the howl of the jackal."

However, the simple way of life is not identical to these minimal, human accoutrements. It is not only a matter of the raw and cooked, the naked and the clothed. The quality of the food and clothing are also important. But in the case of food, simple preparation is seen as being a particular sign of quality. The Kel Ewey have the following to say about their standard meal of *ashin* - a type of polenta made from millet, water and milk, "you don't need any spices, salt or oil. You eat the *ashin* with milk, take a sip of water, get up and you're quite satisfied." Simple needs, not complicated and varied ones are seen as being the ideal. The goal of a Kel Ewey should be to increase his *ehare*, the number of animals he owns, not *tenafliy*, the abundance of goods.

## VI. Non-believers, believers, savages and the civilized

In a comparison of the wild and civilization the Kel Ewey do not consider that the material possession of goods, the 'standard of living' plays an important role. Precisely because of this, moral and religious criteria are all the more important. As strict Moslems, the Kel Ewey see the division between believers and non-believers as being fundamental. This division at least partially marks the difference between civilization and the wild. For a community of believers a mosque and an *aneslem*, an Islamic scholar, are required. This may well be in an area normally defined as bush (*asuf*). There are several religious centers in Aïr which consist of little more than a collection of *aneslem* and their students. Any place where a recognized *aneslem* lives and teaches is no longer the wild, even if it is the most inhospitable place imaginable.

Of course, in practice it is difficult to reconcile a pious with a nomadic life. Just as modern schools have problems in enrolling nomadic children, so do the Koranic schools where the basic precepts of Islam are taught. Timia is an important religious center in Aïr and many think that it is the mosque and the numerous scholars which justify its existence rather than the oasis gardens, the modern school or the authority of the state in the person of the village representative. A number of *aneslem* who run the Koranic schools and play an important role in baptism, marriage and burial live in Timia. During Ramadan, the month of fasting, many people come out of the bush to listen to their instruction. Old people live in Timia in order to be buried by an *aneslem* in a proper cemetery rather than to die in the wilderness. Weddings and births with the following baptism should also only take place in Timia.

Full nomads who live in the bush and belong to no permanent settlement are described by the Kel Ewey as "the people who live outside" (*kel atakas*) or simply as "the people of the bush" (*kel asuf*).[2] At times they are talked about in a positive fashion, particularly the fact that they know a lot about keeping camels. But in the first instance they are seen as people who live far from the Islamic centers and who are thus practically non-believers. The Kel Eweys' criticism of pure nomads is not entirely due to their lax religious practices. These nomads do not conform to the common order and compared with the civilized Kel Ewey they are savages. They steal and lie, they carry no provisions with them, but live like animals from hand to mouth. They often do not eat civilized food, such as millet, but live on wild grasses and fruits. They do not prepare their food properly but leave the spelt on corn and eat their meals half raw. At meal times they do not leave a little on their plates like decent people but as guests, they eat everything up or tip what is left into their trouser pockets. They do not observe sexual and marriage taboos, but marry their sisters and sleep with their daughters. They avoid contact with other people and hide in the wild like the barbary sheep.

In the literature there are numerous indications that the other Tuareg describe the Kel Ewey with contempt as Hausa, blacks or even slaves since they share many racial and cultural characteristics with the Hausa. This can mean that the Kel Ewey are considered to be savages. Many Tuareg call the

---

[2] It would be interesting to investigate where these nomads draw the line between bush and civilization. In fieldwork concerning the Fel Ferwan, the French ethnologist Casajus (1987) showed that for these nomads who live to the south of Agadez the spatial representation of the wild and civilization is not made up of bush and permanent settlement, but rather the bush and the tent. *La tente dans la solitude* is the title of the book, in which, once again *asuf* has the two-fold meaning of both solitude and bush. See also Klute (1992).

Hausa *awennan*.³ *Awennan* means savage or gone wild and is normally used for animals which have reverted to the wild (camels, donkeys). However, the Hausa consider the Tuareg to be savages. In this respect, the situation has scarcely changed since Barth's time.

The Hausa and Tuareg both consider themselves to be civilized and the others to be savages. Is the same true of the relationship between Europeans and the Tuareg? The fact that Europeans consider the Tuareg to be savages and barbarians is hardly surprising given their understanding of civilization. But is it possible to turn this relationship between civilized and savage around? Yes and no. Concerning religion and morals, the Europeans are *akafer*, non-believers at a lower level of civilization. People who eat pork are hardly better than animals. The Tuareg also consider other European behavior to be savage, e.g. public displays of intimacy between man and wife, clothing which exposes the body, the consumption of raw salads and tomatoes. We saw above how Annur, Barth's informant considered Europeans to be savages because of their weapons.

The case of material culture is different. All are aware that Europeans have more goods and are technologically superior. And all feel that modern technology is pushing back the frontiers of the wild. The speed at which a vehicle can cross the bush reduces the meaning of solitude. The effects of technology are , however, more far-reaching. The noise and exhaust fumes of vehicles drive away the demons who represent an essential element of the wild. The completely artificial world in which the Europeans live makes it highly unlikely that they are savages. For if the wild cannot be identical with any definite area, it is also inconceivable for it to exist without its own space.

## VII. Dead desert and living nature

When Henry Barth on leaving Rhat in 1850 entered the real desert for the first time, he marked on his map a "sad, desolate, stoney plain with isolated granite peaks, few or no animals and hardly any vegetation." However, he

---

[3] This is not true for the Kel Ewey. They use the neutral term *atefen* to describe the Hausa.

seems to ascertain rather different emotions in the Kel Ewey accompanying him, "The aspect of this uninterrupted plain seemed to inspire our companions" (Barth 1890, Vol.I:117).

This sentence would seem to be convincing since we are all accustomed to seeing the Tuareg and Arabic Bedouins as "sons of the desert." But does Barth here really reflect the emotions of the Tuareg or simply his own prejudices? When the caravan reaches a valley six days later after crossing the desert, Barth once again notes the enthusiasm of the Kel Ewey, but now for "a richer vegetation" (p. 120). This joy seems to me to match reality rather more closely than the former enthusiasm for the desert. At least it is more in tune with the emotions of the Kel Ewey, whom I accompanied in 1980 on a caravan through the desert.

The seven-day march through the Tenere desert to Bilma is extremely strenuous. The caravan travels for 16-18 hours a day without halting. Even tea is prepared and drunk on foot. For the Kel Ewey *tenere* means any arid plain, devoid of vegetation, i.e. any desert. The fact that the area between Aïr and Bilma is simply called the *tenere* is due to the particularly harsh character of this part of the desert. There are no trees, no grass, no pieces of wood, no animals. *Tamattan*, death is the first thing that the Kel Ewey associate with *tenere*, since there is no life there due to lack of water. But the desert is not only dead, it also kills those who cross it, or at least this danger is ever present. They must bring their own food and water and fodder for the camels. Any carelessness can lead irrevocably to death. Unlike the bush, here it is impossible to live off wild plants in an emergency and look for the next water hole.

Whereas in the bush a Tuareg can easily find his way by topography and vegetation, in the desert there is the very real and lethal threat of losing one's way. At night one must take one's direction from the stars and during the day from one's shadow. In contrast to the bush one cannot hope to come across a herdswoman who might be able to give directions or help out with food and water. The desert is quite simply a wilderness without human beings or any other form of life. Only demons live there who lead people astray. It is this absolute wilderness which causes most Tuareg to panic, even when they are familiar with the rules of orientation, "when you can look in every direction without seeing a mountain or a tree or a human being or any other living creature, then you lose your head."

How can a caravan cross the desert under these conditions? It must have a *madugu*, a guide who walks at the head of the caravan and who not only knows the rules of orientation, but who also has the calm and equanimity not to lose his head in the desert. He concentrates only on the desert, he looks straight ahead, keeping his eye on the sky and his own shadow; he pays no attention to what is happening behind him in the caravan and scarcely talks to anyone.

Some caravan guides have a close relationship with the desert, just as we so generally, but wrongly suppose all nomads to have. Our caravan guide, Khada, made the following remark about his predecessor Archi, "He was a desert fox. He loved the desert and felt at home there." This comment illustrates Khada's admiration for Archi but also underlines the difference between them. For he feels in no way at home in the desert, despite the fact that he is an experienced guide. When I once told him that people in Europe call the Tuareg "sons of the desert" he laughed about such a foolish notion. He himself, and most of the others think that the desert is primarily hostile to man and any other living thing, "A march through the desert is like a war. You never grow used to it and feel relaxed."

While the guide must keep an eye on the desert and its dangers, the rest of the caravan has to overcome hardship and fear by worrying about the desert as little as possible. The others leave the job of orientation to the guide and instead talk almost continuously in order to forget the desert around them. Never have I heard so many stories and so much gossip as during the Bilma caravan! However, it is only possible to lose sight of the desert if the caravan has a certain minimum number of people so that one can successfully concentrate on the inner life of the caravan. If it only consists of a handful of people and 30 to 50 camels, then this is difficult to do. No-one can then be enclosed within the caravan, but each finds himself on the edge, i.e. in direct confrontation with the desert. Conversation is quickly exhausted with only a few people. Long periods of silence descend on the caravan when each individual is directly exposed to the heat and the desert. A large caravan, however, achieves the incredible; no matter how small it may really be, it, nevertheless, creates a mobile oasis of civilization in the boundless desert.

Against the background of the desert the bush now acquires quite a different quality to that which has been described so far. It is no longer a case of the division between human civilization and the wild but rather of the fundamental difference between dead desert and living nature. The more that nature is threatened by the desert, the more the Kel Ewey are aware of this. The *tenere* is not once and for all a separate entity from the lively bush but can encroach on its space at any time. During any drought formerly fertile valley can become, at least temporarily, desert. Living nature is not a given fact of life, but is always at risk and is therefore considered to be a precious gift.

As far as I know, there is no word in Tamajegh for nature in the sense in which I here use it to compare it to the dead desert. We must also look for other key concepts if we wish to understand the way of thinking of the Kel Ewey. Rain and water are the essential requirements for life and since there is often a lack of both in Aïr, one is more aware of them. This is particularly true after a year of drought as can be seen in the following tale told by a herdswoman after the drought of 1984/85, "The first rains. We took the goats to the trees. The *terakat* tree is the first to come out when it has drunk from the rain. And the *tasar* bush which the goats particularly like. The trees come out before the grass is green. The first rain. We go to where it has just rained, a day here, a day there. We're happy. We trill and sing. The first rain. We only trill, we don't have to boss the goats around. Trill and sing. Today it's raining, today we're going to Tagheris, there's good grazing there. The goats stand on their hind legs and eat the *terakat tree*. The rain pours down, you can hear thunder in the distance, the goats bleat worriedly... you walk and trill at the same time, you have no worries. It's raining, you go up into the mountains with them, today they don't eat the grass, they stand on their hind legs and eat the bushes. When you rest at midday, they jump from stone to stone, like kids. They are full and jump about. They all run, some this way, some that. Some stand on a tree stump, others on rocks. The herdswomen are happy, they call their goats, they trill. They call their favorite goats" (Spittler, 1989a:58).

It is obviously unimportant for this herdswoman in her relaxed and happy frame of mind that she is alone in the bush with her goats. She does not see her surroundings as wilderness now. The goats are company enough for her, the trees are alive for her, she does not mind the pouring rain and the thunder; on the contrary, they make her trill and sing.

*Albaraka* is an important concept meaning blessing or fertility. *Albaraka* is granted but also withdrawn by Allah. If he gives people and animals his blessing, then they are fertile and multiply. If a blessing lies on a particular area, then one finds lush vegetation, the goats give a lot of milk, the cheese is particularly good. According to the Kel Ewey Aïr is a blessed land and has the advantage over other regions. The elevation, climate, water, special vegetation, the quality of the animals are all of benefit to the people in terms of strength and health. When Barth established 140 years ago that, "Aïr is one of the healthiest countries of the earth" then this matches the opinion of the Kel Ewey today.

The Kel Ewey have a particularly highly developed perception of nature, since their very existence is anything but a matter of course. The experience of the desert gives the Kel Ewey a special feeling for life. Between the dead and the potentially lethal desert and the living, life-giving bush lies a far deeper division than that between civilization and the wild. Faced with the lethal desert the contrasts between human beings and the rest of nature are less significant and the common interests of human, animals and plants play a far more important role.

*Acknowledgements*

This article is a translation of "Wüste, Wildnis und Zivilisation - Die Sicht der Kel Ewey". *Paideuma*, 35:273-282, 1989. Translation by Heather Kempson. I would like to thank the Frobenius Institut, Frankfurt (Main), for their generous permission to publish this translation of the original article. - I also thank the German Research Council (Deutsche Forschungsgemeinschaft) who funded my field work on the Kel Ewey since 1980.

## References

Barth, H. ([1857] 1890). *Travels and Discoveries in North and Central Africa.* Vol. I. London, Ward, Lock & Co.

Casajus, D. (1987). *La tente dans la solitude. La société et les morts chez les Touaregs Kel Ferwan.* Paris, Maison des Sciences de l'Homme.

Grimm, J. and W. (1956). *Deutsches Wörterbuch*, Vol XV. Leipzig, Hirzel.

Klute, G. (1992). *Die schwerste Arbeit der Welt. Alltag von Tuareg-Nomaden.* München, Trickster.

Spittler, G. (1989a). *Handeln in einer Hungerkrise. Tuaregnomaden und die große Dürre von 1984.* Opladen, Westdeutscher Verlag.

Spittler, G. (1989b). *Dürren, Krieg und Hungerkrisen bei den Kel Ewey* (1900-1985). Studien zur Kulturkunde, Vol. 89. Stuttgart, Franz Steiner.

# WERE THE CROW INDIANS CONSERVATIONISTS?

Fred W. Voget

## I. Introduction

Concern in the industrialized West for the way in which improper management of natural resources leads to destruction of ecosystems prompts a closer look at the ways in which preindustrial societies managed their resources. This chapter surveys the economic practices of the Crow Indians to see if their relations with the natural world were guided by conservation principles.

The Crow Indians shared a buffalo-hunting and horse-raiding culture with the Blackfeet, Sioux, Cheyenne, Arapaho and other Northern Plains tribes. The Crow ranged from southern Alberta to the Wind River Mountains in Wyoming and from the Absaroka Range in western Montana to the Black Hills of South Dakota, but the Yellowstone River basin and the Big Horn Mountains constituted the core of their homeland. During the historic formation and efflorescence of Plains Indian Culture, which followed introduction of the horse and expansion of trade and warfare, the Crow probably numbered no more than eight to ten thousand. In 1883-1884 they moved to their present reservation in southcentral Montana, settling on lands carved from their original homeland. In 1986 the tribal roll listed a population of 7,615, of which 3,783 were males and 3,822 were females (Voget, in press).

## II. Sustained yield: a measure of conservation practice

A principle of sustained yield offers an appropriate measure of conservation practices. Under sustained yield any hunting people expectably would seek to control the cropping of game to assure a constant replenishment. Disturbance of environment would be minimal, and efficient collection of game would be matched by efficient use and consumption.

Sources available do not address the issue of conservation. Nonetheless, the reports of explorers, traders, Indian scouts, military officers, Agency officials, interested laymen, and ethnographers do provide descriptions and observations of hunting techniques and uses of game animals which permit judgements regarding conservation, or its absence.

### III. Gods, men, and animals

The Crow learned their attitudes concerning animals and their uses from the gods. First Worker, or Old White Man above, had created the earth from mud brought from below flood waters by his spirit 'brother', a hell diver. After shaping the earth, First Worker created humans and also animals for them to eat. However, in more detailed and popular accounts, two co-workers were earth's creators. In one version, Sun and Old Man Coyote worked together, while in another, Old Man Coyote, accompanied by Little Coyote, played the dominant role of a creator-trickster and live-in mentor to the Crow (Curtis, 1970,4:52-54; Lowie, 1918:14-19; 1935:122-131).

The world had not been created solely for the Crow, for the gods had surrounded them with mortal enemies. At the very creation, the world was imperfect, and though demigods descended from the sky to rid earth of monster spirits who threatened to devour all living things, the world still was filled with spirit beings dangerous to the Crow. The star gods themselves were dangerous, for, like the Sun, they thrived on flesh.

First Worker and earth's co-creators out of pity had made strong mystical powers available to the Crow in order that they might control the dangers which threatened their survival. God-like spirits were on hand to convey specialized powers which would allow individual Crow to see things at a distance, control the movements of game, cure sickness, and confuse enemies with a foggy cloud. By fasting in the pristine purity of mountain peaks and canyon heights, and offering a gift of flesh in the form of strips of skin or finger joints, a suppliant usually received a gift of special power and the protective friendship of a spirit benefactor. Spirit patrons, or medicine fathers, possessed two bodies. In his vaporous form a medicine father appeared to a Crow visionary to be a man, a person like himself, who seemed to be advancing through a cloud. On departing a medicine father assumed his original animal form by which he was known for a special sacred power (Lowie, 1935:239-241; Nabokov, 1970:62-64; Voget, 1984:40-49, 63-74).

Of all the creators, Old Man Coyote was viewed with special fondness by the Crow. He was no stern moralizing god, but an amiable rascal who enjoyed the body's pleasures, to which all were susceptible. Mention of Old Man Coyote always brought a near uncontrollable laughter and a sparkle to Crow eyes as they recalled Od Man Coyote's cunning maneuvers to satisfy a gluttonous appetite for food and women. His appetite was so insatiable that he spared no deception, and he was exceedingly selfish with food. When living among the Crow, he had tried to marry his own daughters, and he had succeeded in having intercourse with his mother-in-law. No Crow son-in-law would ever think of talking to his mother-in-law except through a third person! All such adventures ended in humiliation for Old Man Coyote, and he had to change himself into his coyote form and run off to escape the Crow when they discovered his bold escapades with his daughters and his mother-in-law (Lowie, 1918:41-43, 49-51).

For all his foibles, Old Man Coyote was a powerful god who had brought the Crow forth from a hole in a tree by striking it with his medicine stick. His adventures demonstrated that animals and birds were created to serve Crow needs. He told buffalo to eat and drink as he intended to kill and eat them. Elk and deer likewise were to be eaten, while otter were to furnish blankets and beaver perfumes. He wrung the necks of many birds, and he seemed not to care when Porcupine did away with a helpful buffalo.

He showed the Crow how buffalo could be tricked into running blind over a precipice; for, to satisfy his own voracious appetite, Old Man Coyote persuaded a herd of buffalo to close their eyes while racing him to a precipice, and to their deaths. Old Man Coyote also taught crow to run antelope along a sloping ridge where people could rise up and frighten them with robes and drive the antelope into a corral (Lowie, 1918:17-20; 1935:122-131).

Old Man Coyote's teachings about the uses to which buffalo and other game could be put were thorough and efficient measured by Crow usage. *Tanned buffalo* hides provided robes, bed blankets, tipi covers, soft bags, pad saddles, saddle blankets, mittens, leggings, moccasins, and winter clothing for both sexes. *Rawhide* was transformed into shields, ropes, lariats, bridles, whip lashes, thongs for ceremonial use, and box-like containers for storing food and medicines. Moistened rawhide was perfect as a binding for wooden saddle frames and for attaching handles to stone mauls and war clubs, for the hide as it shrank, tightened joints and held them in place. *Buffalo hair* made strong ropes and stuffing for saddles, digging sticks, and pillows. Sinew provided a tough thread for sewing and strong cord and rope loops through which hides could be drawn for softening. *Bones* provided arrowpoints, fleshers, arrow straighteners, dishes, hoes, knives, porcupine quill smoothers, gaming pieces, sled runners, and marrow for eating. *Buffalo horn* was manufactured into spoons, cups, arrowheads, and points for javelins used in the hoop game. When softened, the horn was split and shaped into a recurved bow strengthened with sinew backing. Sinew backing also was applied to wooden bows. Teeth were strung as necklaces and used in ceremonial rattles. *Buffalo skulls* served as altars in ceremonies and for cutting off of finger joints as offerings. Suppliants also drew buffalo skulls attached to skewers in their backs. *Buffalo heads* were sometimes roasted and the brains eaten. Brains also were used in combination with liver and other ingredients for tanning. *Tails* supplied knife scabbards and handles for war clubs and stiff papillae made tongues good hairbrushes. *Paunches* were useful as water carriers and for cooking with hot stones. The grass contents of paunches were eaten and also fed to ponies. In winter, the paunch of a fresh killed buffalo warmed hands and averted frostbite. *The pericardium* was handy for carrying water, and dried *udders* were readily converted into dishes. The *gall bladder* furnished an excellent condiment for raw liver, and the yellow gallstones could be ground for paint. *The scrotum* made a tough stirrup cover, *hooves* softened to a serviceable glue, and *buffalo chips* provided fuel, punks for making fires, and powder to keep infants dry (Clark, 1982:84-86; Lowie, 1922:201-210).

Buffalo were the favorite food animal of the Crow, and during the winter days and weeks when hunting was not practicable, they depended heavily on dried buffalo meat in their parfleches to carry them through. Buffalo also were prominent in Crow ceremonies. Sacralized buffalo hides were used to make Eagle's nest at the top of the Sun Dance tipi, and sacralized tongues were distributed to contributors to the performance of a ceremony. Suppliants drew buffalo skulls or heads attached to their backs when seeking a spirit patron, and buffalo skulls rested like guardians on each side of a pledger of a Sun Dance as he slept (Lowie, 1915:1-50; 1935:297-326; Voget, 1984:112-113, 116-117).

Efficient use and storage practices are important to sound conservation. Old Man Coyote's insatiable appetite did not encourage conservation of any kind. His approach, revealed in a tale of ant men hunters under his command, was to slaughter the entire buffalo herd and bring back every hide, bone with marrow, and piece of meat so he could gorge himself and sleep it off. In 1850 trader Denig (1930 46:504, 509) reported that buffalo hunting Indians commonly alternated between times of plenty and of scarcity. When meat was plentiful, they were inclined to indulge themselves, inviting each other to feast as many as ten times a day. He considered the Indians 'very improvident,' and their eating habits soon exhausted their small supplies. Earlier, in 1805, Larocque (Wood and Thiessen, 1985:209) also commented on the wasteful use of meat. The Crow took only the choicest cuts, and within two to three days were out of meat, despite a successful hunt. Larocque was amazed at the number of buffalo killed by the Crow in their hunts.

The Yellowstone River and Big Horn Mountains ecology undoubtedly encouraged an expectation that animal food sufficient to sustain life would be available during each season of the year. There were limits, too, as to how much dried meat could be prepared and transported in camp movements. Crow families made use of five to six horses when moving their tipi poles, lodgecovers, and other household equipment, including tanning stakes, dried meat, children, infants, and puppies or cub bears. Decorated saddle bags behind a woman's saddle were so heavy with gear that the long fringes almost swept the ground.

Neither the behavior of gods who established the world order, nor relations the Crow developed with the environment stimulated conservation attitudes. Children grew up without conservation attitudes, for during the winter months they listened wide-eyed to adventure tales in which Old Man Coyote displayed his cunning ways and powers, and revealed attitudes towards animals which they observed in the behavior of their parents. Hunters sang medicine songs to draw buffalo to them, and during a run they tried to kill as many as they could (Curtis, 1970,4:111-114).

## IV. Maintaining a cycle of growth and increase

The Crow told tales about Old Man Coyote only during winter's long nights, for winter was the proper time to recall those creative and power-filled moments when demigods walked the earth and camped out with the Crow. In reaching back to the creation, the Crow may have sought to remind spirits of the seasonal wish dreams granted individual Crow to ensure the healthy growth of their maternal 'clan children', and to influence the change from an icy and dormant earth to an earth warming with the promise of growth and increase. Symbols of birth, growth, feeding, increase, and prayers for health and long life may appear in any Crow ceremony. Candidates for adoption into the Tobacco or Sacred Pipe societies represented respectively children to be born, or eaglets to be fed. In ceremonies women moved green willow shoots up and down to indicate growth and increase. Paternal relatives used their dream blessings to bring 'clan children' safely through each year. In spring and summer they generally dreamt of yellow leaves and winter's snows, while in fall and winter they had visions of green foliage and ripening berries (Lowie, 1924:325-365; 1935:237-255, 274-296).

Despite a concern for the yearly renewal of life, the Crow possessed no public ceremony in which they controlled earth's renewal or the replenishment of buffalo and other animals so essential to life. Mother Earth was the source of life and increase, but no goddess to be worshipped. Animals crept from earth's burrows and caves each spring, just as buffalo at their creation had clambered out of a hole in the ground. Intervention in earth's processes, however, was a private and not a public capability. Men with a gift of power from a guardian spirit, or medicine father, were the ones who controlled the weather and turned migrating buffalo in the direction of the Crow camp. The nature of this power permitted the owner to loan and even to sell it up to three times before his relation with his medicine father was severed.

In the fall, when frost touched the ground, an owner who dreamt of his rock medicine assembled a select group of rock medicine owners for a grand feast on buffalo pemmican enriched with plenty of fat. He also invited twenty young braves and a war captain with an outstanding record. In their festive mood they signaled to the gods their happiness at having plenty to eat and the enjoyment of life together. Warriors recited coups and sang medicine songs for victories to come, while an honored paternal relative of the host distributed pemmican loaves and prayed especially over a loaf shaped like a bear. Bears in early fall danced festively among the mountain berry patches and stuffed themselves with sweets. During their fall feasting, Crow with bear power exhibited indwelling spirit guardians after rubbing their faces on a bearskin drawn over a post. The Crow apparently included bears in their good luck wishes; for bears enjoyed good eating in the fall, and then they went to sleep in Mother Earth's caverns and bestirred themselves just in time for spring's awakening (Lowie, 1924:349-360; 1935:258-268; Wildschut, 1975:98-103).

When in spring Thunderbird flashed eyes of lightning and hurled his voice in rolling waves, he signaled that spirit beings once again were active. The Crow now knew that it was time, as the moon drew full, to open their medicine bundles and with tobacco prayers to renew friendships with their spirit patrons. They looked forward to the planting of their sacred tobacco which linked them to earth's growth and increase, and gave them victories over enemies. So long as they possessed the seed and flowers of Holy Tobacco, they would thrive as a people (Denig, 1953:51-59). That was the promise conveyed with the gift of tobacco medicine to a chief of long ago. Rock medicines also stimulated growth and increase as the many pebbles lining mountain streambeds and the growing number of stony fragments along mountain trails demonstrated. Owners of rock medicines, when opening their bundles in the spring, looked forward to an increase in their rock 'children' and to more beads and earrings than worshippers in the fall had placed there as offerings.

## V. Hunting strategies and conservation

Control over the number, kinds, and ages of animals to be killed is essential to any conservation policy. Aside from individual stalking of game, the Crow, as other Plains tribes, obtained their game by organizing cooperative hunts. July and August were poor for buffalo hunting as rutting brought turmoil to the herds and the quality of flesh and hides deteriorated.

All cooperative hunts were directed by a man selected because he had been given a medicine gift to influence the movements of buffalo and also to control the movements of winds. Camp police assisted the hunt leader in organizing and regulating the hunt. Punishment for private hunting before the communal hunt was severe. Police could confiscate a poacher's kill, destroy his property, and disqualify him from the hunt. The immediacy and severity of punishment discouraged the irresponsible startling of the herd and its movement to a distant location. The respect and authority commanded by a band or tribal chief was integral to cooperative hunting, and for apportioning animals felled by a cliff jump or when impounded. No provision existed for a deputized leadership during a chief's absence, as on a war raid, and small hunting groups usually took over, especially during fall and winter when the Crow made winter camps in the lee of the mountains.

Cooperative hunting took the form of a controlled charge, surround, cliff jump, and impoundment. A controlled charge was used when the buffalo were clustered in relatively large herds of several hundreds. The surround involved encirclement of the herd, while impounding required a box canyon formation into which the herd could be driven and then confined with a barrier of posts, logs, and brush. A cliff jump might require the building of a barrier for containment if the drop were insufficient to disable the animals outright. Buffalo were lured and directed down a converging path lined with rock and timber barriers from which women, children, and old men could rise at a timely moment, and, with waving buffalo robes and shouts, frighten and confuse the buffalo as they streamed to destruction.

The horse brought significant changes in that hunters now could manage much larger herds and could assemble several thousand buffalo by uniting separate herds numbering several hundreds. When set in motion, buffalo usually ran several miles before slowing to a halt, and the horse enabled Crow hunters to sustain pursuit and make a kill.

Except for impoundment, Crow hunting tactics did not permit a controlled kill, but there is no indication that the Crow ever spared animals to achieve a balance between consumption and reproduction. Actually, personal kills were modest, ranging from several to perhaps as many as fifteen buffalo during a surround or controlled charge. A cliff jump might produce a herd kill of thirty to a hundred or more. In a tribal hunt in which some five thousand buffalo scattered over a twenty square mile area were rounded up, the estimated kill came to five hundred, or about ten percent. The Crow feasted at the kill site for upwards of a month while women tanned hides and dried meat (Lowie, 1922:210-212). Over a period of twenty years trader Denig (1930:410) observed no decrease in the number of buffalo killed in the vicinity of the Fort Union post near the junction of the Yellowstone and Missouri Rivers. He estimated an annual kill of 150,000 throughout their trade area, not counting natural deaths by drowning, etc.

While the Crow, as other plains societies, made use of buffalo hides and other parts in some eighty-two ways, there was no ritual obligation to make full utilization of the meat. The amount of meat left on each animal probably varied according to season and family need. During the summer when buffalo were plentiful, the Crow may have left behind as much as one hundred and fifty pounds of good meat on each buffalo slain, if Tixier's estimate for Osage practice is accepted (McDermott, 1940:197).

Nature conspired against conservation by making the meat of cows more tender, tastier, and easier to dry than the meat of bulls. Cowhides also were thinner and easier to tan. In a fall hunt, the Crow often sought cows of two to three years for prime buffalo robes since the hides did not require splitting in order to be tanned. The meat of many of these cows was left behind as Crow appetites preferred more mature and fatter cows for eating and winter provisions (Curtis, 1970:112-113). Older people usually wore the split bull robes while young men sported the whole tanned hides.

Hides were valued more than meat. Hunters who left meat for others always claimed the hide. After 1840 the fur trade raised the value of hides, for the Crow were not regular suppliers of meat to trading posts, nor were they a part of the buffalo tongue trade which satisfied the gourmet tastes of traders situated at posts along the Missouri River and city dwellers in St. Louis. When buffalo in large numbers approached Hidatsa villages in North Dakota around Christmas time in 1804, "Hunting and eating became the order of the day," according to trader McKenzie (Wood and Thiessen, 1985:233-234). Indian hunters killed many buffalo but returned "only with the tongues."

## VI. Ceremonial use of buffalo

Buffalo skulls, heads, hides, and tails were important when Crow fasted for power and cured disease, but the most concentrated use was made by a mourner who pledged a Sun Dance to obtain the right and power to kill enemy in retaliation. A fasting mourner usually received dream instructions to raise an imitation of Sun's own medicine tipi; and there, avoiding food and water, he should dance for power. The dance lodge required a man with eagle medicine to consecrate a nest for Eagle, Sun's own messenger, near the top of the tipi. Construction of the nest required the hides of two bulls ceremonially slain, and the hunter and butcher were instructed to leave nothing behind except the heads, backbones and hooves. The meat was distributed to old men and women who assembled to verify that the two buffalo had been killed with an arrow that did not make two holes in the hide (Lowie, 1915: 26-29). Buffalo tongues, duly sacralized, were necessary to repay those who performed special services in the construction and consecration of the lodge, such as the twenty young men who had drawn the twenty poles for the lodge site. The tongues were collected ceremonially and might number from several hundreds to a thousand or more. Other than tongues, little meat was taken. The meat left behind in all likelihood was an offering to Sun, whose appetite for flesh was well-known and respected.

## VII. Summary and conclusion

Oral traditions and literature indicate that the Crow Indians did not practice a philosophy of conservation with regard to buffalo and other game animals on which they depended for food. The following appear influential in their lack of concern for a sustained yield policy with regard to food animals:

1. The gods who ordered and regulated the world had created animals for the Crow to eat and use according to their needs, and by their own behaviors the gods demonstrated that conservation was not important to animal use.

2. Spiritual beings existed who came to the aid of the Crow with power to influence the movements of animals and to control winds and weather which disrupted hunts.

3. From their own experience Crow knew hungry times in any year but seldom starvation. Their homeland was well stocked and they usually could count on getting enough buffalo, elk, or deer during winter and early spring to extend their limited supplies of dried meat and Indian turnip flour.

4. The percentage of animals killed in band and tribal hunts was so small that local herds were not depleted significantly even though the Crow killed more cows for food and hide purposes than bulls. The general availability of game did not discourage individual hunters from taking as many buffalo as possible according to their needs and skill. Interband visiting, fraternal adoptions, and Sun Dance ceremonies all were made possible by the abundance of buffalo meat available in the summer hunts. As for indulgent feasting, that was Old Man Coyote's habit; and Crow well knew that plenty of food supplied the lubricant for feelings essential to good social relations. Invitations to feast built friendships, while stinginess aroused negative feelings and hostile actions.

5. The ceremonial use of buffalo made no provision for conservation. Crow were extravagant in their use of buffalo tongues, especially in the Sun Dance, to reward those performing sacred services, and there is no suggestion that the meat of these buffaloes was used. In one recorded instance, the meat of two buffalo bulls slain ceremonially was distributed to old people who wished to participate in the good luck which followed the prescribed slaying of the animals. The two hunters

were forbidden to eat any of the meat because the two bulls belonged to Sun (Lowie, 1915:26-28).

6. Cooperative hunting techniques, with the exception of impoundment, did not offer the controls which could encourage a selective slaying of animals by number, age, and sex and development of a policy which balanced consumption with reproduction.

## References

Clark, W. P. ([1884] 1982). *The Indian Sign Language*. Lincoln, University of Nebraska Press Bison Book.

Curtis, E. S. ([1909] 1970). *The North American Indian, The Apsaroke or Crows* (20 Vols.), Vol. 4:3-126. New York, Johnson Reprint Corporation.

Denig, E. T. (1930). "Indian Tribes of the Upper Missouri, The Assiniboin." In J. N. B. Hewitt (ed.). *Smithsonian Institution, Bureau of American Ethnology, Forty-Sixth Annual Report*. Washington D.C., pp. 395-628.

Denig, E. T. (1953). "Of the Crow Nation." In J. C. Ewers (ed.). *Smithsonian Institution, Bureau of American Ethnology Bulletin* 151. Washington D.C., pp. 3-74.

Larocque, F. (1985). *Francois-Antoine Larocque's 'Yellowstone Journal'*. Edited by W.R. Wood and T.D. Thiessen. Norman, University of Oklahoma Press, pp. 156-220.

Lowie, R. (1915). "The Sun Dance of the Crow Indians." *American Museum of Natural History Anthropological Papers*, 16:1-50.

Lowie, R. (1918). "Myths and Traditions of the Crow Indians." *American Museum of Natural History Anthropological Papers*, 25:1-308.

Lowie, R. (1922). "The Material Culture of the Crow Indians." *American Museum of Natural History Anthropological Papers*, 21:201-70.

Lowie, R. (1924). "Minor Ceremonies of the Crow Indians." *American Museum of Natural History Anthropological Papers*, 21:325-65.

Lowie, R. (1935). *The Crow Indians*. New York, Farrar and Rinehart.

McDermott, J. F. (ed., 1940). *Tixier's Travels on the Osage Prairies*. Norman, University of Oklahoma Press.

Nabokov, P. (ed. 1970). *Two Leggings: The Making of a Crow Warrior (manuscript of William Wildschut)*. New York, Thomas Y. Crowell, Apollo Edition.

Voget, F. W. (1984). *The Shoshoni-Crow Sun Dance*. Norman, University of Oklahoma Press.

Voget, F. W. (1990, in press). "Crow". In *Handbook of North American Indians*. Plains Vol. Washington, Smithsonian Institution.

Wildschut, W. (1975). "Crow-Indian Medicine Bundles." In J. C. Ewers, (ed.). *Contributions from the Museum of the American Indian Heye Foundation* 17. New York, Museum of the American Indian Heye Foundation, pp. 1-178.

Wood, W. R. and Thiessen, T. D. (1985). *Early Fur Trade of the Northern Plains*. Norman, University of Oklahoma Press.

# PAWNEE VIEWS OF NATURE IN THE CENTRAL PLAINS: THE HISTORIC AND PREHISTORIC DATA

Patricia J. O'Brien

## I. Introduction

The focus of this study is the Pawnee Indians, and their view of nature. A view, it will be argued, effected by the dramatic features of their environment within the North American Great Plains. This paper will focus on the Pawnee's 'invention of nature' using three different avenues of information. The first is the logic of the historic Pawnee thought. The second is the character of the Central Plains as a natural environment, an ecological setting. The third is the relationship between Pawnee mental constructs and that ecological setting. This interrelationship is essential to understand Pawnee cosmological views of nature.

The data for this presentation comes from ethnographic and historic documents, but also from the archaeological record. In combination these data will be used to reconstruct lost Pawnee religious and cosmological concepts. This is possible because by employing Pawnee dualistic thinking, one can use their logic to predict the archaeological record. For example, a description of a Pawnee Morning Star sacrifice allows one to identify material culture elements in the archaeological record that would survive such an event. This data could then be used to establish the antiquity of such a rite.

## II. Background concepts

In Pawnee theology *Tirawahat* (the Universe-and-Everything-Inside) existed with *Tirawa* (the All-Powerful), as their highest deity, and his spouse *Atira* (Vault-of-the-Sky), and the other gods (Dorsey, 1904:3). *Tirawa* created thought, and in so doing (by thinking it) created the separation of the earth and the heavens, and positioned the star deities at the cardinal and semi-cardinal points. Some of these stars in their turn created humans in their image - specifically Morning, or Great Star and Evening, or Bright Star. For this reason a Pawnee man looked within himself to philosophically organize his life, and it is from within himself, with the blessing of Heaven, that his *vision* of his life came. The universe continued its seasonal round because the Pawnee willed it through the performance of specific rituals that revitalized the universe and all things in it. Indeed, the importance of this concept is commented upon by Blaine (1990:47), who noted that in the 1870s and 80s, when the Pawnee could no longer go on the traditional hunt, they saw the universe becoming unbalanced.

From these notions the Pawnee recognized a rhythmic alternation of the cosmic powers: winter-summer, day-night, male-female, the cycling of the stars, sun and moon, the succession of the powers of the south with those of the north, and the east with the west. From these concepts a logical sequence of ceremonies was developed.

*Tirawa* placed the gods as go-betweens between humanity and himself, and they are the Powers in the Heavens (Dorsey, 1904:3-5). The first one positioned was the Sun, in the east, and the next was the Moon in the west. Evening, or Bright Star (identified with Venus) who is the mother of the Skiri, and controls crops was put in the west while Morning, or Great Star (identified with the planet Mars), who is a warrior and created people through his union with the second deity, was stationed in the east. Next *Tirawa* placed the four stars identified with the semi-cardinal points in their positions. The Big Black Meteoric Star, who controls animals, especially buffalo, was associated with the northeast pillar pole position. Next the Yellow Star as assigned to the northwest, followed by the White Star in the southwest place, and finally the Red Star, associated with the southeast pillar pole position, who controls the coming of day and animals, was assigned. The next force created was the four powers of the west - Thunder, Lighting, Wind and Clouds, who obey Evening Star. The sixth was the Corona Borealis, the circle of stars that represents the chiefs, who watch over the people, and the seventh was two beings (stars) in the north who send snowstorms, and drive the buffalo to the people. The eighth was the Wolf Star who invented death, although wolves also help people. The ninth, the North Star, is the chief of the heavens, and must not move. In the tenth order of creation came Black Star who controls animals. Finally, *Tirawa* placed the sun, Morning Star's brother, and the moon, Evening Star's sister, in the heavens. The sun is the father of the people, the moon the mother. Morning Star gets heat and light from the Sun while the Moon watches over women and cornfields.

There are also Doctors' (medicine men) and Warriors' powers. They are Water Monster who taught man the secrets of animals, Mother Cedar Tree who saved the people from destruction, Moon who gave power to people through dreams, Sun who gave great power to men through visions, Loons who fly close to the heavens and teach men the secrets of doctors, and Buffalo Skull and Bears who taught men their special secrets.

Associated with these gods and powers was an elaborate ritual cycle that was acted out over the year. The most common item used in these rites was medicine bundle - fundamentally a portable ceremonial center within which were kept the sacred paraphernalia. Historically, medicine bundles were named; being called Evening Star bundle, Yellow, Red, White and Big Black Meteoric star bundles, Skull, North Star, or Morning Star bundles. Bundles contained a variety of sacred objects including special ears of corn, pipes, rattles, feathers, bird and animal pelts, and each item in a bundle had some symbolic role in the ritual of the specific bundle.

### III. Pawnee logic

A number of years ago Claude Lévi-Strauss suggested that it was the nature of the human mind to create dualistic structures. While this paper will not address that issue, it is ethnographically reported that the historic Pawnee have a complicated ideology whose highly developed logic is dualistic in its structure. Weltfish (1965:255) has observed, "Few ceremonial acts of the Pawnee were so obscure that they could not be understood in terms of his 'logic of the universe.' A rhythm of alternation of cosmic powers was a very important phase of that logic. The winter and the summer, the night and the day, succeeded each other in a never-ending round. The powers of the east followed those of the west. As these two rhythms were combined, the semicardinal directions ran their biennial course - northwest, southwest, northeast, southeast - and for each of these a sacred bundle took charge of the tribe in its turn through the alternate seasons. In many functions of his life, including the household, the Pawnee followed this alternating principle. As he valued these alternating rhythms of the universe, he also followed a pattern of rotation of power and responsibility in all phases of his life, particularly in his political life and in his appeal to the cosmos." The importance of this dualistic nature is commented upon within Pawnee mythology itself for when Tirawa has just finished creating the first human, a woman, he asked the gods how she might be made happy and to increase (Dorsey, 1906:13-14). The Moon observed that he had made everything in pairs so he should make a mate for the first woman; thus, he made man her mate.

This dualistic ideology even applied to mundane matters, for Weltfish further notes (1965:10-19) that the Pawnee viewed a lodge as being divided into two duplicate halves: a northern and southern sector. Household activities were alternated between these halves. There were two meals served per day, and each was served to all lodge members by the alternate sides. This meant there were at least two adult women in a lodge. Actually the historic Pawnee lodges were quite large, and had 30 to 50 people living in them. Often there were two groups of women associated with each half, and their activities were focused on three 'stations'. The central one for mature women, the western one for young women, and the eastern one, near the entrance/exit, for the old women. Symbolically old women were on their way out of life.

This north-south dualism was reflected in the gardens too, as each woman, or groups of women, supplied food to the household from their own gardens, and the foodstuffs were dried and preserved in their own storage pits. This pattern was reflected in general household work, and even in the repair of the structure. When a lodge roof was in need of restoration the women of the north repaired their half, and those of the south theirs. This pattern of organization reflects the Pawnee philosophic penchant for dualisms, and was carried to the point where these ladies would stay at different houses while the roof repair was underway.

The symbolic importance of this dichotomy is associated with the Ground-breaking Ceremony, which was performed before the women could begin to plant their crops. While this ritual was carried out by the men it was instituted by a woman who had a vision, and women played a major role in it. The woman visionary was seated on the north side while four prominent female guests who supplied buffalo meat and corn, were seated on the south. Later during the ritual those four women were seated two to the north and two to the south.

Chamberlain (1982), Fletcher (1904), Murie (1981) and Weltfish (1965) record the Pawnee focus on the sky and its elements (stars and planets, sun and moon, clouds, lightning, wind, and thunder), and the earth and its elements (people, animals, vegetation and especially Mother Corn). It will be argued here that the Pawnee selected these elements because they are a conspicuous aspect of their natural environment, the Central Plains of the Great Plains of North America.

Fundamentally, the Pawnee structured a cosmological system around the natural features of the Central Plains. In addition to the sky and the earth birds are important components of this system because they link the sky to the earth, and tie the people to the gods. The most important birds recorded in the late 19th and early 20th centuries, particularly in the bird oriented Hako ceremony, were eagles, owls, woodpeckers, ducks and wrens (see Fletcher, 1904). Significant too, were animals, and especially plants and trees. The most important plant was Mother Corn, the most important trees were Mother Cedar, green year around, and box elder, cottonwood, willow and elm. The last four trees were symbolically placed at the semi-cardinal points, and represent the pillar stars. These trees are the dominant species in the region.

Chamberlain (1982:97, fig.22) has diagramed this dualistic ideology to show how it is related to the structural features of the earthlodge, and how a lodge is a miniature of the universe - the floor, the earth, the dome-like roof the sky (fig. 1). Derived from this dualism is the notion of the sacredness of the number four which is, of course, a dualism of a dualism.

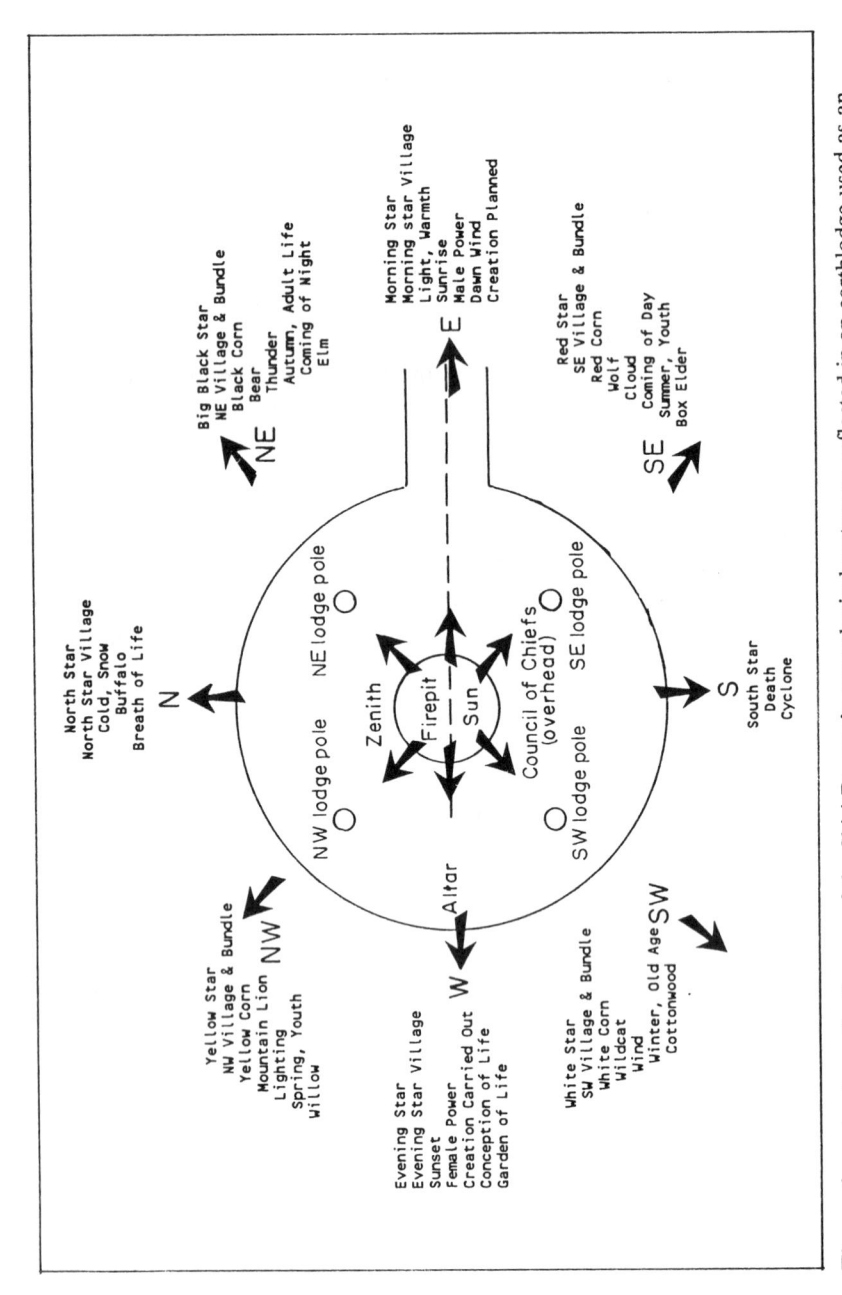

**Figure 1.** A schematic diagram of the Skiri Pawnee's cosmological system as reflected in an earthlodge used as an astronomical observatory (from Chamberlain 1981:fig.22)

By using Chamberlain's diagram in association with the literature on Pawnee ceremonialism, including cosmological myths, we can see not only their logic, but we can predict elements which were lost in the 18th and 19th centuries as they suffered the ravages of disease, depopulation, and the loss of land and resources. We could even propose archaeological models to test these predictions. For example, as mentioned, birds are important in this system, and archaeologically we would search for the remains of birds, especially their wings, talons and claws, which were ceremonially important. Because of the significance of the layout and orientation of a lodge we would seek evidence of the ancient astronomical alignment of buildings.

Historically, eagle skins, talons, feathers, claws and wings were all important ceremonial objects. Symbolically they were signs of authority, but most importantly they represented knowledge coming from *Tirawa*, they represent *Tirawa's* power, or they represent fire. The eagle is the Chief of Day. The eagle is also the symbol of Morning Star, the warrior. Warriors when they went to war painted a bird's claw on their faces, and there is also a Bird's Foot constellation in the heavens. Finally, when a maiden is sacrificed to Morning Star she wears a hawk on her head. By the way eagles, hawks too, are very dramatic birds on the plains. They fly high in the sky, and dive upon their prey like a lighting bolt. As befits sky birds, they nest in the tallest trees.

The owl too is important, and owl feathers and skins were often worn by priests and doctors. The owl is a messenger, he teaches individual Pawnee how to worship *Tirawa*. In the doctor societies some doctors were owl dancers. Owls also represent the four powers of the west that do not sleep: Thunder, Lighting, Wind and Clouds. During the sacrifice to Morning Star the four priests who are keepers of the four pillar star bundles each have two owl skins on their costumes. Finally, owl skins are emblematic of chiefs while those of eagles and hawks symbolize warriors. The owl is Chief of the Night, and has the power to help and protect people at night.

On the Plains owls are large predatory birds who also nest high in the trees, and they hunt silently at night. Owls are linked to the Four Powers that Never Sleep: thunder, lighting, wind, and clouds. The noise of Thunder rolls across the Plains while Lighting cracks the sky, and is especially dramatic at night. The Wind is ever present in the west, roars in storms, can be bone freezing, and bents all things in its wake. Clouds are great white puffs, moody streaks of black, gold or orange, or paint the sky a dull gray. These elements are dramatic on the Central Plains, and they quite consistently occur together as the weather changes. When they are not present the sky is a pure blue while at night the stars seem touchable.

The bluejay (*kiriki*) is the carrier of prayers to the sky, to *Tirawa*. The bluejay's skin or feathers are often tied to two pipes: a red one devoted to the sun and a black one for the moon. Some warriors when going on the warpath carry the bird on their head so it may carry their prayers for success aloft. Thus, the bluejay is the messenger between man and *Tirawa* carrying both prayers and sacrifices. Finally, blue feathers symbolize the clear sky.

Bluejays have a conspicuous coloring, and although they nest in trees, they spend a great deal of time feeding on the ground. Jays have a loud, raucous call which would make them good symbolic messengers - especially carrying petitions from raucous humans.

The woodpecker had the special protection of *Tirawa* and the Thunders because this bird cries out fearlessly during storms, and builds his nest in decaying trees. The woodpecker is the Chief of Trees, and can avert away from man the disasters of tempest and of lighting. The woodpecker is the protector of the life of men.

The woodpecker - there are 7 species on the Plains - lives and nests in the hollows of trees. The red-headed woodpecker, looking like a scalped warrior, is especially important in war symbolism as is its conspicuous noisy, but rhythmic pecking. Also on the flat Plains any tall standing object has the natural capacity to function as a lighting rod. Indeed, averting lighting from humans. At the same times lone, tall trees are conspicuous points on the featureless landscape and were often points on trails.

The ducks are significant, and have great powers. The head and skin of a mallard are part of the two sacred wands used in the Hako ceremony, a ceremony dealing with birds. Because the duck migrates it knows the pathless air and water as well as being at home on land where it knows the streams and springs of the earth. The duck is the Chief of Water.

The mallard's green iridescent head and feathers are used to symbolize the natural traits of all ducks. Their ability to fly to all parts of the world, to travel over water, to swim on water and to dive beneath water. Their migratory pattern reflects the great alternating dualism of winter and summer, and autumn and spring. Also their migratory abilities mean the birds know the unknown paths of earth.

The wren is the smallest and weakest bird, but its loud and cheerful song, which is sung conspicuously to the rising sun, is viewed by the Pawnee as evidence that all humans, even the most insignificant, can be happy.

## IV. Archaeological data

As mentioned at the beginning, this chapter argues archaeological data both documents the antiquity of Pawnee thought, but it can also be used to reconstruct aspects of it lost with Euroamerican contact. Data from the C.C. Witt site, a lodge and burial mound dating A.D. 1300, illustrates how the archaeologist can predict the type of artifact assemblage necessary to document the antiquity of Pawnee religious concepts: Data like the lodge floorplan with its 4-interior support posts, and near its west wall the 4-post pattern of an old altar. The lodge was so aligned, on a north-south, east-west axis, that at A.D. 1300, the rising vernal and autumnal equinox sunlight shone through the entrance, crossed the fireplace and struck the altar near the west wall (O'Brien, 1986:941-942). In so doing, the sunlight crossed over a storage pit located directly in front of the entrance.

Unique aspects of this altar is that it is not placed beside the west wall, as reported historically, but rather just in front of it. Therefore an ancient priest could sit behind it, and open a medicine bundle while the sun shone directly upon it. This specific position on the lodge floor in historic times was a sacred area called the Garden of Evening Star. Also in the historic period the most common piece of religious apparatus resting upon the altar, was a bison skull. No buffalo skull was found on the Witt altar, so we cannot determine whether a skull was removed from the building before it burnt, or if altars did not have bison skulls in prehistoric times. Clues that bison were not as important in prehistory before the arrival of the horse and gun is suggested by Holder (1970) who documents that all the ancient

Caddo-speaking horticulturalists were deeply dominated by an ideology, which emphasized Mother Corn.

Thus, both the layout of the Witt lodge as well as its orientation point to the reflecting aspects of Pawnee religious thought: the notion that the equinox sunlight should illuminate the altar, and the four star pillar posts as representative of the semi-cardinal points ideology (fig. 2).

From the floated entryway pit were recovered a variety of faunal remains (Brown, 1981), but particularly bird wings including the right wing of a red-headed woodpecker, the left wing of a bluejay, the distal portion of the right wing of the rare long-eared owl, and the right and left wing of a woodpecker - species unidentifiable. The symbolism of these birds has been discussed, and all are common in the Central Plains. Also recovered were four right and left wings of northern bobwhite quail, but present too in the same storage pit was a gar jaw, and a snapping turtle carapace. In another pit in the lodge four gar skulls were found. On the lodge floor just north of a 4-post altar was found the right talon of a bald eagle. No other parts of these creatures, suggesting their purely economic use, were found. Additionally, though not a bird, a gar jaw is an important element in the Pawnee Four Pole Ceremony, a ritual whose function is to renew the original federation of the villages (Murie, 1981:107). These materials have been interpreted by O'Brien (1986) as the remains of a prehistoric medicine bundle, and she argues the lodge belonged to a prehistoric priest.

Very significant for the assertion that one can reconstruct Pawnee cosmology from archaeological data, are the wings of the bobwhite. Though birds are important symbolic elements in Pawnee religion, as discussed earlier, no mention is made in Pawnee cosmology of bobwhite. The presence of four pairs of bobwhite wings with other sacred paraphernalia suggests that in the prehistoric past, the Pawnee had a symbolic role for the bobwhite.

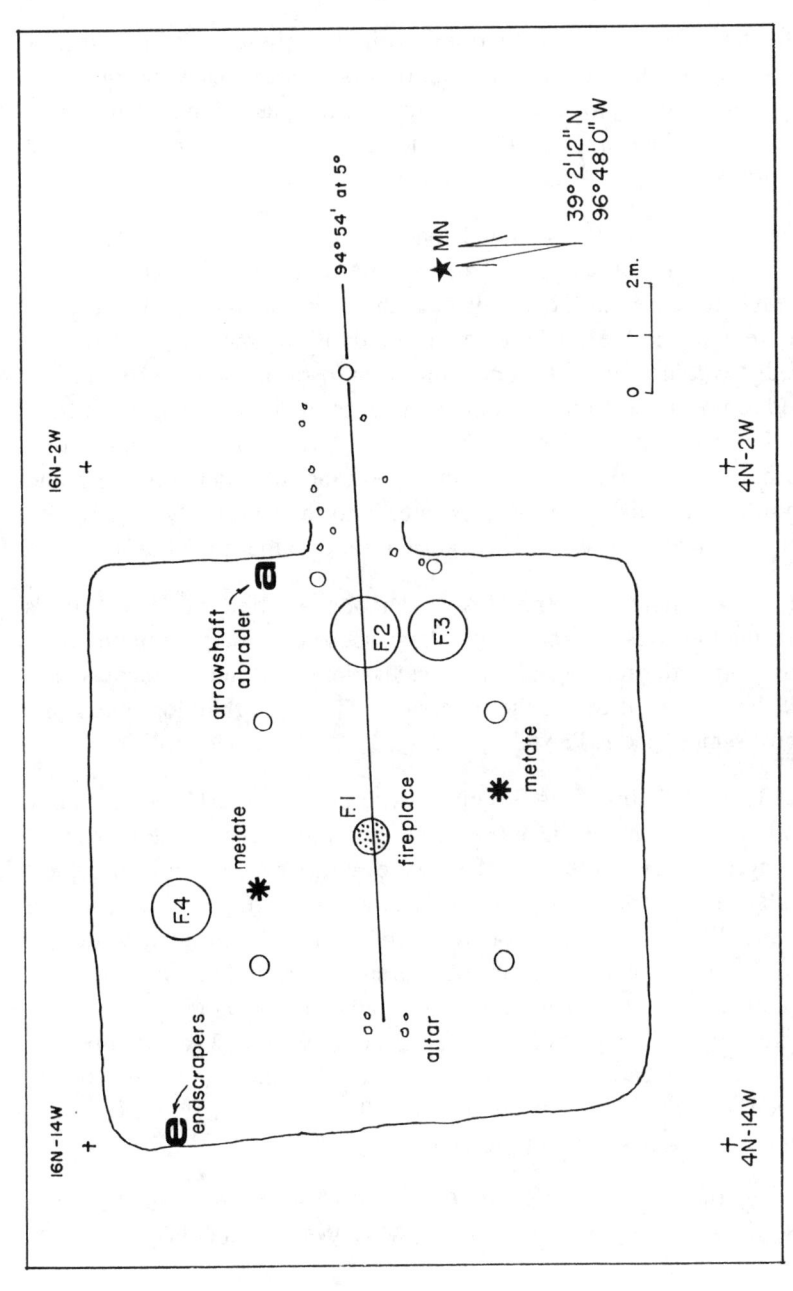

**Figure 2.** Floorplan of the C.C. Witt earthlodge showing the four-post altar, storage pits, fireplace, and equinox alignment at A.D.1300. Also indicated are the locations of a cluster of endscrapers, two metates, and an arrowshaft abrader.

Because the bobwhite is a ground-living bird the presence of its wings in association with others of ritually important sky birds raises the question, "were ground birds important at some time in the past in this cosmology?" This question is logical, given the Pawnee dualistic view, for ground-birds would complement sky-birds.

Fletcher writing in 1904 has noted that the turkey was important to the Pawnee in the past, and says its feathers were used instead of those of the brown eagle to represent the female element in the Hako rite; a white eagle feather represents the male element (1904:173). She (1904:279) also observed a ceremonial shift from using deer to bison, which she thought reflected a movement from one environment to another on the part of the ancient Pawnee. Historically the Pawnee have myths that they came from the south. It could also reflect the rising importance of bison in the 18th and 19th centuries as horses were incorporated into their lives. Hyde (1951:39) too mentions deer were sacrificed in ancient times rather than buffalo.

Hyde (1951:24) notes that the Hako ceremony is a bird ritual with birds representing the gods and the people. Its purpose is to increase the number of children in both present and future generations, and thus to increase the Pawnee themselves. If that is the function of the ritual, than logically some birds must symbolize the Pawnee.

Fletcher (1904:173) discusses the turkey at a point in the Hako ceremony where there is a "Song of the Woodpecker and the Turkey". She notes that "long, long ago," the turkey's feathers were used where the brown eagle's feathers are used today. The song explains why. Sometime in the past the turkey and the woodpecker both desired to be the 'protectors of the children of the human race'. Since children are symbolized as eggs, and turkey's lay many eggs, and also have more tail feathers than any other bird, the turkey argued they should be assigned this task. The woodpecker admitted it produced fewer eggs, but argued their eggs were better protected since their nests were in the trees. The turkey's nest, being on the ground, its eggs were subject to predation.

Turkeys, by the way, lay between 10 to 15 buff eggs (Bull and Farrand, 1977:631) or 8 to 15 (Udvardy, 1977:620) while woodpeckers lay only 4 or 5

(Bull and Farrand, 1977:508, 646). Bobwhite quail lay 10 to 15 white eggs (Bull and Farrand, 1977:493).

Because of the danger to the eggs the woodpecker prevailed, and the turkey was deposed. Also the brown eagle was put in the turkey's place because it was not quarrelsome, was gentle and cared for its young, and because of its strength protected them better (Fletcher, 1904:173).

Not surprising, this suggests that the Pawnee were aware of ground-living birds, and that at some time in the past had at least one in their cosmology, the turkey. Although Fletcher does not ask why the turkey was a female element, or why the change occurred, an obvious answer, given the Pawnee's logic, would be the earth is female, and the turkey is a ground-living bird.

Thus, archaeological data point to the importance of ground birds in the prehistoric past, an aspect which was lost in the 18th and 19th centuries. In fact O'Brien and Post (1988) argue that bobwhite quail were the symbol for the Pawnee as a people, and models of human behavior, especially parental behavior.

In the Central Plains the major birds who spend much of their time on the ground, are the bobwhite quail, prairie chicken and turkey. The prairie chicken has a striking courtship pattern in the spring, and lives in undisturbed grassland (Bull and Farrand, 1977:494-496). The turkey is polygamous, the male struts and gobbles to hold his harem, and the birds live in open woodlands and forests with some natural clearings. Many Indians considered the bird stupid and cowardly (Bull and Farrand, 1977:631-632). The bobwhite, unlike other pheasant-like birds, is highly social, forming families in the spring and coveys of families in the fall (Udvardy, 1977:533-534). In fact it is suspected that the bobwhite was chosen because of its 'human-like' qualities.

For example the shape, and the mode of construction, between the earthlodge and quail nest are very similar (O'Brien and Post, 1988:493). Also significant is the annual cycle and spatial distribution of quail (Rosene, 1969:57-101) which starts in the spring with the establishment of nesting territories by males to attract a mate. The new territory and mate are then defended from single males. The young are presocial at birth, and follow their parents about the territory. Territories abut each other, and in the fall family units and unmated males coalesce into coveys. The coveys forage and roost together through the late fall and winter. Patterns of covey territorial defense are the same as nesting territory defense with the older male(s) defending the area. Covey areas are also spaced like nesting territories, but with a proportionally larger area being claimed. With the arrival of spring the covey breaks up into nesting pairs.

This pattern of dispersal and coalesce is reflected in prehistory for in the past earthlodges, individual farmsteads, were spatially separated up and down the rivers and streams. The Indians raised crops, collected wild plants, and used the animal resources located nearby. However the presence of selected small numbers of bison bone tools suggests that they hunted bison on the high plains, carrying the meat, hides, and selected bones back home. Such hunts were very likely conducted by a number of isolated farmstead households coming together. Thus, an annual alternating cycle of communal coalescence and breakup into family units would have been displayed by the Indians and the quail: pairing in the spring to farm and coalescing in the autumn to hunt. This pattern of hunting in the fall or winter is quite an old for the both the Caddo and Wichita had such a complementary system before hunting with the horse became important (see Bell, Jelks and Newcomb, 1974:343; Wyckoff and Baugh, 1980:252).

The war paint of the Pawnee, a black or dark brown line painted over the eyes, matches the dark marking around the eyes of the male bobwhite. The *pariki* (hair scalplock) of the Pawnee, symbolic of them as a people, matches the raised crest of the fighting quail.

The behavior of the bobwhite (Leopold, 1977:67-70, Stoddard, 1936: 15-67) is highly social and gregarious, except in the nesting cycle; in the fall and winter they group into coveys and their behavior appears highly organized; in early spring their behavior changes when pairing occurs, and the males become aggressive and they remain so to the end of the breeding cycle. When the young are hatched parents and chicks form a firm social group, as summer gives way to fall family groups form coveys. Bobwhites of either sex also have a strong tendency to adopt and rear lost or orphaned chicks or even a brood. When flushed, their main concern is to re-establish the group. Quail imitate one another, and this disciplined behavior is learned by the very young when imitating parents. Single birds appear uneasy, distracted, and give out a loud assembly call. Indeed, the need to reassemble at roosting time is so great, it appears the birds will do so even if it is dangerous. The imitative tendency pervades life and the birds follow each other even when feeding. Leadership seems to be a manner of one bird (male or female) going off and being followed. If the bird is not followed it returns to the group. The birds are cooperative in sharing a good food supply, or in calling out in danger. Through the year the cocks have sentry duty, but especially after pairing. He guards the hen while she feeds, builds the nest, and incubates the eggs. After the young are developed a cock is still most likely to perceive danger and to give warning.

If one has ever watched a covey of quail in the autumn they clearly look like small people, busily going about their tasks and assignments. From the behavior of these highly social birds, and given the Pawnee habit of symbolizing bird behavior, it would be easy for the Pawnee to isolate patterns of human social interaction and ethics to serve as symbolic models of Pawnee behavior: fidelity of pairs, children imitate their parents, parents care for and protect the young, any adult in society cares for orphaned or lost children, leadership is for the good of the group, males protect females and the young, food is shared by all, and the importance of the group is paramount.

Thus, the four pair of bobwhite wings recovered from the Witt lodge belonged to a prehistoric priest, and were part of the religious paraphernalia of that cleric. Just as the Eagle symbolized the warrior and Morning Star; the Owl, the messenger from *Tirawa*; the Bluejay, the messenger to *Tirawa*; the Woodpecker, the protector of humans; the Wren, the symbol of human cheerfulness, and the Duck, knower of the unknown paths and knowledge, so O'Brien and Post (1988) proposed that the bobwhite quail were one of the bird elements of the ancestors of the historic Pawnee, maybe the South Bands, and that the quail were the symbol for the people themselves, and particularly the symbol of parental behavior. In the Pawnee system the quail should logically be the Chief of People.

Associated with the lodge, about a quarter of a mile due south of it, was a burial mound in which were recovered the highly scattered and rodent gnawed remains of 13 individuals: 6 adults, 3 adolescents - one a 13 year old girl, and 4 children (West and Sager, 1991). Also present were over 32 arrowheads and fragments belonging to four types. These materials we have interpreted as representing the remains of at least one Morning Star sacrifice around A.D. 1300 (O'Brien, 1991).

The sacrifice of a captive maiden by the Skiri Pawnee in the early 19th century shocked and horrified European and American observers of the Plains Indians. The painting of this young woman half red and half black, the tying of her to a scaffold, and then shooting her full of arrows reminded some students of Indian life of the sacrifices of the Aztecs.

This ritual has since its earliest reporting fascinated the serious scholar of Plains Indian life because of its uniqueness, and because it was completely embedded into a complex religious theology. It was essentially a fertility ceremony in which Morning Star (Mars) has a sexual union with Evening Star (Venus), and from that union came the whole human race. The human sacrifice is a symbolic re-enactment of that event. It is a way for the Pawnee to revitalize and fertilize all the universe, and to repay Morning Star for his manifold gifts to mankind.

The ritual began when an individual man had a vision to make the sacrifice. After consultation with the priests that man went out from his village with his warrior friends to capture (unharmed) a young woman of appropriate age from an enemy tribe. The young woman was taken back to the village, and was kept in the company of the responsible ritual leaders until the correct time to begin the four day ceremony that culminated in her death.

She was dressed in appropriate garments, symbolically painted, tied to a wooden scaffold whose beams are tree species-coded to the four semi-cardinal points, and at the moment Morning Star appeared in the sky, at dawn, was shot in the heart by the man who captured her, and who pledged the ceremony. He came up from a nearby ravine where he and other men were hiding. A small cut was made with a special knife in her heart, and the small trickle of blood from it was caught upon buffalo meat to be offered to

Morning Star and *Tirawa*. After this was done every Pawnee male had to shoot an arrow into the sacrifice. This included boys as well as male infants in their father's arms.

On completion of the shooting, when her back was full of arrows, all the males circled the scaffold four times, and then were dispersed by the priests. The young woman's body was removed from the racking by four priestly assistants who carried her body about a quarter of a mile from the place of sacrifice. She was laid face down upon the prairie with her head to the east. The four assistant priests sang a final song over her to the effect that her body would now return to the earth because all the animals mentioned in the song would consume her remains. Following the ritual, the men returned to the village, and a general rejoicing occurred. One authority, Ralph Linton (1923), says the arrows were removed from her body after she was cut down from the scaffold, and they were placed into four piles. Unfortunately, he does not mention what happens to them or to her body.

Aside from the role of arrows in the Morning Star sacrifice we have other evidence on the sacred character of arrows which might be applicable to this data. While every man made his own bow and bowstring, only a select number of men (five among the historic Skiri) made arrows. The presence of an arrowshaft abrader and arrowshaft straighters in the Witt lodge suggests a male occupant who made arrows. But more than just an object made by a small group, the arrow symbolically was associated with the eagle who flew high through the air. Every sacred bundle had four sacred arrows, and different colored sacred arrows had different effects. The keeper of the black-arrow brought buffalo, the red-arrow if shot at any danger would overcome it, the yellow and white arrows would bring rainstorms. Arrows had feathers attached to them so they would get straight to heaven, which was the reason feathers were placed on pipestems, to make prayers go straight to heavens. Thus, symbolically arrows are associated with eagles and Morning Star, war and the warrior.

## V. Discussion

From the preceding presentation one can see how it is possible to use the historical and archaeological records to illuminate, and enlarge our understanding of ancient Pawnee religious cosmology, and to document its antiquity. By using the Pawnee's logic and examining the environment of the Central Plains we can explore other questions. In fact it was by using this logic that O'Brien (1987) argued the Morning Star sacrifice was itself dualistic, with a girl being sacrificed to Morning Star and a boy to Evening Star. Historically sacrifices of captive males were reported, but scholars viewed their use as a stop gap measure because a girl was not available at the appropriate time. O'Brien (1987), however, suggested that a male was sacrificed to Evening Star, and a female to Morning Star.

Thus, if we begin to think like a Pawnee we can, in fact, discover gaps in the ethnographic record. For example, given the Pawnee's ideas on birds one can ask, where does the majestic Great Blue Heron fit in this scheme, or the bright red cardinal, or the marsh hawk, which is the only harrier on the Plains and is blue-gray in color? Indeed, one can examine all the common birds of the Central Plains, and ask what their position was within this cosmology. Common birds, besides eagles, hawks, owls, ducks, woodpeckers, bluejays, and bobwhite quail, birds like the loon, or meadowlark, prairie chicken, or turkey, geese, or turkey vulture, chickadee, or titmouse, martins, or larks. Where are they in the scheme of things, and were they even all used?

For example, one myth associates the Golden Eagle with *Tirawa*, but not all Skiri Pawnee agree with that assertion (Dorsey, 1904:342, n.127). Father De Smet (Chittenden and Richardson, 1969:974-988) was among the Pawnee in 1847, and actually witnessed a Morning Star sacrifice. He reported the Pawnee highly venerated a stuffed bird (ibid.:975), and that they decorated themselves with the plumes of the eagle and heron (ibid.:982). He also states (ibid.:985) that, "They ornament their hair with the feathers of the heron, and of the gray eagle, a bird superstitiously venerated by them." This last bit of information allows one to suspect that the marsh hawk may be important as it is the only gray, bluish-gray, rapine on the Plains. The wearing of heron feathers is clearly significant. I suspect that the bird which represents *Tirawa*, is, in fact, the Great Blue Heron, and not the Golden Eagle. I suspect this because all major powers of the universe have a bird symbol. Great Blue Herons are blue in color, are associated with the sky, but they fish in water, and nest in trees. Their eggs are greenish-blue in color, and they usually lay four (Goodrich, 1945:70). The number four is profoundly symbolic to the Pawnee, being, as noted earlier, a dualism of a dualism.

Father De Smet, as noted, pointed out the religious importance of a 'gray eagle'. The marsh hawk is the only gray rapine bird on the Plains, and interestingly is the only harrier. It nests on the ground and families of them gather together on the ground after breeding (Udvardy, 1986: 453-454). Finally, it flies low to the ground as it hunts rather than diving or plunging upon its prey like the other hawks and eagles. Since all the powers of the universe are identified with a bird symbol, and because each has an errand boy bird I suspect the marsh hawk is in fact Tirawa's errand boy. His task is to carry messages from Tirawa to the Pawnee. This he could be seen to do as he skimmed the ground while hunting its small creatures, including the bobwhite quail. Thus, symbolically he was also carrying Pawnee to Tirawa.

Like ducks, the common loon is a migratory visitor to the Plains, (ibid: 145-146). It is a large diving bird, which has been caught in nets up to 200 feet below the surface. That fact, coupled with its high human-like laughing tremolo (Udvardy, 1977:475-476), would surely attract attention. Loons, because they fly close to the heavens know the secrets of doctors, and therefore are one of the seven chief gods of doctors (Murie, 1981:39-40). Loons are probably associated with the constellation Scorpio, and are used as alters (ibid.:40-41). They are set up at the west side of a lodge (ibid.:167). The loon's association with healing is outlined in the myth of the origin of the Loon Medicine Ceremony (Dorsey, 1906:254-261).

Like major powers and gods the animals associated with animal lodges also have birds who are errand people. For example, the magpie and buzzard function thus for the Spring-Hill Lodge (ibid.:245).

Finally, we can ask, if the hawks and eagles symbolize Morning Star, which bird symbolizes Evening Star? It would have to be a ground bird, for the earth is female, but cannot be the bobwhite for they symbolize the Pawnee. I suspect the bird was really the turkey, particularly since the turkey is a very common ground bird in eastern Texas and Oklahoma from whence all Caddo-speakers originally came. I think this is particularly the case because the meadowlark, a ground nesting song bird, is Evening Star's errand boy (Dorsey, 1904:333 n.45), carrying messages from Evening Star to humans. While owls are associated with Evening Star, they symbolize the Four Powers of the West which are under her control: Wind, Cloud, Lighting and Thunder. From the Storms of the Four Powers come Dew, Fog, Mist and Rain (Dorsey, 1904:7). Life-sustaining rain naturally comes out of the west in the Central Plains.

If specific trees are positioned to the four pillars, where do plants fit? Mother Corn we know is color-coded to the four semi-cardinal points: with yellow, white, red and black varieties, but what are the associations of the other domesticates: sunflower, squash, beans and marsh elder? Where do important wild plants like the prairie turnip fit, and especially what of medicinal plants? These questions are important because through Evening Star and the Four Powers That Never Sleep, *Tirawa* gave seeds to women (Dorsey, 1904:7).

Finally, though not discussed here the Pawnee awareness of the geographic aspects of their environment has been explored by Parks and Wedel (1985). They have attempted to archaeologically identify specific sacred places - animal lodges, and to find the locations of historic villages associated with specific medicine bundles.

## VI. Conclusions

If all these proposals and assertions are correct, this study demonstrates several things. First, and most important, it shows how Pawnee thought is powerfully linked to features of the natural environment of the Central Plains. It shows how that cosmology is pervaded by dualisms, which are themselves embedded in nature, with the most fundamental being earth and sky.

Second, it demonstrates the antiquity of the Pawnee's complex religious ideology, and how we have the means of reconstructing aspects of it that have been lost in the wake of the dramatic depopulation and cultural changes that occurred in the 18th and 19th centuries. Additionally, since the

Pawnee live in Oklahoma further researches on their dualistic philosophy are possible.

Third, it reveals that the archeologist has the ability to reconstruct some intangible aspects of society. It also suggests that they have a more important role than generally assumed in documenting the ancient religious ideas and systems of non-literate people, and that they have the potential for studying changes in religious thought, and illuminating historically obscure religious concepts.

## References

Bell, R. E., Jelks, E. B. and Newcomb, W. W. (1974). *Wichita Indians*. New York, Garland Publishing.

Blaine, M. R. (1990). *Pawnee Passage:* 1870-1875. Norman, University of Oklahoma Press.

Brown, M. E. (1981). *Cultural Behavior as Reflected in the Vertebrate Faunal Assemblage of Three Smoky Hill Sites*. Unpublished M.A. thesis, Department of Anthropology, University of Kansas.

Bull, J. and Farrand, J. Jr. (1977). *The Audubon Society Field Guide to North American Birds: Eastern Region*. New York, Alfred A. Knopf.

Chamberlain, V. D. (1982). *When Stars Came Down to Earth: Cosmology of the Skiri Pawnee Indians of North America*. Anthropological Papers No. 26. Los Altos, Ballena Press.

Chittenden, H. M. and Richardson, A. T. (1969[1905]). *The Life, Letters and Travels of Father Pierre-Jean De Smet, S . J. 1801-1873*. 4 Vols. New York, Francis P. Harper. (Kraus Reprint, New York).

Dorsey, G. A. (1904). *Traditions of the Skidi Pawnee*. New York, American Folklore Society. Memoir No. VIII.

Dorsey, G. A. (1906). *The Pawnee: Mythology*. Washington DC., Carnegie Institution Publications, No . 59.

Fletcher, A. C. (1904). *The Hako: A Pawnee Ceremony*. Washington D.C., Twenty-second Annual Report of the Bureau of American Ethnology, Part 2.

Goodrich, A. L. (1945). *Birds in Kansas*. Report of the Kansas State Board of Agriculture, LXIV, no. 267. Topeka.

Holder, P. (1970). *The Hoe and the Horse on the Plains*. Lincoln, University of Nebraska Press.

Hyde, G. E. (1951). *The Pawnee Indians*. Norman, University of Oklahoma Press.

Leopold, A. S. (1977). *The California Quail*. Berkeley, University of California Press.

Linton, R. (1923). *The Sacrifice to the Morning Star by the Skidi Pawnee*. Chicago, Field Museum of Natural History, Anthropological Leaflets, No. 6.

Murie, J. R. (1981). *Ceremonies of the Pawnee; Part I: The Skiri and Part II: The South Bands.* Edited by Douglas R. Parks. Washington D.C., Smithsonian Contributions to Anthropology No. 27.

O'Brien, P. J. (1986). "Prehistoric Evidence for Pawnee Cosmology." *American Anthropologist,* 88 (4):939-946.

O'Brien, P. J. (1987). "Morning Star Sacrifices: Contradiction or Dualism?" *Plains Anthropologist,* 32 (115):73-76.

O'Brien, P. J. (1991). "Evidence for the Antiquity of Women's Roles in Pawnee Society." In M. Kornfeld (ed.). *Approaches to Gender Processes on the Great Plains.* Plains Anthropologist, 36 (134), Memoir 26:51-64.

O'Brien, P. J. and Post, D. M. (1988). "Speculations About Bobwhite Quail and Pawnee Religion." *Plains Anthropologist,* 33(122): 489-504.

Parks, D. R. and Wedel, W. R. (1985). "Pawnee Geography: Historical and Sacred." *Great Plains Quarterly,* 5:143-176.

Rosene, W. (1969). *The Bobwhite Quail: Its Life and Management.* New Brunswick, Rutgers University.

Stoddard, H. L. (1936). *The Bobwhite Quail: Its Habits, Preservation and Increase.* New York, Charles Scribner's Sons.

Udvardy, M. D. F. (1977). *The Audubon Society Field Guide to North American Birds: Western Region.* New York, Alfred A. Knopf.

Weltfish, G. (1965). *The Lost Universe: Pawnee Life and Culture.* Lincoln, University of Nebraska Press.

West, D. L. and Sager, R. D. (1991). "The Dentition of the Smoky Hill Burials from the Witt Mound." In M. Kornfeld (ed.). *Approaches to Gender Processes on the Great Plains.* Plains Anthropologist 36(134), Memoir 26:65-68.

Wyckoff, D. G. and Baugh, T. G. (1980). "Early Historic Hasinai Elites: A Model for the Material Culture of Governing Elites." *Mid-Continental Journal of Archaeology,* 5(2):225-288.

# THE ACTION-CONSTITUTIVE MEANING OF NEWARK: THE FORMS THAT COUNT

A. Martin Byers

### I. Introduction

This essay interprets the large-scale embankment earthworks of the Central Ohio Valley, attributed to the Middle Woodland Period, in terms of the perceptual and action experiences of the world that their builders/users must have had - if we are to make sense of these monumental constructions. It is argued that in building and using these earthworks the responsible social populations constituted and realized their collective experiencing of the world, what is termed their 'umwelt'. The object of their 'umwelt' was the tangible world of their senses which they constituted as Nature. Hence the intelligibility of these earthworks is established by demonstrating they were used as the medium through which the builders/users constituted and reconstituted their 'umwelt' experiences in action, thereby discharging their sacred duties to Nature.

Underwriting this experience-oriented interpretation of the earthworks is a pragmatic or action-constitutive approach to characterizing the nature of material cultural meaning. This stands in strong contrast to the orthodox archaeological view, namely, that material cultural meaning is used to mediate a type of 'silent' speaking about the world, a view that is here termed referentialism. This treats material cultural meaning as based on the 'stands for' referential relation. The action-constitutive view favored in this essay treats material cultural meaning as based on the 'counts as' constitutive relation. This necessitates understanding material culture as an essential constituent element of the activity which it is habitually used to mediate. The meaning and sense of prehistoric monuments are then articulated as serving the Intentionality of a people that can only be satisfied by the use of the appropriate range of material things to constitute their sacred collective actions, actions which discharge their duties to Nature.

Figure 1 is a depiction of the prehistoric embankment earthworks of Newark as they would have been seen in the early 1840's from a bird's eye vantage point. Even though the geometrical regularities of the site do not hit the ground-level observer as immediately as they do from the overhead view, Newark must still have been an impressive site to the newly arrived American pioneers in the late 1700's. For example, today the large Circle-Octagon feature in the upper left hand corner currently incorporates a full nine-hole golf course. In particular, knowing the fact that the geometrical features of this site were constructed of earth fill by a people who at the time of construction practiced foraging and lived a largely semi-nomadic way of life must color our visual experience of them. Indeed, it ought to generate in our seeing them a mixed experiential sense of awe and puzzlement. Why would a people, apparently quite limited as to the amount of surplus labor that they could mobilize, direct what capacity they were capable of mobilizing to such an endeavor. From a Western outsider's perspective, drawing on a World View that characterizes preindustrial nomadic social populations as subsisting at the close-to-starvation level, the construction of Newark would seem to be so very pointless.

The site is located in the center of the small central Ohio city from which it derives its name. However, the Newark site is not unique. It is only one example of about fifteen similar 'geometrical' embankment earthworks, many of them found in south-central Ohio. Approximately 100 km to the southwest of Newark is a cluster of such earthworks, two 'classic' examples of which are the High Bank Works (fig. 2) and the Liberty Works (fig. 3). These are only about two km from each other on the east bank of the Scioto River where the Paint Creek joins it. On the west bank of the Scioto, opposite High Bank and Liberty Works, is the small city of Chillicothe, the seat of Ross County, Ohio. In numerical terms Ross County contains the largest concentration of these geometrical type earthworks, although others are found further south, east and west. For example, the Scioto continues due south from the Paint Creek about fifty km to join the Ohio at Portsmouth -which is the site of another major clustering of geometrical earthworks (fig. 4).

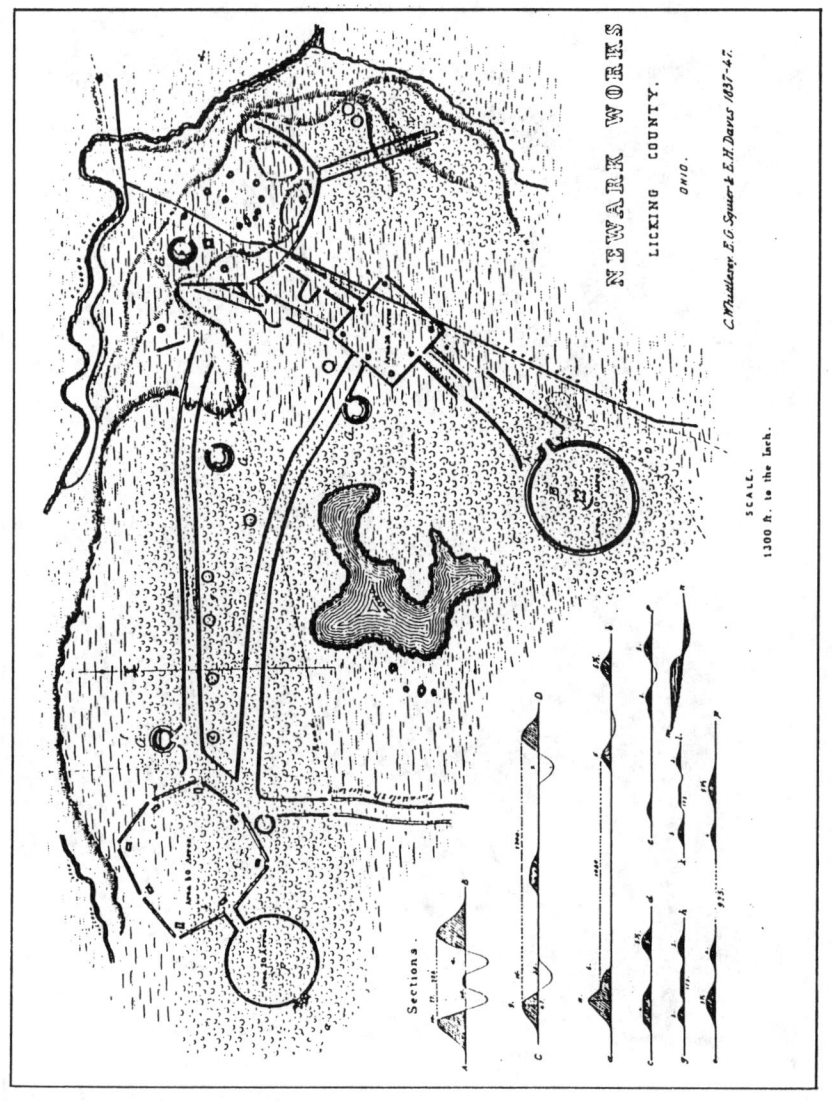

**Figure 1:** Newark - Sacred Dual C-R Motif type (Squier and Davis, 1973:Plate XXV).

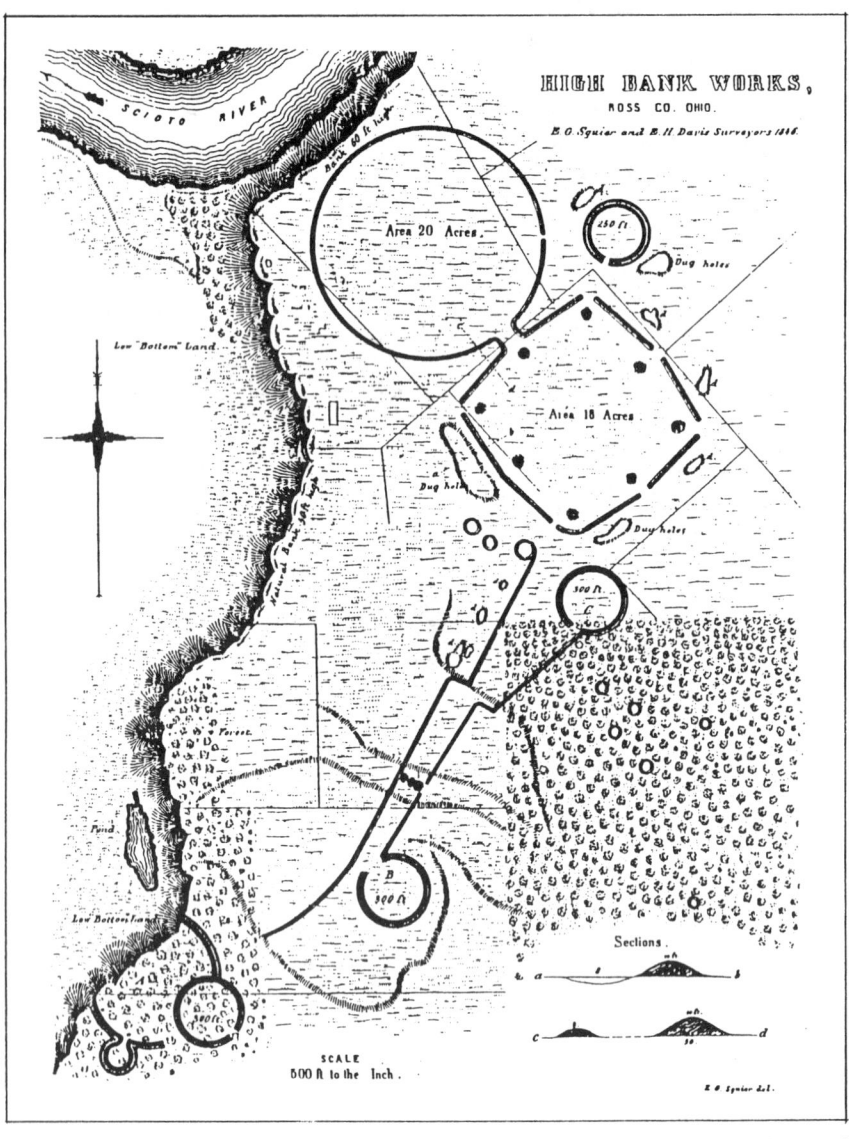

**Figure 2**: High Bank Works - High Bank C-R Motif type (Squier and Davis,1973:Plate XVI).

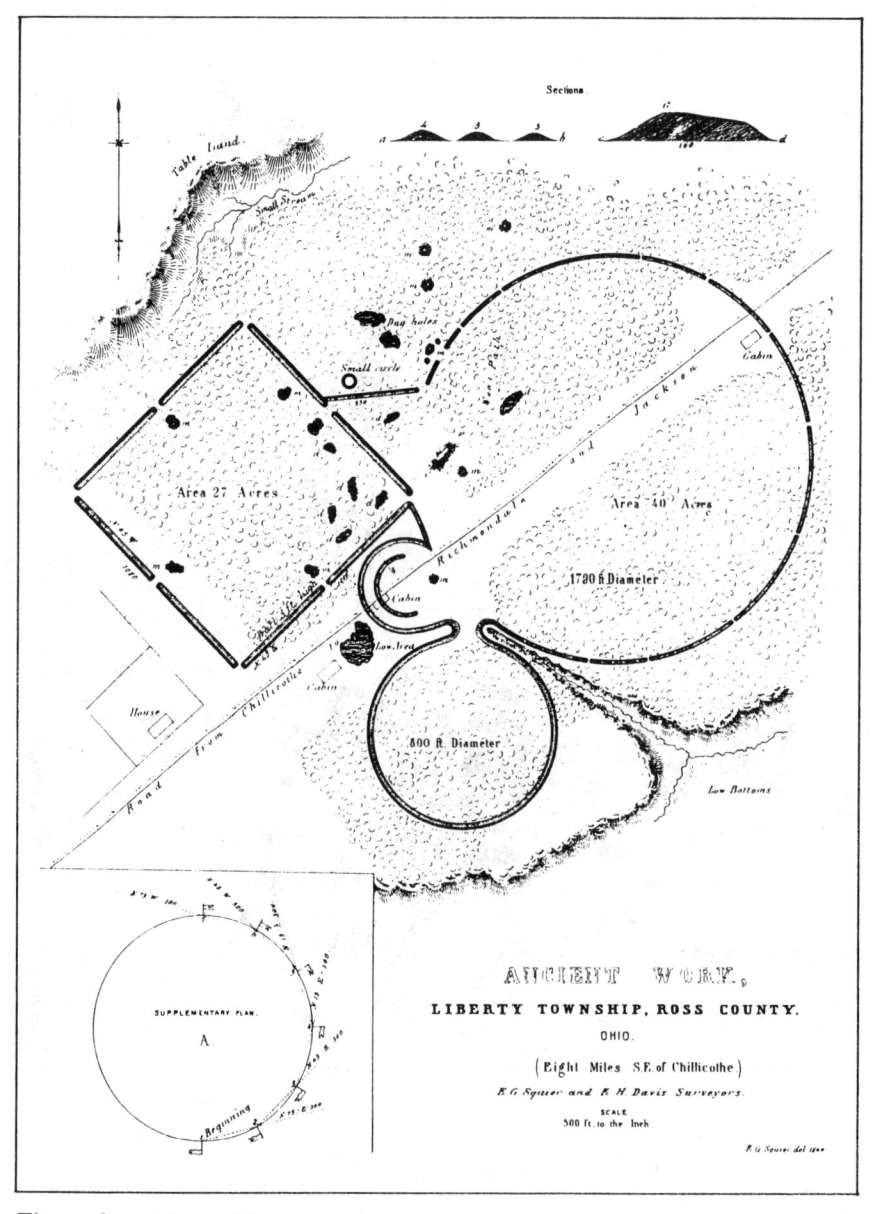

**Figure 3**: Liberty Works - Paint Creek C-R Motif type (Squier and Davis, 1973:PlateXX).

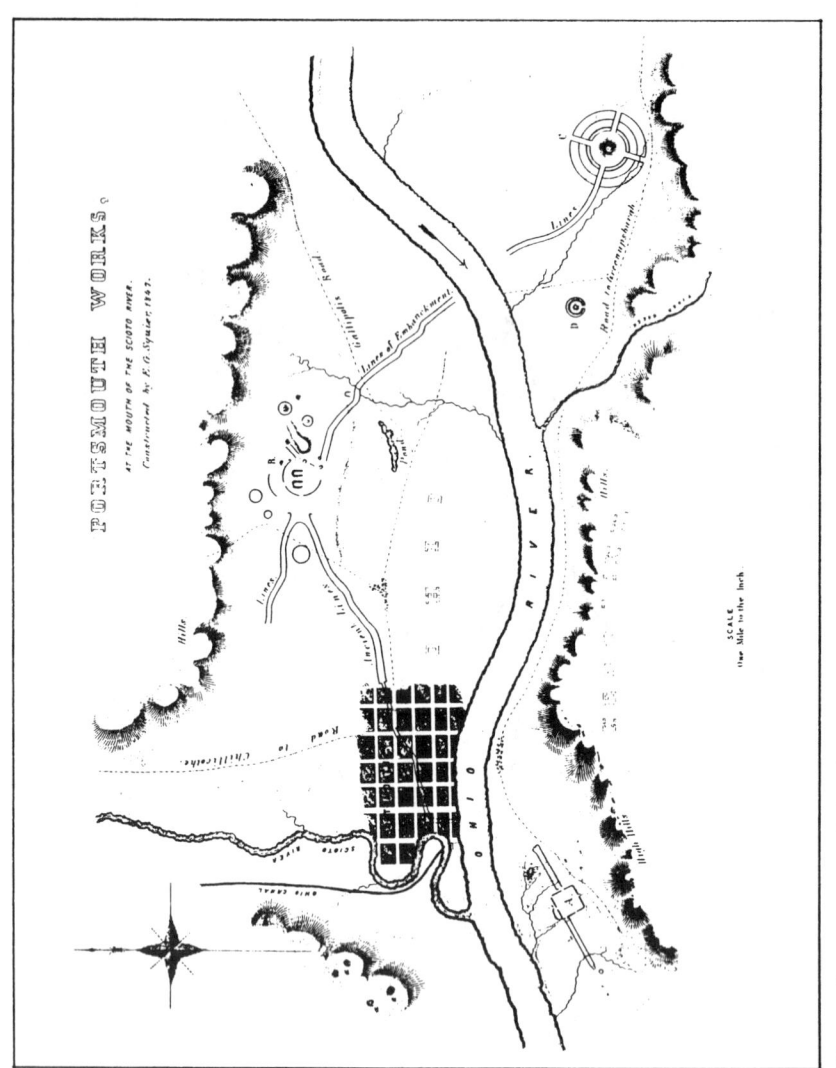

**Figure 4:** Portsmouth (Squier and Davis, 1973: Plate XXVII)

Collectively, these and similar Ohio Valley earthworks are attributed to the prehistoric Ohio Hopewellian culture, which is dated between 100 B.C. and A.D. 500 (Fischer, 1974; Greber, 1976, 1979, 1983). Figures 1, 2, 3 and 4 are taken from the published work of two amateur archaeologists, E. G. Squier and E. H. Davis (1973). Its full title is *Ancient Monuments of the Mississippi Valley Comprising the Results of Extensive Original Surveys and Explorations*. It was originally published in 1848 as Volume One of the Smithsonian Contributions to Knowledge Series. It includes bird's-eye view plats of all the major geometrical sites of the Central Ohio Valley, as well as many non-geometrical and sub-symmetrical embankment earthworks of the same magnitude in south-west Ohio and central Kentucky. Accompanying these plats are fairly extensive and detailed descriptive and interpretive commentaries of the sites by the authors. This makes it one of the earliest comprehensive publications of prehistoric archaeology in North America.

Almost all of these features have embankments made of earth fill, although a few are found made of piled field stone. The average height of the embankments ranges between 1 m to 2 m and their widths between 2 m to 10 m. However, some are larger, reaching up to 5 m in height. For example, the embankments forming the neck gateway of Circle E in fig. 1 (lower center, also referred to as the Fairground Circle) are about 5 m high and the contiguous borrow trenches from which their earth fill was procured have almost an equal depth (Squier and Davis, 1973; Wright, 1990). The areal dimensions of these symmetrical to sub-symmetrical earthworks often incorporate between 20 to 40 acres. The Newark Circle-Octagon (fig. 1, upper left), for example, has embankments that average 2-3 m high. One of its attached features, the so-called Observatory Mound that is tangent to the southwest sector of the circumference (this Mound will figure prominently later in the analysis of this site), is a monumental earthwork in itself. It is 5-6 m high by 50 m long. The Circle has a diameter of 322 m and the attached Octagon is a transformed 322 m square. And this magnitude is not unique as many of the earthworks required the construction of embankments totalling 5-8 km or more in length (Essenpreis and Mosley, 1984). For this reason alone the earthworks can be fairly characterized as monumental in size.

## II. The meaning of material cultural features

The point of this essay will be to interpret Newark in terms of the meaning that it held for its builders/users. Clearly, given the standard western world view of prehistoric and preindustrial peoples that I touched upon above, and given the empirical fact that Newark (and other similar sites) exist, then the requisite surplus labor was successfully mobilized and directed. It follows that we must admit the inadequacy of our western world view about how cultural others perceive their world. I shall start from the following presumption. In the understanding of those peoples responsible for Newark (and other sites), physically acting in the manner that such construction necessitated made incredible sense to them. To understand why, we must start at the beginning and ask how these earthworks served to satisfy the socio-culturally constituted sensibilities of the responsible populations.

In saying 'start at the beginning' I am not taking a temporal but a structural position. Some archaeologists have accounted for large scale construction of this order in political ideological terms, an impression management process by which the rulers entrench their power (Trigger, 1990). The problem with this is that it begs the question. Why, precisely, would building earthworks, rather than pyramids or platforms, count as impressive actions, worthy of a people's admiration of their leaders? Even when a 'practical' explanation can be given, e.g., the Great Wall of China, there is almost always, in such massive construction programs, a surplus of patterning and size that cannot be accounted for in such utilitarian terms. In other words, in order to explain human production and use of material things, we must first establish the meaning, in terms of intentionality, that they hold for the producers/users.

I shall follow Searle (1983) in my treatment of meaning, considering the latter as the set of structural rules and representations that is internal to the intentionality which the construction and use of the earthworks served to satisfy. A central element of such satisfaction was the felicitous performance of intentional material actions that conformed to these rules. Amongst other stipulations, the rules determined what forms of material things must be present and used in mediating forms of behavior that would both be and count as satisfying the intentions with which they were performed, that is, would constitute fully felicitous material actions. Hence, Newark manifests meanings, i.e., the content of the intentions its construction/use satisfied, the wants it fulfilled, the beliefs it realized, and the perceptions it re-constituted. These must first be established before we can move to the political, etc., level of explanation. For example, even the Egyptian pharaoh, if he really wanted to exercise impression management, had to order construction that made sense to the people.

This intentionalist perspective on the meaning of things, monumental constructions in particular, is not reductionist - in the sense that given a certain belief, certain monumental construction was necessary. Rather, it presumes that in any given instance of construction we have manifest before us the outcome of a balance of forces - political, economic, social. Hence, the construction of Newark, for example, was a contingent event. It could have been otherwise - if the particular balance of internal interests and powers of the community had been otherwise (Bhaskar, 1979; Giddens, 1976, 1979, 1981, 1984).

### 1. The action-constitutive view

In these terms, then, one could say that the meaning of an action is the structural content of the intention with which it was performed. When the structural rules of meaning are shared, they constitute part of that complex intersubjective reality we term a people's culture. What I have implicated here is the claim that the nature of the meaning of *material cultural* items is best characterized in action-constitutive rather than referential terms. Whereas the latter form of rules conventionally structures the meaning of things on the basis of the 'stands for' relation, the former does so on the basis of the 'counts as' relation. Reference is most characteristic of language. For example, in English the semantic force of a word such as 'cat' relies on its conventionally 'standing for' 'that four legged animal over there'. In contrast an objectification that is grounded on the 'counts as' conventional relation has non-referential constitutive generative force. For example, the meaning of the Christian cross is the part of the *content of the intentionality* that its regular (1) use-in-action and (2) perception-in-use serves to satisfy. (1) and (2) are simultaneous, of course, for the actors must regulatively self-monitor perceptually the actions they perform in order to constitute them as felicitous. In this view, material culture is not merely a physical medium to bring about intended material transformations; in virtue of human self-reflexivity and symbolic capacity it is an essential constituent element of the activity it is regularly used to mediate (Byers, 1991, 1992. As the object is rule-governed in use, its form and objective properties are also rule-governed in production. The meaning just is the content of the intentionality that its use is intended to serve.

In this sense, in virtue of holding/wearing the cross, both in his own perceptual experience and that of his parishioners, the priest is endowed with sacred force, i.e., a virtual power derived, in their shared understanding (religious culture), from the highest creative authority of the universe, the Christian God. Hence, in uttering certain standard sounds, the latter are virtually transformed so as to count as an act of blessing. Just as material artifacts have endowment or *ascriptive power* to transform both the speech and non-speech actions of their possessors, so monumental features, such as, Newark, are taken by their builders to mediate power-based properties that endow those who behave in their context with virtual properties so that their behaviors count as fully felicitous performances of the intended (religious, ceremonial) actions. In short, I shall argue that the nature of the meaning of monumental features such as Newark is best understood in 'elocutionary' or speech action-constitutive terms rather than 'propositional' or referential force terms.

Now the acronym, IFIDS, standing for Elocutionary Force Indicating Devices, refers to the grammatical conventions that constitute utterances as the speech actions they are (Austin, 1962; Searle, 1969, 1979, 1983). Unfortunately we have no equivalent term when speaking of the action force of material cultural meaning. Therefore, I have coined the acronym, ACFIDS, short for Action-Constitutive Force Indicating Devices, to serve in referring to the range of properties that material things are made to possess by their producers so that they will have action-constitutive force in use (Byers, 1992). We can speak of the ACFIDS as the rules of style that characterize a material cultural assemblage - in whole or in part. And style, as the objective patterning of material cultural things, just is the material manifestation of the ACFID rules, norms and standards. In the absence of things that manifest the appropriate range of patterning, i.e., ACFID style, realizing action that is fully felicitous will be impossible and the Intentionality of the subjects will be frustrated. Life will be experienced as truncated and incomplete.

## 2. World view and the 'Umwelt'

On theoretical grounds I shall argue that prehistoric, monumental features such as Newark derive their ACFID force from the 'World View' of a people, the latter being orally realized as the content of the beliefs which they might express if asked to explain the 'meaning' of Newark. The world view, as a set of representations, constitutes the content of those beliefs that have the physical world as their object. This set stipulates and delineates that range of events, processes and things - both as manifested and as 'hidden' - of the objective physical world that go into making up a people's natural world, the latter constituted in their understanding as Nature. In this view Nature is that part of the objective world that a people *construct* or constitute in their understanding as *relevant* or meaningful.

Now, in any particular cultural community, it would be quite surprising to find the world as Nature being fully/absolutely isometric with the physical world (not to mention how this could be proved). Clearly, as a constitution of reality, part of Nature will be properties that are not tangible to human perception, e.g., sacredness, capacity to be owned, etc. I shall treat the latter as being materially mediated by those physical elements of the objective world that constitute the tangible aspects of Nature. Hence, intangible properties may be fully constituted as part of the world view and exist only in the instances of actual perceptual/action experiencing of a people. In short, in virtue of the world view, a preindustrial people characteristically *act* upon and *see* the objects of their perceiving/acting, namely, the objective world, as being 'sacred' (Douglas, 1966, 1970, 1975). For them Nature is immanently sacred and they phenomenologically experience it as such.

Using a visual term, 'world view', to refer to a cultural structure of natural representations of the world is confusing. But it is standard practice in Anglo-American anthropological thought. Attempts to circumvent this by terms such as 'cosmos' and 'universe' does not help for these reduce to synonyms in practice. As a result there is a tendency to dissolve the perceptual and action experiencing of the world, i.e., the phenomenology that we have of the world, into the world view beliefs themselves so that our perceiving/acting and our believing can be at radical odds. But I think this must be avoided. The perceptual experiencing of the physical is constitutively structured by the very same set of structural representations that underwrite our beliefs about the world. But we can, at any moment, constitute mentally a particular belief about the world that does not require its object to be present to our senses. But to have a real and veridical visual perceptual experience of the sunset, we must have present to our eyes - *as a causal element of that experience* - an actual 'setting' of the sun (Searle, 1983). Similarly, we can contemplate acting in the world without doing so. But in order to actually experience the action, we must have present the objective elements that we causally manipulate as part of that action. In this sense, following Searle (ibid), neither beliefs nor perceptual/action experiencing are mutually reducible. Rather, they both rely upon internal structuring. And these structures are not the same - although a set of ACFID rules of action manifested in material cultural style *presuppose* a certain determinate range of world view structures.

For beliefs and perceptions, world view structures constitute these mental properties. For actions (and possibly wants), it is rules, i.e., norms, standards, conventions, that stipulate the range of behaviors and objective transformations that must be obtained for the intention (to act) to be satisfied. Because of this irreducibility of different forms of intention (beliefs, perceptions, wants, actions, etc. Searle, 1983) another term is needed to refer to the collective perceptual/action experiencing that a people - in virtue of their shared world view - will characteristically have of and in their physical world. This on-going experiencing I will call their 'umwelt'. It has as its object the very same range of physical events, processes, and things as does the world view and it is because of the latter that the former is possible. That is, world view and 'umwelt' have the very same object as their object, namely, Nature.

In these world view and 'umwelt' terms then, two peoples living in the same physical world who do *not* share the same *type* of world view structures will experience that world quite differently. That is, they constitute or construct their experiencing of the world as Nature differently. It is not that they physically live in two different worlds - for they do *not*. I take the realist perspective that the objective world exists independently of the observing/acting humans (Benton, 1977; Bhaskar, 1978, 1979). But the two peoples will have two different experiences of that self-same world, i.e., they will have two different 'umwelts' and, therefore, they will act in the world as two different Natural realities.[1]

## III. An action-constitutive interpretation of the meaning of Newark

*The central thesis*:

The Newark Circle-Octagon was constructed as part of the material realization of a prehistoric monumental episode. It was built so that its formal properties would be congruent with the very same sacred structural powers that sustained the world. This means that the structural content of the construction intentions presupposes certain determinate world beliefs. Hence, the builders performed their construction activities so as to ensure that the objective properties of Newark would be congruent with the very structural forces that they believed to be immanent in the world. In this way they endowed the Newark Circle-Octagon with action-constitutive force, the same creative and reproductive force that was immanent in the world. The model argues that Newark was a monumental iconic warrant essential for the generation of fully felicitous world renewal ceremonies (Wright, 1990).

For reasons that will become clear, I shall call this the Rectification Model. I will present three lines of empirical evidence to confirm its validity. The first is based on what I will call the *C-R Motif analysis*. It provides the empirically founded background knowledge for establishing the rules governing the earthwork forms. The second, I term the *astronomical alignment analysis*. The third line of evidence will reconstruct the building

---

[1] I find this 'umwelt'-Nature model of how human populations materially situate themselves to be fully compatible with Bargatzky's ecological view (1984) of how local human populations culturally construct (or continually reconstruct/ reproduce) their on-going interactions with the physical environment.

sequence of what I refer to as the Feature A/Observatory Mound Complex. This analysis will lead to the establishment of specific rules that governed the construction activity. These rules will give us a sense of the builders' 'umwelt' experiencing in their construction and will bridge the gap between the intentions of the builders and the basic world view structural principles on which they were drawing. In this complex, cumulative process of evidence construction, I will be able to confirm the claim that the real meaning of Newark was to serve as a monumental iconic medium, i.e., a locale that was endowed - via the construction process itself - with the same sacred properties and powers that were immanent in the natural world. This is the critical sensibility underwriting the construction. In action-constitutive terms, in the absence of the appropriate material contexts, namely, Newark and its equivalents, the populations that were responsible for their construction would have experienced themselves as incapable of discharging their sacred obligations that constituted them as part of Nature (Byers, 1987).

**1. The C-R motif analysis**

One of the conclusions of my formal analysis of these large sites (Byers, 1987) was that, despite their apparent complexity, they are based upon a simple Circle-Rectilinear complementary oppositional configuration. I refer to it as the C-R configuration and, when treating it as rule-governed, I refer to it as the C-R Motif. The C-R element consists of a circle junctured to a rectilinear. The circle element is usually made of a single and unbroken circular embankment with no asymmetries built into it.[2] The rectilinear is always a regular polygon - often a 'perfect' square or octagon. The Newark Circle-Octagon is a classic example of this C-R configuration. But there is another numerically more common and complex C-R motif configuration. This is represented both at Liberty Works (fig. 3) and at Seip (fig. 5), which

---

[2] However, there is one important exception to this patterning. The circular element of the Newark Circle-Octagon *does* have a distinctive asymmetry, referred to as the Observatory Mound (figure 1, southwest sector, and figure 7). Accounting for this feature is an important element of the third analytical step, the Construction Sequences. And it must be accounted for because, in terms of the C-R Motif analysis, it is anomalous.

is about 25 km west of the Scioto on the lower reaches of the Paint Creek (see Map 1).

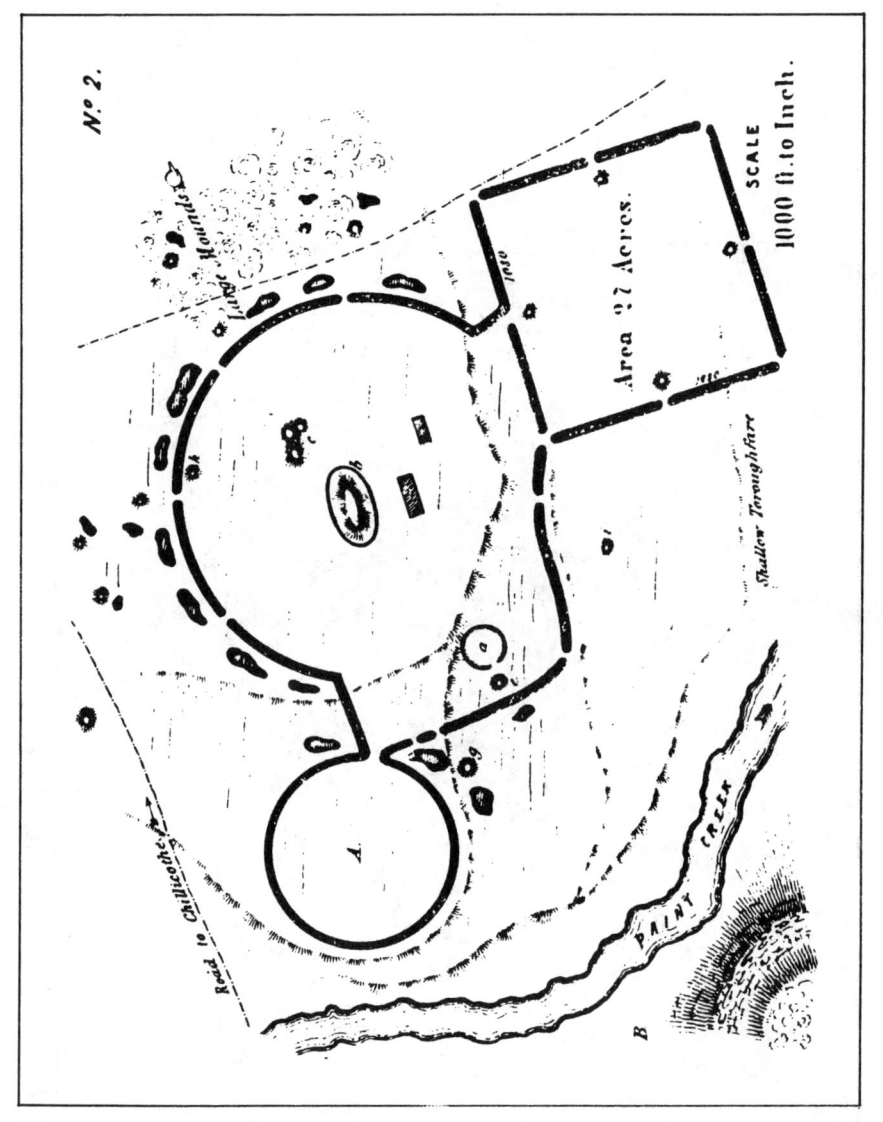

**Figure 5**: Seip - Paint Creek C-R Motif type (Squier and Davis, 1973:Plate XXI, no.2).

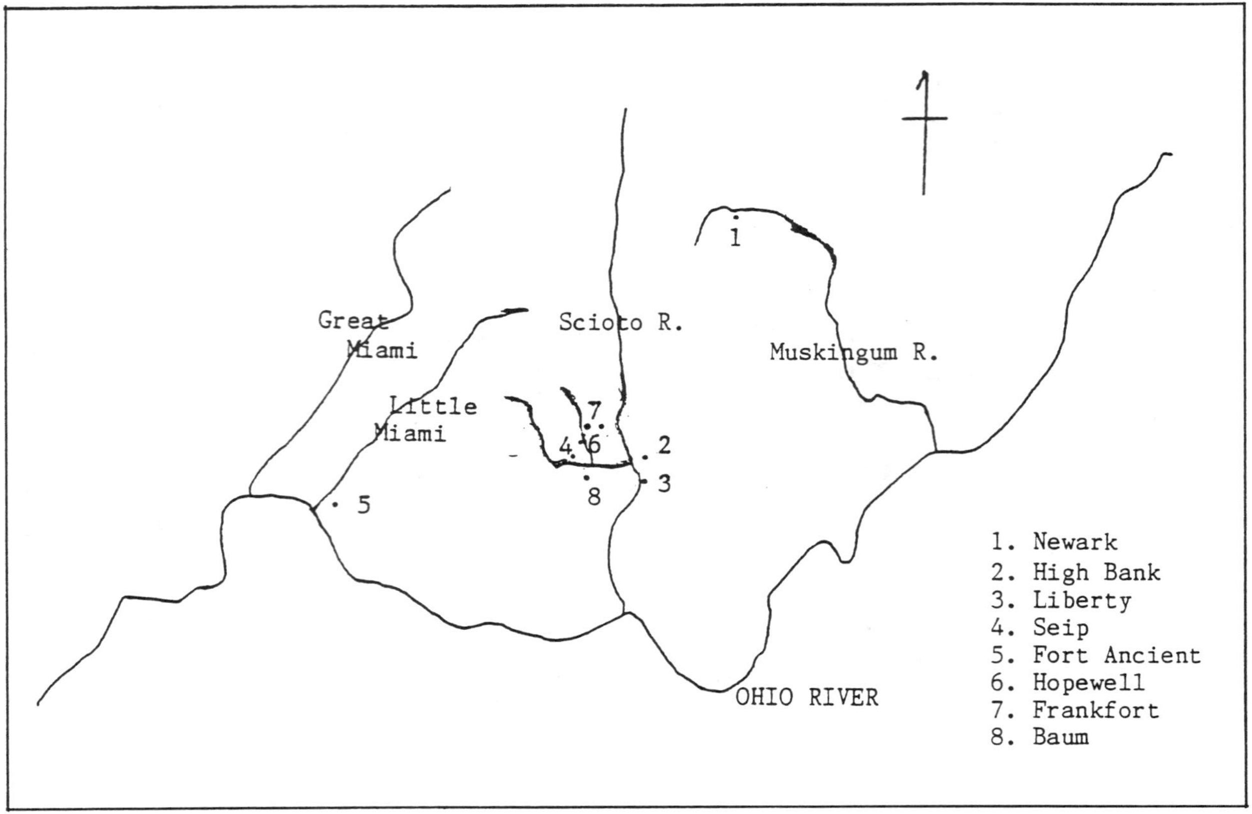

**Map 1 :** Map of Sites Mentioned in Essay

1. Newark
2. High Bank
3. Liberty
4. Seip
5. Fort Ancient
6. Hopewell
7. Frankfort
8. Baum

The differences between High Bank and Liberty Works have established grounds for constituting two C-R Motif types, the High Bank C-R Motif and the Paint Creek C-R Motif. The C-R element of the former is directly junctured by a narrow neck, the *aggregation neck*, while the equivalent element of the latter (e.g., Liberty Works and Seip) is constituted by a large inner circle, which I refer to as the 'infix' element. The rectilinears of the two types vary. For the Paint Creek type it is always a square. For the High Bank type it can be either a square, octagon, rectangle or trapezoid. Although in both cases the corner and center positions of the rectilinears are usually left as open gates, characteristically the High Bank Rectilinear has a mound set back from each gate about 10 m. However the Paint Creek Square has similarly positioned mounds only at the center or medial gates. This brief summary overview of the contrasting attributes constituting the two C-R motif type variations certainly does not exhaust their important observable properties. But it is sufficient for the current purposes for it establishes empirical grounds for my later speaking about the C-R Motif rules.[3]

I interpret the C-R patterning as manifesting a duality of a binary oppositional nature. A second duality is constituted by the patterning of the local distribution of the two motif types. Usually one type is found relatively close to the other type (e.g., within a few kilometers). (Usually there will be only one 'local' High Bank C-R Motif type while there will be two or more Paint Creek types.) All this establishes reasonable grounds for claiming the existence of a *compound* C-R configuration, which I have termed the Dual C-R Motif. Since Liberty Works as a Paint Creek variant and High Bank Works as a High Bank variant are only about 2 km apart, together they constitute a Dual C-R Motif.[4]

---

[3] See Byers (1987, 1992) for more comprehensive descriptive summary and analysis of these two types.

[4] It turns out that most of the complexity in the formal properties of these embankment earthwork sites actually derives from being variations of the Dual C-R motif (Byers, 1987).

## 2. The astronomical alignment analysis
### 2.1. The observatory model

Hively and Horn (1982) painstakingly re-surveyed the remaining elements of the Newark site, particularly the Newark Circle-Octagon (fig. 1). They confirmed that Whittlesey, a local surveyor under commission to Squier and Davis, was surprisingly accurate in his survey. Their subsequent analysis established several remarkable findings. First, the Circle and the Octagon are based on the same unit measure. This is the Observatory Circle Diameter (the OCD unit), which is 322 m. The attached Octagon is a transformed square, ACEG, the sides of which are also 322 m. For this reason they hypothesized that it was the basis of the Octagon.[5] They used one of the simplest geometrical procedure (fig. 6) to show how ACEG could be transformed into an octagon. They predicted that this method should generate vertices fitting square BDFH.[6]

Although the Newark Octagon actually does fit their predicted model fairly well, as they pointed out, more important was their establishing that the actual Octagon is slightly asymmetrical. This is most pronounced in the fact that two sets of opposite sides, BC/FG and EF/AB, lack the requisite parallelism of a symmetrical octagon. They attributed this to the placement of vertex F 6 m too close to the center of the Octagon. However, the other vertices, H, B and D, are precisely where they ought to be. But they also established that there were several other 'mistakes' resulting in a series of subtle asymmetries in the Octagon lay out. Less astute workers may have

---

[5] Hively and Horn (1982) consider that the OCD unit was a measurement that had particular significance for the builders as it governs the total lay out of the major features of Newark. Not only does this unit underlie the Circle and Octagon, the linear distance between the center points of the latter and the center points of the Fairground Circle (E in Figure 1) and the Wright Square (large square northeast of E) is 6 OCD units each. They speculate that this cannot be coincidental. I tend to support them. Furthermore, I consider the sharing of the OCD unit by the Circle and the Octagon as empirical grounds confirming this C-R Motif as manifesting a unity based on the principle of complementary opposition.

[6] This procedure was based on using the diagonal of square ACEG as the radius and the vertices as the centers to make four sets of intersecting arcs. They hypothesized that these four points should coincide with the vertices BDFH. As they have clearly demonstrated in a more recent analysis, this is not the only procedure for constructing an octagon which builders of embankment earthworks used (Hively and Horn, 1984). Marshall (1978, 1985) has suggested another method. These alternatives, however, have no bearing on the establishment of intentionality as such.

simply fobbed this off as the sloppiness of 'primitive' geometricians. Instead, they used these 'errors' as grounds to conclude that the asymmetries were intentional.

They then established that, but for these asymmetries, a number of key events of the lunar cycle that are now marked as alignments embedded in features of the Octagon would *not* be so marked (table 1, section A). These lunar events are quite specific. They are the four maximal and four minimal south and north horizon risings and settings (i.e. the 'turning points') that the Moon makes in the course of its 18.6 year cycle. They confirmed this hypothesis by demonstrating that but for each of the asymmetries a particular turning point alignment would not be embedded in the Octagon features. I consider this to be strong evidence for their claim, making it the most reasonable accounting of the asymmetries. On these grounds, then, the asymmetries were intentionally generated and the intention was to embody in the Octagon the lunar cycle alignments. They concluded that these features must have been built with the purpose in mind of monitoring the movement of the Moon through its regular cycle, "Thus, an observer standing at the entrance to the avenue where it leaves the Observatory Circle would see the Moon rise in the avenue only when it was between the maximum and minimum northern extremes. Moreover, the 18.6 year cycle could be easily and precisely monitored by noting the position of the monthly northern extreme rise point as viewed from the south end of the avenue" (Hively and Horn, 1982:13).

Hence for them the intelligibility of the Newark Circle-Octagon is grounded on its being intentionally built as a lunar observatory. They even, very cautiously, suggest it could have been used to predict some of the years of the lunar eclipses. From this they further deduced that not only the Newark Octagon but possibly the whole of the Newark embankment earthwork site was built with this lunar monitoring in mind.

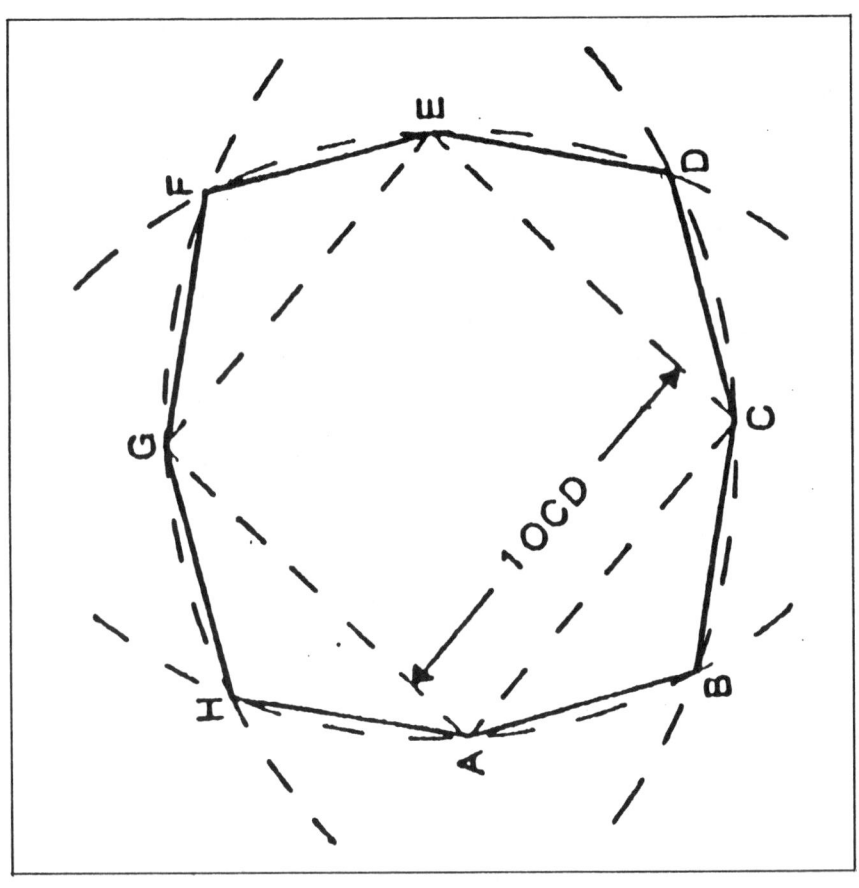

**Figure 6**: Hypothetical Construction of the Newark Octagon (Hively and Horn,1982:8). The dotted lines show a method which may have been used to construct the Newark Octagon. First a square (ACEG) of side 1 OCD (321,3 m) is laid out; then circular arcs of radius $\sqrt{2}$ OCD are drawn with centers at the vertices A, C, E and G. The intersections of the circular arcs locate the remaining vertices B, D, F and H.

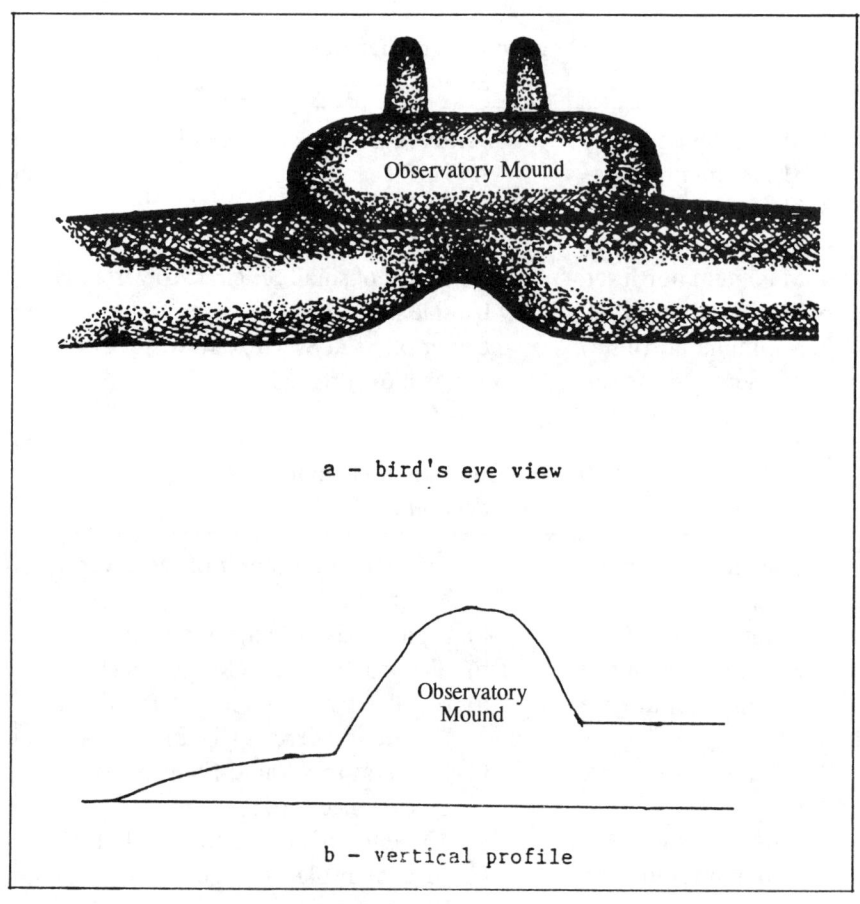

**Figure 7:** Bird's-Eye View Feature A/Observatory Mound Complex.

| Octagon Lunar Alignments<br>Section A | |
|---|---|
| 1. Maximum north rise | vertex A to vertex E - axis of Octagon |
| 2. Minimum north rise | side GF |
| 3. Maximum south rise | side AB |
| 4. Minimum south rise | vertex G to vertex D |
| 5. Maximum north set | a) center of small SE circle to vertex H |
| 6. Maximum north set | b) side EF |
| 7. Minimum north set | center of small SE circle to vertex A |
| 8. Maximum south set | vertex F to vertex H |
| 9. Minimum south set | side CB |
| Extra-Octagon Lunar Alignments<br>Section B | |
| 10. Maximum north rise | axis of circle from center of Observatory Mound to neck |
| 11. Minimum north rise | a) avenue axis of Fairground Circle |
| 12. Minimum north rise | b) diagonal of Circle-Octagon neck |
| 13. Maximum south rise | a) parallel displacement of Newark and Fairground Circles (fig. 8) |
| 14. Maximum south rise | b) Observatory Mound-Fairground Circle tangent (fig. 8) |
| 15. Minimum south rise | a) NW entry of Square to N end SE side |
| 16. Minimum south rise | b) parallel displacement of Octagon and Wright Square (fig. 8) |
| 17. Maximum north set | parallels at NW side of Square |
| Minimum north set | NONE |
| 18. Maximum south set | FH to tangent Observatory Circle |
| Minimum south set | NONE |

**Table 1:** Set of Minimum-Maximum Lunar Rises and Sets. (From Hively and Horn 1982: Table 2 [modified].)

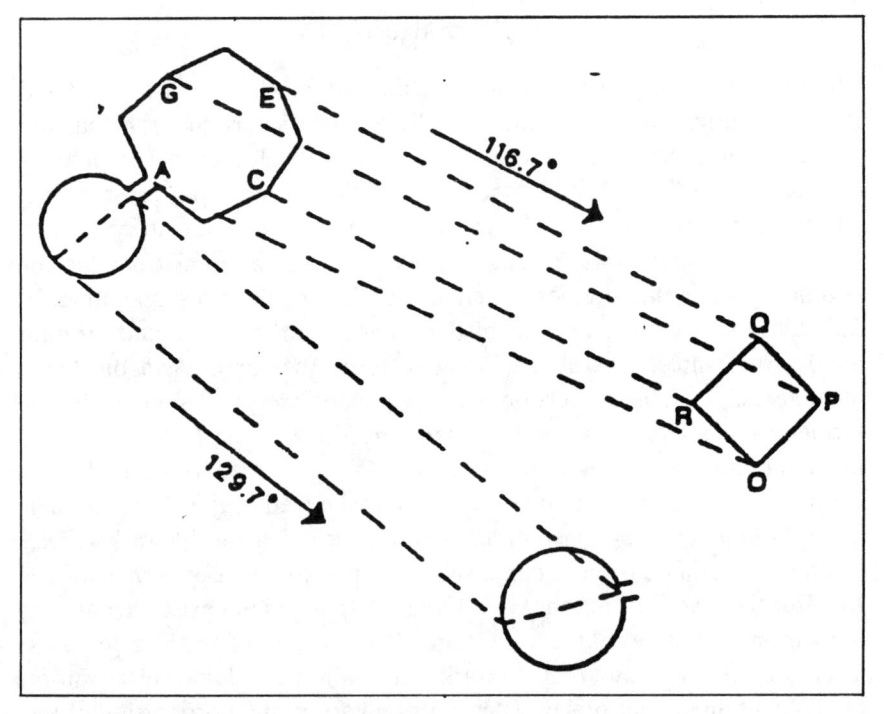

**Figure 8:** Parallel Displacements showing Extra-Octagon Alignments: Nos. 13, 14,16, (Hively and Horn, 1982:S6)

## 2.2. Critique.

I find this study very refreshing and useful. Both much of their method and their conclusions are stimulating. I fully accept their conclusion that the noted asymmetries of the Octagon were intentional. I even accept their conclusion that 'lunar consciousness' has much to do with the construction. But their interpreting Newark as a monumental lunar observatory used to monitor the lunar cycle, presumably to constitute a ritual calendar for regulating the cyclic ceremonial activity of a lunar cult, is disappointing. In fact, they pushed their analysis of the lunar alignments by demonstrating almost a complete extra set, what I term the Extra-Octagon lunar alignments. As table 1, section B shows, there are just as many Extra-Octagon lunar alignments as there are embedded in the Octagon. But if lunar monitoring was the purpose of the Octagon, then why should this surplus exist? As all eight lunar events are embedded in the Octagon, then all the other features constituting Newark, including the Newark Circle, could be eliminated without diminishing the monitoring effectiveness of the site. But the reverse is not the case. If the Octagon did not exist, then two of the turning points would not be marked in the rest of the site features. Therefore, their claim that Newark was built as a lunar observatory, mediating a lunar cult practice, accounts only for a small proportion of the actual patterning they observed.

But can we say at least that the Octagon was built in the manner it was just so as to monitor the lunar cycle? This is unlikely. Even if we ignore the surplus of monitoring needs that the Extra-Octagon alignments implicate, if mediating monitoring intentions was of primary and pressing importance then why would a people even consider realizing such a labor intensive monumental effort? There are many other adequate and less laborious methods to construct a lunar monitoring facility. Hence, the Observatory Model is inadequate. It does not account for the majority of the empirical patterning that is its interpretive object.

Hively and Horn, implicitly taking a referential stance, presumed that the alignments were built to 'point at' the Moon as a mode of monitoring its cycle. But in action-constitutive terms we must 'reverse' the intentionality. The asymmetries were constructed to ensure that the Moon would 'point at' the Octagon, *during the critical turning points of its cycle*. In this parasitic manner the Octagon was intentionally endowed with the same powers that animated the lunar cycle. Thus Hively and Horn's empirical findings are extremely important. Here is demonstrated a 'classic' mode of preindustrial societies 'fitting' their material activities to Nature (Douglas, 1966, 1970, 1975). In terms of the 'counts as' symbolism underwriting human material culture, the 'Umwelt'-Nature relation is necessarily immanent in the patternings of the monumental feature and its objective physical relations and orientations to the physical world.

This patterning is not unique. Astronomical alignments of major features have been noted by many archaeologists. Particularly Mesoamerican archaeologists have argued for their significance (Aveni, 1975; Aveni, Calnek, and H. Hartung, 1988; Townsend, 1979; Van Zantwijk, 1985). We can understand their careful solar, lunar, and/or Morning or Evening Star, etc., alignments - plus many other objective properties they were made to have - as ensuring congruency of these features with the sacred powers of the objects which thereby 'pointed' at them. In this manner, their builders/users constructed monumental sacred 'machines' whose objective properties were intentional constructed so as to make them congruent with the same sacred powers as animated the astronomical bodies. Similarly, immanent in Newark, I shall now empirically demonstrate, are the sacred structures that constitute the creative powers of the Nature that was the object of the builders' 'umwelt'.[7]

## 3. The construction sequence analysis
### 3.1. The feature A/observatory mound complex

It is critical at this point to note that of all the circle elements of the known C-R Motif sites only the Newark Circle deviates from the norm as defined by the earlier C-R Motif analysis. This abnormality is largely the Observatory Mound. Given the normal C-R Motif attributes as established by this analysis, I can quite properly ask, "Why, in this single instance, did the builders fail to realize the C-R symmetry that, according to the C-R

---

[7] A fuller account of the ACFID or action-constitutive theory of the nature of material cultural meaning can be found in Byers (1991, 1992).

Motif configuration, they ought to have realized?" This failure is particularly telling since, *in our view*, there seem to be no obvious physical constraints that would have prevented the normal C-R pattern. To explain this anomaly the Rectification Model focuses attention on both the Observatory Mound and its associated features. These latter are the *two low parallel embankments* that jut out from under the Mound. I refer to them as Feature A (fig. 7).

### 3.2. The Squier-Davis construction scenario

Squier and Davis (1973), back in 1840, were quite impressed by the Observatory Mound. But they also noted Feature A and accounted for it in the following manner, "(The Circle) encloses no mounds, but possesses a remarkable feature in the line of the wall, at a point immediately opposite the entrance. This consists of a crown work (...), which is wholly unlike anything heretofore noticed. It would almost seem that the builders had originally determined to carry out parallel lines from this point; but after proceeding one hundred feet, had suddenly changed their minds and *finished the enclosure*, by throwing an immense mound across the uncompleted parts. This mound (...) is one hundred and seventy feet long, eight feet higher than the general line of the embankment, and overlooks the entire work. It has been called the 'Observatory,' from this fact (1973:69, emphases added. See figures 1 and 7)."

On-site inspection supports Squier and Davis' description. The features definitely taper-off as they extend in a southwest direction away from the base of the Mound. As embankments go, they are puny. Where they jut out from the base of the Mound, they are less than a meter high and they taper off as they extend away. They certainly are much lower and narrower than the embankment of the Circle where it joins the Mound on the inner side. Nevertheless, it would be unreasonable to claim that Squier and Davis were not correct in their hypothesis that these two embankments were originally part of the Circle. If this is the case, then the embankment of the Circle would have been subsequently enlarged by additional earth strata.[8]

---

[8] An excavation of this protected feature would be invaluable as it would definitively confirm this analysis. There is good empirical evidence that some of the earthworks

I will presume that the emphasis in the above quotation, "finished the enclosure," refers to the completed Circle-Octagon - as we now see it. If this is the case, then the construction sequence can be inferred in this manner.

1. First, the Octagon was built.
2. To this was added the aggregation neck at vertex A, as now found.
3. The Circle was then built leading from the aggregation neck.
4. As the builders completed the Circle, they decided to add Feature A.
5. After building these two low embankments, Feature A, about 30 m long, they changed their minds.
6. To rectify their having built on Feature A, and as their final construction step of the Circle, they built what is now called the Observatory Mound *over* it.

### Critique

I agree with only the main clause of step 6 of the Squier-Davis construction scenario. That is the Mound was added *after* the low embankments were built. Immediately this scenario reveals a very interesting fact - the covering of these embankments. Why were the embankments left in place? This is an important question since, quite apart from the Observatory Mound, their presence appears to constitute a breaking of the C-R Motif norms. The C-R Motif analysis has empirically grounded what attributes the C-R Motif earthwork should manifest in order to count as being properly constructed. Can these two embankments, Feature A, be accounted for in terms of the C-R Motif analysis? Yes. In this view it becomes immediately clear that Feature A is a typical example of the High Bank C-R *aggregation neck*. But this interpretation makes the Newark Circle-Octagon truly unique (anomalous). It is the only High Bank C-R Motif earthwork known to have not only the Observatory Mound feature but also to have *two* aggregation

---

with substantial embankments were actually constructed in cumulative stages (Essenpries and Mosely, 1984; Riordan, 1986).

necks, namely, Feature A and the current one juncturing the Circle and Octagon, which I will now call Feature B.

According to the C-R Motif analysis, since we know that a High Bank C-R motif requires only *one* aggregation neck to juncture the circle and rectilinear elements, Scenario 1 makes no sense. It would entail adding on Feature A when the total earthwork was near completion. Given the C-R Motif analysis, we know that such an addition would have been superfluous. In the absence of any overriding constraint, there would have been good reason *not* to build Feature A at all. But its very existence is evidence to the contrary. Although correct in the Feature A/Observatory Mound sequencing, by claiming that the Mound was the final step in the building of the Newark Circle-Octagon, Scenario 1 fails in its over-all sequencing of that C-R construction.

### 3.3. The feature B construction sequence

What this critique suggests is that Feature A was built because the Circle was actually the *first* and not the second step in the construction of the Newark Circle-Octagon, as suggested by Squier and Davis. And this seems quite logical. There are two possibilities. (1) The Circle was started as one of the embankments of Feature A. It was then extended in a great embankment arc to form the Circle and terminated where it started, thereby completing Feature A. (2) Alternatively, it was started in the northeast sector, diametrically opposite where Feature A was to be built, and built in two large arcs. In either case, when Feature A was constructed, there was a sudden change of plan. In the original plan, of course, the Octagon would have been built from Feature A, thereby placing it to the southwest of the Circle, diametrically opposite from where we in fact now find it. The change of plan, then, was to actually build it on the northeast side of the Circle, where we now, in fact, find it. Feature A would have been abandoned; in this case by covering it with a mound of earth which we now identify as the Observatory Mound. This would have required, however, that part of the embankment Circle diametrically opposite Feature A be opened by removing the embankment wall so as to connect the current aggregation neck, Feature B. At that point, as the final step, the Octagon was built. I will call this the Feature B Construction Scenario.

### Critique

As established by the critique of the Squier-Davis Scenario, the Feature B Scenario is correct with respect to the Circle being built *before* the Octagon. But it has a fatal flaw. If part of the embankment of the Circle was able to be removed so as to open a space for the attachment of Feature B, why was Feature A, the previously constructed neck, closed simply by being covered with earth to form a mound? According to the C-R Motif analysis the rules should have generated a symmetrical Circle. On these grounds, then, the builders should have had good reason to remove Feature A and fill in the gap in the Circle so as to make a smooth embankment in its place. Certainly, removing earth from an embankment - according to the Feature B Scenario - was quite possible and doing so would have been no more labor consuming than either opening the embankment of the Circle diametrically opposite for Feature B or doing what they did, that is, covering Feature A.

In other words, the Feature B Scenario grounds the existence of two construction practices and results in a puzzle. If removal of fill from an embankment was possible, then why not eliminate Feature A? The fact that Feature A was covered and not destroyed grounds the conclusion that the Feature B Scenario is internally contradictory. Because Feature A was not removed, then it is impossible that Feature B was built by first removing earth fill from an already completed Circle.

### 3.4. The rectification construction scenario

This scenario hinges on sustaining the Circle-Octagon construction sequence of the latter scenario while reversing the construction sequence of the Circle. But given that the Feature A/Observatory Mound Complex is the result of avoiding removal of Feature A, then the *very first step* in the building of the Newark Circle-Octagon must have been Feature A. Accordingly, the Newark Circle-Octagon was started by both sides of

Feature A being built simultaneously as two low parallel embankments starting at its far south-west end, where it now 'peters out.' The parallel embankments of Feature A were then opened and extended in two great embankment arcs on the northwest and southeast sides to form the Circle. But, before these two arcs were junctured in the northeast to form the Circle, as initially intended, a change of plan occurred, leading directly to closing Feature A by covering it with a mounding of earth. Diametrically opposite Feature A and its mound of covering earth, Feature B, the new aggregation neck was built. The Octagon was then added to complete the Newark C-R Motif as we now see it.

## Critique

The construction sequencing of the Feature A/Observatory Mound Complex was established by the Squier-Davis Scenario and empirically confirmed by the findings of C-R Motif analysis. But this same C-R Motif analysis, by identifying Feature A as being a normal aggregation neck, revealed this scenario to be mistaken in its sequencing of the Newark Circle-Octagon project. The Feature B Scenario corrected the former scenario through reversing this sequencing to establish the Circle as having been built prior to the Octagon. However, using the normative knowledge of the symmetry requirements grounded by the C-R Motif analysis, this scenario was shown to be based on an anomaly. If it were adequate as a construction sequence, then only the subtractive mode of construction rectification should have been used, thereby eliminating any reason to build what, as a matter of empirical fact, exists, namely, the Feature A/Observatory Mound Complex. The Rectification Scenario, therefore, grounds the conclusion that the latter Complex is best interpreted as the result of avoiding disturbing the order of an earthwork embankment. In other words, it grounds an intentional *avoidance* practice.

Based on this crucial finding of an avoidance practice - no easy fact to empirically ground - this Construction Sequence analysis leads to the conclusion that only *one* rectification mode was possible, this being the addition of earth fill.[9] Since the Rectification Scenario uses the same empirically grounded knowledge about the C-R Motif as do the first two scenarios, while resolving the anomalies and contradictions of these models, it follows that, until a better model is presented, judged in the same terms, it must be accepted as the most reasonable explanation of the data.

### 3.5. The implications of the rectification model: The nature cult

The major implication of this model is that there are now empirically grounded reasons to conclude that an avoidance practice was a *generative intentional cause* of the patterning of the data. That is, the literal deconstruction of embankment earthworks was an unacceptable mode of construction rectification. This leaves only two possible alternatives by which the builders could make modifications to past constructions: (1) rectification by adding soil to previously built features; (2) 'going around', i.e. circumscription.[10] But avoidance practices always presuppose the exercise of *proscriptive* rules and these implicate structural principles that would ground the nature and sensibility of these rules, thereby bridging the gap between the structural rules of intention and the representational contents of beliefs.

The proscriptive rule that this avoidance practice realized can be most reasonably stated as a negative directive with the following propositional content, "It is forbidden to disturb the physical order of an embankment earthwork - no matter in what stage of construction it is."

Since intentional earth procurement entails disturbing the natural order, then the structural content of that intentionality would presuppose beliefs

---

[9] It also establishes that, in fact, a change of plan occurred, namely, to build the Octagon on the side opposite from that initially intented. This implicates many of the construction complications that make Newark such a complex earthwork. However, I cannot pursue further analysis in this essay. A full interpretation of the construction sequence of Newark - in total - is given in Byers (1987).

[10] Circumscription as a form of rectification would account for the 'lobed circle' at Liberty Works (figure 3). Inside this element there is an incomplete circle embankment, suggesting that it was abandoned when partially completed. I interpret this as meaning that the C-R Motif was then constructed with the infix being built around (circumscribed) it. Circumscription also accounts for the irregular in the circularity of the infix at Seip (figure 5).

about the nature of the world. By drawing on the cosmological theory of primitive society developed by Douglas (1966, 1970, 1975) I shall argue that the nature of this property was *sacredness* and the latter was experienced by the builders as immanent in the natural stratification of the world. It is in and through the material act of disturbing this natural order that the transformative and immanent power of sacredness is released. Hence, in their view in the material action of procuring the earth fill with the intention to build an embankment earthwork they necessarily released the essential creative properties of the earth, thereby literally endowing this material fill with the same properties. Only if we posit some such reality can we make sense of the Feature A/Observatory Mound Complex. In virtue of the sacred nature of Feature A, and any *embankment*, secondary disturbance was forbidden. Such secondary disturbance of a sacred embankment would pollute the sacred state of the world. Therefore, the procuring and placement of earth in the construction process was itself a form of congruence-construction.

Earthwork construction exercised a deep structural principle that I will term the *sacred earth principle*. This principle is profoundly positive, even though it was discovered because it underwrote the proscriptive rule and its avoidance action. Its positive nature is what made earthwork construction an incredibly sensible material activity for the society to undertake, suggesting a *prescriptive* rule, "Actively build earthworks, in the appropriate manner and form, so as to transformatively mediate material actions that will count as discharging sacred 'umwelt' duties."

I would argue that, since according to the Scenario Analyses, Feature A was sacred even before the Octagon was constructed, the real source of the Circle-Octagon sacred ascriptive powers must have been founded on the earth procurement practice and the sacred earth principle that it realized in action. And because this sacred ascription was independent of lunar alignment construction, the latter would be a secondary form of sacred congruency. Hence, the alignments ascribed the *aspect* of the sacred world order under which the Newark Circle-Octagon was understood to be participating, namely, the *lunar aspect*.

## IV. Newark and the Hopewellian 'Umwelt'

What is now required is to apply the sacred earth principle to establish the meaning of the C-R Motif as a total configuration. The primary implication of this structural principle is that it clearly grounds the nature of the complementary opposition underwriting both the C-R Motif and the Dual C-R Motif as sacred. As the Newark Circle-Octagon is a High Bank C-R Motif type, then, given the findings of the Observatory Model, this variety can be appropriately termed the Lunar Motif. The Paint Creek C-R Motif should be the complementary Solar Motif. It is not surprising, therefore, that Hively and Horn (1982) comment on the fact that the Wright Square, the (Paint Creek) square east of the Octagon, has alignments embedded in it that 'point to' the summer solstices. They also point out that other Paint Creek Squares, such as at Liberty Works (fig. 3) and Baum (fig. 9), have the same directional orientation as the Wright Square. Indeed, according to N. Greber (personal communication, 1986) this is also probably the case for Seip (fig. 5). On the North Fork of the Paint Creek drainage are the sites of Frankfort (fig. 10) and Hopewell (fig. 11).[11] Hence, Baum, Frankfort, Seip and Hopewell, all within a 10-20 km radius of each other and within the Paint Creek drainage system, were intended by their builders to be taken as Solar Motif sites.[12]

---

[11] Without a doubt the former is a Paint Creek C-R Motif type, although the Hopewell site clearly deviates from the norm. A closer examination reveals that it possesses the two requisite elements to constitute it as a Paint Creek Motif: the C-R element and the infix juncture. The latter is the large C-Form embankment to which the Paint Creek Square was added as part of the final stage of the construction of the site (Byers, 1987).

[12] Portsmouth (figure 4) is probably a variant of the Paint Creek C-R Motif (Byers, 1987).

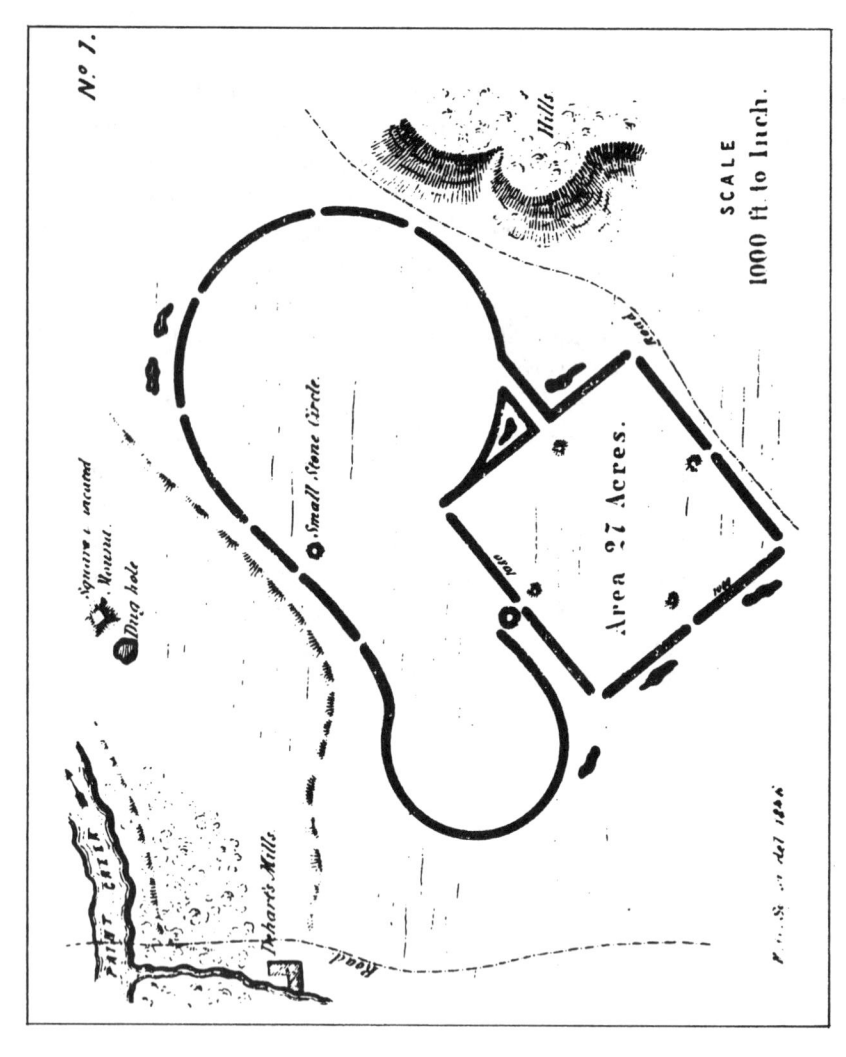

**Figure 9:** Baum - Paint Creek C-R Motif type (Squier and Davis, 1973: Plate XXI,no.1)

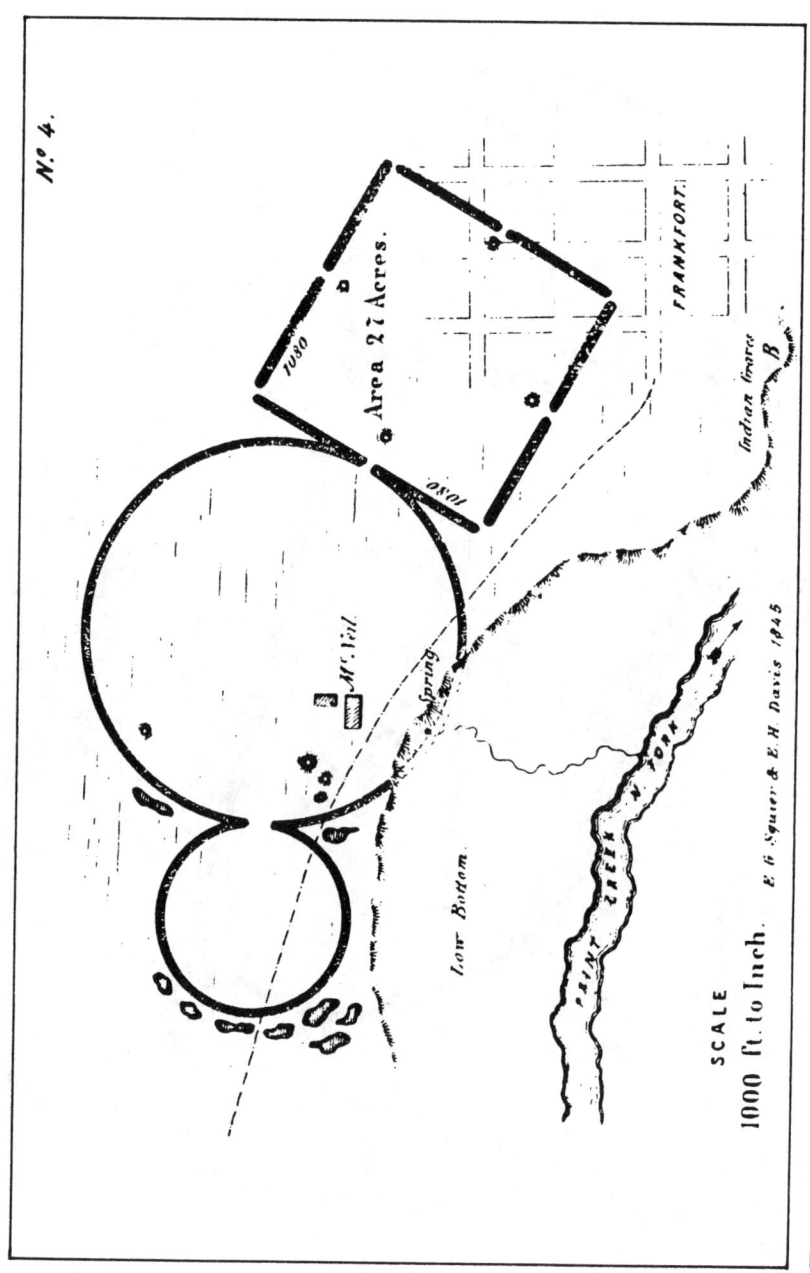

**Figure 10:** Frankfort - Paint Creek C-R Motif type (Squier and Davis, 1973:Plate XXI, no. 4).

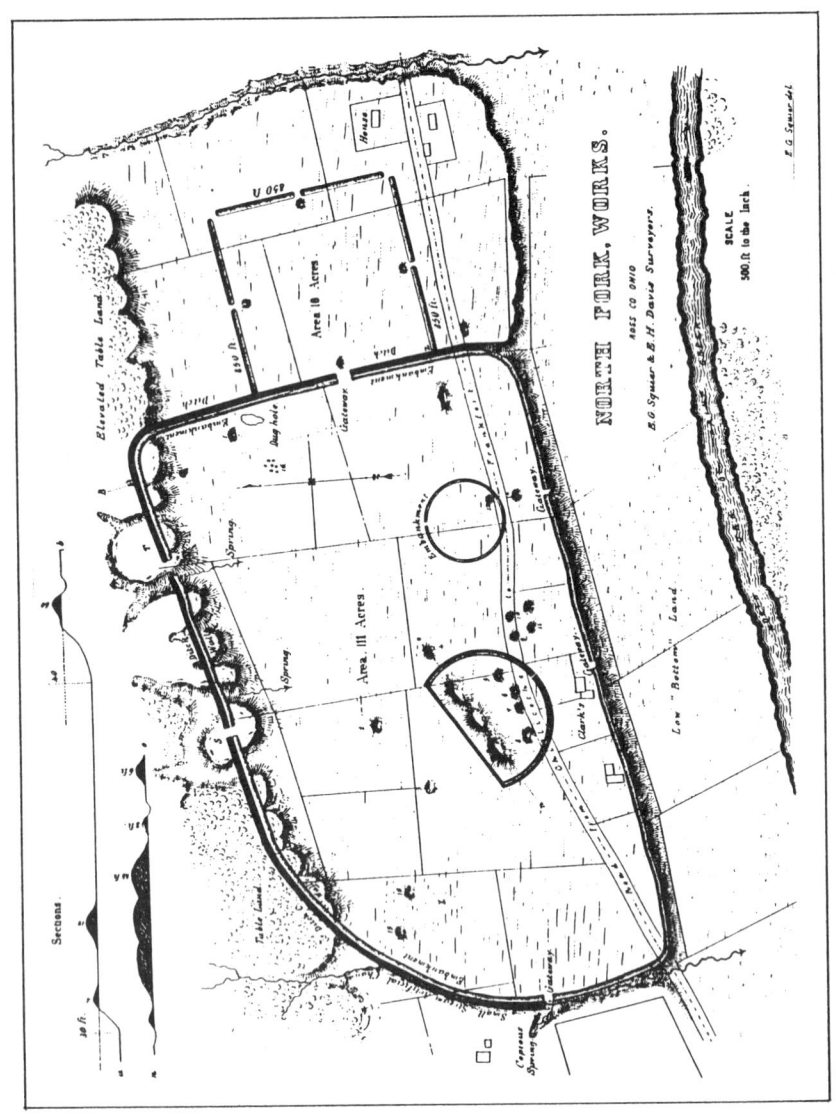

**Figure 11:** Hopewell - Paint Creek C-R Motif type (Squier and Davis, 1973:Plate X)

But this does not account for the total C-R Motif itself, only the rectilinears. What was the point of the circle and juncture elements? To pursue the empirical fact that the solar and lunar alignments are embedded in the rectilinears, and the latter mark the critical rises and sets of these bodies at the horizon of the earth, they are most reasonably interpreted as representing and participating in the powers of the Underworld.[13] The principle of sacred duality, then, grounds the circle element as the Heavens. The structurally equivalent juncturing elements, viz. the aggregation neck and the infix, would represent and participate in the Middle World. This is that part of the world occupied by living humans and which is the material interface binding/separating the Heaven/Underworld duality. The C-R Motif, then, is a monumental iconic symbol that realizes in material form the sacred vertical stratigraphy of the world view structures.

As the embankments of the earthworks are constructed of the sacred earth itself, they necessarily participate in the sacred nature of the world. Given the sacred stratification of the world, it is not surprising, to note that typically the circular element of the C-R Motif was made of surface stratum earth and the rectilinear of deep stratum earth. The pattern of structural congruency would be:

| A | (stands to) | B | (as) |
|---|---|---|---|
| Surface Stratum | : | Deep Stratum | :: |
| Circle | : | Rectilinear | :: |
| Above | : | Below | :: |
| Heaven | : | Underworld | (Byers, 1987) |

Now what I have laid out here can be read in two related ways. From the point of view of the 'umwelt' as a shared collective experiencing of the world, this is the set of structures they drew upon in constituting their action and perceptual experiences. The causal object of their on-going 'umwelt'

---

[13] North American Indian beliefs almost universally claim the astronomical bodies rising from under the world, the Underworld, through great eastern caves, fly into the sky, the Heavens, and set into great western caves. They then pass through the Underworld to rise again in the east (Aveni, 1975; Aveni, Calnek and Hartung, 1988; Van Zantwijk 1985; Wright, 1990).

experiencing, of course, would be the objective physical world, which they would constitutively experience as Nature - a living sacred complex entity of which they were an integral element. Hence, in looking at and acting in Newark the builders would experience themselves seeing/participating in the essential structures of Nature. Here are displayed in one integrated site both the vertical Heaven/Middle-World/Underworld stratification and the temporal solar/lunar cycle that, together, constitute the essential sacred spatio-temporal order of the physical world as Nature.

It is because Newark is a Dual C-R Motif site that its layout is so complicated.[14] It is because Newark is here interpreted as manifesting the *Sacred* Dual C-R Motif that I cannot agree with Hively and Horn's claim that 'lunar consciousness' *exhaustively* underwrote the intentionality of Newark. Theirs is only a partial interpretation and it does not ground the necessity of a lunar cult, as such. Rather, the Rectification Model implicates interpreting Newark as the sacred locale of a Nature cult, the totality of the world as they conceived and constitutively experienced it to be. In such a Nature the lunar powers play a necessary but incomplete role. Hence it made incredible sense to the builders of Newark to construct this site as we now see it for it was a monumental material feature that was built just so as to be congruent with the sacred *totality* of Nature. This construction activity ensured that the material behavioral interventions it mediated would be transformed into the intended ceremonies of Nature-Renewal (Wright, 1990). Through its mediation the people of Newark experienced themselves as fully discharging their sacred duties to Nature, thereby intentionally pursuing repute and honor and, largely unintentionally, reproducing the very social structures that mediated this activity and made it necessary (Bhaskar, 1979).

## V. Conclusion

But such monumental features are never exhaustively accounted for in world view/'umwelt' terms only. That is, I do not want to leave the

---

[14] Furthermore, as I more fully discuss in Byers (1987), it was precisely to achieve this task that the sudden change of plan entailing the Feature A/Observatory Mound rectification was required.

impression that the Hopewellian monuments can be fully accounted for in ideal terms - as if the builders/users were simply driven by a blind commitment to a religious belief. Rather, without begging the question, the Rectification Model establishes reasons that would make earthwork construction politically, economically and socially worthwhile. Taking a non-reductive position, I presume that presupposed in this interpretation of Newark is the possibility (indeed, probable certainty) that alternative 'umwelt' strategies existed simultaneously with the one actually manifested in this particular record. For, although we now have empirical grounds for the existence and the exercise in action of the sacred earth principle, and the manifestation of one strategy directed towards satisfying 'umwelt' goals, the very same principle could as logically ground competing alternative (and thereby contradictory) strategies.

In such a case, these would promote the regular enhancement of the sanctity of Nature by way of actively *avoiding* earthwork construction practices altogether - and such complete avoidance could presuppose the very same world view and 'umwelt'. As I pointed out earlier, beliefs/knowledge (about a world) and intentions (to act in that world) are irreducible forms of Intentionality (Byers, 1992; Searle, 1983). The Hopewellian beliefs and intentions necessarily share the same world view structures. But the content of the former are world view representations; of the latter, world view structural rules and principles. Hence, any given set of material actions must *presuppose* a determinate set of the beliefs, but the reverse is not the case. Although world view constrains the range of possible forms of behavior that realize it, within these limits which forms of behaviors will count as fully felicitous actions realizing these beliefs is historically contingent. That is, the Hopewellian world view could as easily ground complete avoidance of earthwork construction as it could ground the actual practices that Newark, we now know, entailed. Given this non-deterministic view of the belief/action relation, it is interesting to note the irregular distribution of monumental features across the Midwest at this time. Large areas have no similar monumental features, suggesting that although possessing the type identical world view, many neighbors of the central and south-central Ohio Hopewellian peoples intentionally avoided monumental construction. Hence, monumentalism is as much a political as a religious social strategy. The political implication that such construction entails may partly account for the rather sudden halt (around 500 A.D.) to all such construction in the central Ohio Valley.

*Acknowledgements*

I wish to thank AMS Press Inc., New York, for their making Squier and Davis' classic study *Ancient Monuments of the Mississippi Valley* more widely available through their reprint policy. - I used Newark as a substantive example of a different theoretical concern with respect to monumentalism in a paper recently published in the *Journal for the Theory of Social Behaviour* (Byers 1992). I wish to thank the Editor, Dr. Charles Smith for permission to draw on that reconstruction for this article. - I wish to thank the Editor of *Archaeoastronomy,* Dr. C.L.N. Ruggles, for permission to use figures 4 and 5 from the article by R. Hively and R. Horn (1982). I also wish to thank the authors, Ray M. Hively and R. Horn, for permission to use these figures.

## References

Austin, J. L. (1962). *How to do things with words.* Cambridge, Massachusetts, Harvard University Press.

Aveni, A. F. (1975). "Possible astronomical orientations in ancient Meso-america". In A.F. Aveni (ed). *Archaeoastronomy in Pre-Columbian America,* Austin, University of Texas, pp. 163-190.

Aveni, A. F., Calnek, E. E. and Hartung, H. (1988). Myth, environment, and the orientation of the Temple Mayor of Tenochtitlan. *American Antiquity,* 53(2):287-309.

Bargatzky, T. (1984). "Culture, environment and the ills of adaptation. "*Current Anthropology,* 25(4):399-415.

Benton, T. (1977). *The philosophical foundations of the three sociologies.* London, Routledge and Kegan Paul.

Bhaskar, R. (1978). *A realist theory of science.* New Jersey, Humanities Press.

Bhaskar, R. (1979). *The possibility of naturalism.* New Jersey, Humanities Press.

Byers, A. M. (1987). *The earthwork enclosures of the Central Ohio Valley: A temporal and structural analysis of Woodland society and culture.* Ph.D. dissertation, State University of New York at Albany. Ann Arbor, University Microfilms.

Byers, A. M. (1991). "Structure, meaning, action and things: The duality of material cultural mediation". *Journal for the Theory of Social Behavior,* 21(1):1-26.

Byers, A. M. (1992). "The action-constitutive theory of monuments: A strong pragmatist version." *Journal for the Theory of Social Behavior,* 21(1):1-44.

Douglas, M. (1966). *Purity and danger.* New York, Praeger.

Douglas, M. (1970). *Natural symbols*. London, Barrie and Jenkins.

Douglas, M. (1975). *Implicit meanings: Essays in anthropology*. London, Routledge and Kegan Paul.

Essenpreis, P. S. and M. E. Moseley (1984). "Fort Ancient: Citadel or coliseum?" *Field Museum of Natural History Bulletin*, 55(6): 5-10, 20-26.

Fischer, F. W. (1974). *Early and Middle Woodland settlement, subsistence and population in the Central Ohio Valley*. Ph.D. dissertation, Washington University. Ann Arbor, University Microfilms.

Giddens, A. (1976). *New rules of sociological method*. London, Hutchinson.

Giddens, A. (1979). *Central problems in social theory*. London, MacMillan Press.

Giddens, A. (1981). *A contemporary critique of historical materialism*. London, MacMillan Press.

Giddens, A. (1984). *The constitution of society*. Berkely, University of California Press.

Greber, N. (1976). *Within Ohio Hopewell: Analyses of burial patterns from Several Classic Sites*. Ph.D. dissertation, Case Western Reserve University. Ann Arbor, University Microfilms.

Greber, N. (1979). "A comparative study of site morphology and burial patterns at Edwin Harness Mound and Seip Mounds 1 and 2". In D. S. Brose and N. Greber (eds). *Hopewell Archaeology: The Chillicothe Conference*, Kent, Ohio, Kent State University Press, pp. 27-38.

Greber N. (1983). *Recent excavations at the Edwin Harness Mound*. Liberty Works, Ross County, Ohio. Midcontinental Journal of Archaeology. Kent, Ohio, Kent State University, Special Paper No. 5.

Hively, R. and Horn, R. (1982). "Geometry and astronomy in prehistoric Ohio". *Journal for the History of Astronomy. Archaeoastronomy Supplement*, 13(4):1-20.

Hively, R. and Horn, R. (1984). "Hopewellian geometry and astronomy at High Bank". *Journal for the History of Astronomy. Archaeoastronomy Supplement*, 15(7):85-100.

Marshall, J. A. (1978). "American Indian geometry". *Ohio Archaeologist*, 28(1):29-33.

Marshall, J. A. (1985). "An atlas of American Indian geometry". *Ohio Archaeologist*, 37,(2):36-49.

Riordan, R. V. (1986). *The Pollock Works: Chronology and construction of a hilltop enclosure*. New Orleans, Louisiana, The Society for American Archaeology, paper presented at the 51st annual meeting.

Searle, J. R. (1969). *Speech acts*. Cambridge, Cambridge University Press.

Searle, J. R. (1979). *Expression and meaning*. Cambridge, Cambridge University Press.

Searle, J. R. (1983). *Intentionality*. Cambridge, Cambridge University Press.

Squier, E. G. and Davis, E. H. (1973). *Ancient Monuments of the Mississippi Valley Comprising the Results of Extensive Original Surveys and Explorations*. Washington, D. C., Smithsonian. Reprint, originally published 1848, *Smithsonian Contributions to Knowledge*. Vol. I.

Trigger, B. G. (1990). "Monumental architecture: A thermodynamic explanation of symbolic behavior". *World Archaeology*, 22(2): 119-132.

Townsend, R. (1979). *State and cosmos in the art of Tenochtitlan*. Washington, Dumbarton Oaks.

Van Zantwijk, R. (1985). *The Aztec arrangement*. Norman, University of Oklahoma Press.

Wright, G. (1990). "On the interior attached ditch enclosures of the Middle and Upper Ohio Valley". *Ethnos*, (1-2):92-107.

# WHAT 'NATURE' MEANS FOR A SOUTH-WEST COLOMBIAN INDIAN

Franz X. Faust

## I. The subject

In this article I treat the problem of whether a similar concept of nature exists for the Occident, on the one hand, and the Indians of South-West Colombia on the other. I will also consider what role this concept plays in the daily lives of these people.

A current distinction made in the occidental culture is that between the terms 'Culture' and 'Nature'. Taking into account the definition of culture as, "the acquired knowledge people use to interpret experience which generates a behavior" (Spradley, 1981:6), we may state that the basis of culture is acquired knowledge, or tradition.

Generally, human groups consider themselves to be formed by tradition; by their history, and so people understand themselves as a cultural society. The specific tradition which creates the cultural identity of groups of people delimits them against other societies with other traditions. This is a problem of ethnicity. But the tradition also delimits them against non-human space in which there are non-cultural norms; a space which in our every day terminology is called 'Nature'.

It is a universal feature of human beings in general, to conceive of themselves as being conditioned by culture. Hence in the following text the central question is not whether the South-West Colombian Indians differentiate between 'space of culture' and 'space of no culture', but where they make this differentiation and how this specific form of limitation influences their everyday life.

## II. The ethnic groups

I will deal with the concepts of two communities which belong to two different ethnic groups: the community of Puracé from Coconucos ethnic groups and the group of Rio Blanco which belongs to the Yanaconas. These two neighboring groups live in the north western part of the Macizo Colombiano, which is a mountainous area of volcanic origin where the central and oriental cordilleras of the Colombian Andes come together. They live at an altitude of 2,000 meter and 3,000 meter where the climate is cold. They cultivate potatoes, maize, corn, *ulluco, majua,* coca and other products, as well as breeding cattle and sheep.

Linguistically these two groups descend from different ancestors. The Coconucos belong, like the actual Totoro and Guambiano, to the linguistic group of the Chibchas, although we can also see an influence of the Paez, Quechua languages. The Yanaconas live at the northern tip of the Quechua in the Andes.

Nowadays the Coconucos and the Yanaconas use the Spanish language in their everyday life. In the case of the Coconucos the Spanish idioms have replaced the native ones totally, whereas among the Yanaconas there are still individuals who know how to speak the local Quechua. This change of language has not affected their auto-identification as Indians, which is very strong in both groups. Thus although the Yanaconas and Coconucos descend from different ancestors and from different linguistic groups and see themselves as ethnically different, the difference in their concepts about the world is so minimal that the expression of these concepts in everyday life is very similar.

## III. The resource of information

The present data were collected while I was a teacher at the Fundación Universitaria and at the University of Cauca from September 1987 to August 1990 in Popayán (Colombia). The research topics were: "The indian groups, their natural environment with its biological and non-biological elements." The research addressed the following points:

1. Ethnobotany with special emphasis on the categories of function the Coconucos use in order to apply a classification to the botanical kingdom. The research was made with people from the Puracé community.
2. Categories of function for geological and geographical features or events observed by the Yanaconas from Rio Blanco.
3. What concepts do the Coconucos and Yanaconas have about animals in their habitat. The research was carried out with people from the Coconucos community of Puracé and the Yanaconas from Rio Blanco.

These concepts are common knowledge for all Indians from the age of 10 years on in both ethnic groups.

### IV. The concept of nature among Coconucos and Yanaconas

As I indicated before, the Coconucos and Yanaconas nowadays speak Spanish. Hence the word 'nature' belongs to their vocabulary, although I only registered this word once when a female Indian teacher from Rio Blanco said that "the nature in the páramos (area with low vegetation on the high, cold mountains) protects itself against 'the human presence'". Let us take this sentence as the beginning of the treatise.

It is a common idea that the páramos protects itself against human presence by several elements such as fog, heavy rain, thunder, and storms. For the common Indian, this defensive force of the páramos is called *jucas*, a word which is translated as 'madre monte' (Mountain Mother) by the Coconucos and 'diablo' (Devil) by the Yanaconas.

The analysis of the word *jucas* shows that the Indian teacher had every reason for translating it as 'nature' because its meaning is very similar to the Western concept.

*Jucas* is an unpersonified quality ('sin cuerpo') which can be found in areas not under human control such as the volcanos, virgin jungle, high mountains, swamps, lakes, rivers. It is also said that all uncultivated plants and wild animals as well as atmospheric elements like fog, rain, wind, ice, and storms belong to *jucas*. The Coconucos and Yanaconas also use the term *jucas* in order to differentiate between culture and nature. Deer belong to *jucas* whereas sheep belong to humans. Everything which belongs to *jucas* occurs more commonly where human influence is less common and where the landscape is much more savage and therefore less accessible for the humans, such as deep jungles, high mountains, and strong rivers.

What has been said so far shows that the concept of *jucas* is, at least to a certain extent, quite similar to our Occidental concept of 'nature'. However, it is also applied to elements of the realm Westerners would call 'supernatural' (Faust, 1989; 1990). Thus 'Cocos', which in the imagination of the Coconucos and Yanaconas live in areas which belong to *jucas*, act as the guards of these places. 'Los cocos' are the spirits of nature. For the Indians the following cocos exist:

'La fantasma negra': which lives in the lakes of the páramos and shows itself as a dark cloud;
'Los cuiches': which is the rainbow and is localized in swamps;
'Los truenos': which live in the rocks;
'Las pumas': women with very large breasts having their home in the páramos;
'La madre agua': who lives in the pools of waterfalls and shows herself in the shape of a snake or a beautiful woman - she is the Queen of all aquatic life;
'Los duendes': little human beings with bandy legs and hands living beside the rivers;
'Los niños auca': skeletons with long teeth living in the rocks beside the waterfalls.

All these beings, which for the Occidentals would be included in the category of the supernatural, represent for the Indians of the Macizo Colombiano the higher concentration of *jucas*. Whenever they talk about these beings, they do so in the same way as they speak about deer, bears and tapirs.

When we continue our reflection on the similarity between the terms *jucas* and nature, we find that these spirits have nothing to do with the supernatural world; quite to the contrary they are among the most natural of things. These cocos extend the concept of *jucas* because 'Los cocos' represent the subterranean world. For the Coconucos and Yanaconas this is the place where the *jucas* is at home and where it lives without any competition. Furthermore, the ancestors continue to live in this subterranean world on the shores of great lakes. The element of the subterranean world is water and water is also an element of *jucas*. For this reason, in the above-ground part of the world, all the springs, lakes and everything replete with water like the woodlands and swamps are full of the quality of *jucas*; they are places where *jucas* is concentrated. But the subterranean world is not only the world of water. It is also the world of the ancestors and all precolombian funerals and all things related to them, like pieces of art in ceramic or gold, are extremely full of *jucas*. Therefore *jucas* has aspects that can hardly be included in our concept of nature. It is also important that *jucas* is closely related to the periods of the moon. *Jucas* is especially strong in the nights after full moon and less powerful in the days of new moon.

The relationship that the Indians have to *jucas* is ambivalent. *Jucas* supplies the water and the most powerful plants for medical use as well as material of animal, plant or mineral origin necessary for their rituals which form part of their life from birth to death. But *jucas* also has the power to punish every violation of the Indian's rules, using the cocos which steal the personal soul of the violator and make him suffer from an illness called 'viento'. This, according to the intensity of the violation, can involve symptoms ranging from insomnia to epileptic fits. What belongs to *jucas* acts in this way because *jucas* is *auca*. The Yanaconas translate the term *auca* into Spanish using 'bravo' (wild) and 'peligroso' (dangerous) as synonyms, while the Coconucos have replaced these terms by another synonym 'hieloso' (frozen). *Auca* or 'hieloso' is everything which steals the personal soul, which is what the cocos of *jucas* do when they bring 'viento'.

We shall now discuss the concept of *auca*. In doing so we shall see that *jucas* which lives in the wild world and in the subterranean world has its counterpart in the development of the human being and his social life. Several steps in life and certain conditions, behaviors and circumstances within social life, raise the danger of causing 'aire', which, just as the 'viento' caused by the cocos, steals the personal soul and produces the same symptoms. Both, 'viento' and 'aire' belong to the same category of 'hieloso' and both are caused by something which is *auca*.

I previously explained that, in the countryside, *auca* comprises all the things which belong to *jucas*. Now I must also explain the *auca* as a threat in social life.

*Auca* for Coconucos and Yanaconas is something omnipresent; it is related to pregnancy, birth, the first steps in life, puberty, sexuality, menstruation, and finally to death and even to the dead. Furthermore, *auca* is all strong emotions like envy, anger or love and every illness. Everybody who is living in a state of strong *auca* is capable of getting the illness of 'aire' or 'viento' and this implies a danger of transmitting 'aire' to other people.

If we look at *aire* with its social *auca* aspects and 'viento' also being *auca* by *jucas* then we see that both forms represent only one complex and thus demand the same behavior. If we continue to compare the similarity of the concept of *jucas* and the Occidental concept of nature, we have to amplify this similarity to all that is *auca*. As a result volcanos, woods, mountains, lakes, waterfalls, swamps, storm, ice rains, cocos, 'guacas' (mounds), birth, sexuality, menstruation, love, envy, anger, death, etc., all fall into this category. To an Occidental, this categorization would seem strange; but, in the end, the accumulated elements have something in common. Neither the volcanos nor the swamps, nor the storms, birth, sexuality, anger, envy or death are controlled or controllable by mankind.

So far, the concepts of *auca* and *jucas* together represent a concept similar to what we call 'nature' but we have to take into account that in spite of their similarity both concepts have very different connotations.

Let us look at how these concepts influence everyday life. When we look at the Indian translation of the term *auca* into the Spanish words 'peligroso' and 'bravo', we might think that Indians also see *auca* and *jucas* as something terrible which can affect their lives and which it is necessary to avoid. It is true that they can be dangerous, but this is only one of their aspects.

In order to understand the way *auca* works we should consider its translation as 'hieloso'; an extreme coldness (frozen). This translation shows us the position of the concepts of *auca* and *jucas* within the general cultural context of the Coconucos and Yanaconas.

Both ethnic groups, like so many American Indians between Mexico and Chile and between the Pacific Ocean and the mountains of Guyana, assign to every thing, fact or event, a certain quality which in the Macizo-Colombiano language is called 'calor' (heat) or 'espiritu' (spirit, soul). These two terms have connotations such as power, strength, hardness, vitality, resistance, and health. A lack of spirit or heat is 'cold' but an excess is 'hot'. This cognitive system assigns to every object, fact and event the specific amount of heat which it should have. The amount of 'calor' involved is so important because it directly influences well-being and health. A person only feels healthy and well if he keeps the right amount of 'calor' for his gender, his age, situation and personality. This is easier if the heat ('calor') is distributed in the right and adequate amount in the surrounding environment.

Let us continue with the role which *jucas* and *auca* play in the well-being of the Coconucos and the Yanaconas. We have already mentioned that the areas of *jucas* and their effects threaten humans with pains which are called 'viento' whereas the *auca* affects the development of life, and in social life it causes 'aire'. 'Aire' and 'viento' belong to the same category of 'hielo' and this 'hielo' steals the personal soul of the people and thus bringing them diseases.

A cold results from a bad influence of *auca*, but it is not necessarily the consequence of meeting something which represents *auca*. On the contrary *auca* is necessary because it brings down the excessive accumulation of 'calor' (heat) which would also cause an illness.

Some examples from everyday life:
- *Birth is full of auca*, but it is necessary to preserve life and it also brings down the heat felt by pregnant women.

- *The first steps of humans are auca*, but the child has to overcome these steps, and the indians show a *very strong* concern if a child does not start to walk in time.

- *Puberty is auca*, but without puberty there would be neither man nor woman, and without this difference the humans would die out.

- *Sexuality is auca*, but sexuality is necessary for reproduction. Furthermore it brings both to man and to woman the necessary cold without which they would get ill. Among Coconucos and Yanaconas, sexuality is regarded as something absolutely necessary for humans from a very early age.

- *Menstruation is auca*, but menstruation is seen as a purification for the woman and brings her the necessary cold; without menstruation the heat of the woman would become to high and she would get ill.

- *Envy is auca*, but envy is a reason for sorcery thus preventing the individual members of the community from accumulating to many goods and personal profits which would result in the disintegration of the group.

- *Death is auca*, but death makes room for new life.

The above examples show us that *auca*, with its coldness, is absolutely necessary for well-being and health, and being unwell only occurs when there is an accumulation of *auca*. For this reason, sexuality and menstruation have an excluding function. For example it is forbidden for a woman who will give birth to carry a baby or a child that is making its first steps. We also have a connection with everything which is related to *jucas* because it is *auca*. Thus neither a menstruating woman nor a woman giving birth can take a bath because water is *auca* and these women are living in a state of *auca*. Somebody who is living in a state of *auca* can not enter an area of *jucas*. This is, for example, the reason why a hunter is not allowed to practice any kind of sexuality before he goes hunting.

It is believed that *auca* is necessary to a certain degree and this influences the way the Coconucos and Yanaconas cultivate their country. Areas of building, cultivating and herding are tamed areas. But the Macizo-Indians can not tame all the territories because the areas of *jucas* give the cold necessary for the countryside and for maintaining the correct balance between hot and cold. If *jucas* disappears, water which is a specific element of *jucas*, disappears, too. This is one of the reasons why the Indians do not influence the vegetation in areas which, due to their topography, are full of *jucas*, such as the 'páramos', rocks, lakes, rivers, ravines, and waterfalls. This concept is so strong that even in areas which were given back to them over the last 20 years due to the 'Reforma Agraria', they do not use all the land for cultivating or herding. In certain areas they let woods grow, thus giving back *jucas* its space again.

Another reason why *jucas* is absolutely necessary for the Coconucos and Yanaconas is that the system of cold and heat in which these Indians divide their world is essentially dialectic. Heat produces cold and vice versa. So the cocos, the guardian spirits of *jucas* places, produce cold but, at the same time these spirits are very hot. Thus the tamed areas, which belong to the humans just as the cultivated country does, are the sources of human illnesses of heat; but the plants growing there are cold and fresh. The illnesses produced in the area of *jucas* are cold pains, but in the same areas plants grow that are full of 'calor', which help against these pains. These plants not only help against the *auca* of the wilderness, but also against the *auca* of life like envy, pregnancy, birth, and menstruation. Thus the Indians always need their medicine and the ritual which accompanies it, both of which are related to these plants out of the region of *jucas*, throughout their life they can only get these plants if they permit the wild vegetation to grow without any human influence.

## V. Conclusion

The word *jucas*, which conveys similar ideas among the Coconucos and the Yanaconas, can be compared with our Occidental concept of nature and the natural. The natural for the Occidental stands in opposition to the cultural, whereas for the Indians there is one space which belongs to *jucas* and another one belonging to humans. To *jucas* belong places like volcanos, ravines, mountains, lakes, rivers, areas of vegetation in the páramos, woods, swamps, the wild plants and animals, atmospheric phenomena like wind, rains, storms, thunder, ice, fog, and the moon in the sky. Contrary to the Occidental concept of nature, the Indians also have the guardian spirits, called *cocos*, belonging to *jucas*. The past which is alive in the subterranean world, represented, for example, by all the funerals, graves of the ancestors, and their treasures, is also full of *jucas*. Something which belongs to *jucas* is related to the adjective *auca* which is translated into the terms wild, frozen and dangerous. *Auca* is not only related to geographical places, types of vegetation and weather, but also to human development and social conditions.

Summing up, we can say that *auca* is everything which is not under human control, like a volcano, or a storm, but also including sexuality and death. *Jucas* and *auca* form part of a system of heat and cold which assigns to every object, fact or event a certain amount of heat or 'espiritu'.

*Auca* takes away the soul and brings cooling that, in a balanced way, is absolutely necessary for well-being. The humans must make room for *auca* and its coldness as well as for the human-controlled things and their heat, in order to be healthy.

Finally, looking back at the similarity of *jucas* and *auca* compared with the Occidental terms of natural and nature, we can say that 'to feel well and healthy' for the Coconucos and Yanaconas means to maintain inside of themselves, as in their surrounding environment, a balance between the cultural, the controlled elements, and the uncontrolled, savage, wilderness of nature.

## References

Faust, F.X. (1989). *Etnobotanica de Puracé. Sistemas Clasificatorios Funcionales.* Hohenschäftlarn, Renner.

Faust, F.X. (1990). "Etnogeografía y Etnogeología de Coconuco y Sotará." *Revista Colombiana de Antropología*, 27:53-90.

Spradley, J.P. (1981). *Participant Observation.* San Francisco, Holt, Rinhart & Winston.

# CULTURE, TECHNOLOGY AND THE RELATION BETWEEN MAN AND NATURE

Antonio Santangelo

The connection between Man and Nature does not appear univocal, since humans are not only adapted to the natural, but also react to and even alter it to such an extent that they rule it and free themselves from it. This process will be considered in more detail.

Glancing over the history of human evolution, the relation between humans and environment became altered with the advent of the genus Homo, but a real emancipation of humans from nature did not occur until recently, and emancipation occurred as a change in quality. To be realistic, humans evaded the objectivity of nature only through a culture producing a modern kind of technology.

This relationship refers to the differences pointed out as far as culture and technology are concerned. Conventionally, the starting point of the hominid lines is placed in the Pliocene. These lines showed comprehensively modified behavior, outdistancing a basically catarrhine ancestral behavior, centered on behavioral patterns tending to occur in non-human primates. The fact that the Pliocene hominids gradually became 'walkers' (Boné, 1983:63; Susman, Stern and Jungers, 1986:184; Senut, 1989:53) led to a series of additional behavioral modifications.

There was adaptation, but also a reaction in prehumans, to the environmental conditions in which they lived. The mechanism of qualitative changes towards bipedalism was based on the ontogenic shift under particular environmental conditions (Vančata and Vančatová, 1987:517), and on the genetic assimilation of the adaptability for bipedalism (Marks, 1989:493). Besides, the fact that walking on two legs must be taught is a further proof of active reaction to the environment, because a morphological disposition to bipedal locomotion, though existing, does not become explicit without any learning. The interconnection between locomotive and, subsequently, behavioral patterns, produced an advance towards new ways of behavior as a whole. The sum of the new ways of behavior are considered as pre-cultural human behavior (Santangelo, 1985, 1987, 1989) and appear as transitional forms of behavior leading towards the human pattern.

This implies a different way of caring for the young, who cannot cling permanently to their mothers any longer (Washburn and De Vore, 1961: 97). The new mother-child relation, limiting the mothers' autonomy, must in return have affected the new setting up of relationships as a whole inside the group, by means of innovating ways of behavior, of providing for the young, preferential bonds and intentional cooperation (Tanner, 1985:145, 151, 213). As a consequence of cooperation the structure of social relations is not to be imagined as hierarchically ordered but rather as egalitarian.

We have suggested that the whole of the behavioral changes occurring in the hominids must be considered as the development of a principle of reciprocity, as a more probable way of forming the new group relation. For this to occur a form of reasoning, as well as a new shaping of the affective moments which are the basis of behavior is needed. Without the emerging of reciprocity, hominid lines, which lack effective canines, would not have been successful. Harvesting, transport and the voluntary sharing of food within the group (Tanner, 1985:151,164) provide short periods in which reciprocity is expressed. This emergent set of behaviors - new for the primate family - could not actually be affected by culture. The hominids' cerebral capacity at this time did not allow any possibility for culture to develop.

Nevertheless we believe that 'the concept of man', due to evolutionary development caused by environmental conditions, can be suggested at evolutionary levels (hominids) which actually have not gone beyond the human threshold. Pre-cultural behavior corresponds to a series of behaviors of the human type, encouraged and lived in this way (by the hominids) without a cultural component. Culture is to be considered as the ability to reflect upon the things and events of life and can be referred to a bio-type which is already human. The accepted meanings and interpretations of what is intended by Culture are various. After Tylor, a lot of them have been added within a century. Kroeber and Kluckhohn, in a very well-known essay

(Kroeber and Kluckhohn, 1972), collected over a hundred definitions and concepts regarding Culture, supplied by different authors, and representing the most different interpretations.

I have argued in some previous works that culture begins as a way of interpreting things which goes beyond mere knowledge (Santangelo, 1987:99; 1989:129). Therefore, in relation to the topic of this argument, it is fundamental to establish the critical evolutionary point at which culture becomes possible. One can investigate the course followed by this ability in its development step by step. In Homo, the structure of the brain evolutionarily went through a process of complexification and/or reorganization which permitted such a change in quality. It is suggested that an intellectual improvement can be dated to 2.3 million years ago and involved only the hominid line of the habilis biotype (Tobias, 1985a:134; 1987:741, 756).

It is interesting to point out that the environmental pressure for change does not justify the necessity of such an advanced cerebralization process, compared with other hominid lines (Jerison, 1973:420, 421). Strictly speaking the operative ability of the primitive hominid brain must be considered sufficient for the processing of information, and for the organization of the ability to cope with the environmental conditions. Therefore a further brain increase by Homo, over the average hominid brain, and the ability for culture, linked to it, was 'something extra' being produced, unnecessary at the moment, to keep pace and compete with other species. This evolutionary stage started with Homo. It is impossible to attribute the ability for culture to lower evolutionary levels. Attributing culture below the human brain would mean that culture was produced before an increase of the brain (Geertz, 1973:30). Moreover, if we adapted the concept of culture to the abilities of limited brains, we would have to cope with great interpretative difficulties about what exactly is meant by culture. The crucial point is that about 2.3 million years ago an event occurred which led rather quickly to an increase in brain quantity; from 450 cc, as in the average Australopithecus to 650 cc as in the habilis biotype (Tobias, 1985b:98). Thereafter further increases also occurred.

Let us proceed with the evolutionary process itself and investigate what, of such great relevance for the human brain, actually happened. Strictly speaking, the morphological scheme of the brain in humans, anthropoids, and hominids of the Tertiary Period is basically the same. It is clear that a complex of shared paleocortical structures, together with affective ones (limbic system) turned out to be very conservative during evolutionary development (Mazzi and Fasolo, 1977:525, 527; MacLean 1973). Over these fundamental structures in the cerebral morphology, mammals and in particular primates developed a cerebral mantle, largely composed of associative structures. Some particular organizations are shared both by humans and higher primates. For example, the Broca area, a center organized for the control of peri-oral muscle movements in higher primates became, at a human level a center of organization for word articulation (Mazzi and Fasolo, 1977:505; Chiarelli, 1984:85-86; Deacon, 1989:368).

Let us turn to the asymmetry of cerebral hemispheres. The asymmetry of hemispheres, in humans with left predominance, is also inferred for the Australopitheci (Tobias, 1989:146; Levy 1978:351). In anthropoids on the other hand, hemispheric laterality is neither constant nor consistent (Denes, 1978:14, 51; Fabbro and Bava 1989:107; Levy, 1978:352-353) and often occurs in the opposite direction to the human one (Levy, 1978:381). Laterality is not a unitary feature, but deals with a mosaic of functions (Fabbro and Bava, 1989:82; Count, 1965). The leftward laterality of the human brain corresponds to a prevailing use of the right hand and is linked to speech. In the human species an expansion of the parietal lobe occurs, whereas in sub-human forms this is much reduced. Above all, however, we must point out that a new area is produced; the angular gyrus, which is situated at a parietal level. The angular gyrus is not present in the alloprimates and is rudimentary in the anthropoids (Crosby and Critchley cit. in Geschwind, 1974:146).

The function of parietal lobes is useful as a major associative area, and the angular gyrus is a new evolutionary form, which is introduced among other associative areas and resumes the link among these (Geschwind, 1974:99, 147; Jerison, 1973:372). The lack of the angular gyrus in alloprimates means that the different cortical units work through the limbic system (Geschwind, 1974:97-98). The angular gyrus shows an operative model for the complex combining of information. The arrangement allows cross-modal associations of the information deriving from sensorial analyzers and from other areas of the brain. The Wernicke area, which is important for the central formulation of speech, is situated in the temporal-parietal lobes and partly coincides with the area of the angular gyrus (Geschwind, 1974:107, 149).

This remark leads us to assume a possible link between an emerging cultural ability and cerebral language skill. The activity of an expanded cerebral mantle, supplied with structural attributes, which must be considered idiotypical for humans, produces a maximal capacity for assembling and processing information in terms of neurological operativeness, up to the point where the word 'neurological' becomes unsuitable and the term 'neuropsychological process' becomes relevant. In addition, the contribution of frontal lobes has to be considered as a possible alteration of the relations existing between the cortical areas and the lower affective stations. In particular, the frontal and pre-frontal areas of the brain are affected by allometric modality of development, compared to other areas (Deacon, 1989:382). The pre-frontal areas in particular became twice the size they would have been on the basis of brain size. The number of existing nervous connections increased, thus reorganizing the whole function. Moreover, frontal area expansion affected the reciprocal proportions with the deep affective structures, and cortical predominance was established over the emotional system (Mazzi and Fasolo, 1977:522, 526; Deacon, 1989:382, 394).

It is clear that we are facing a process which lasted and was developed over a long period, but as a rule, from the habilis biotype on, it is correct to outline a research on culture. The habilis biotype clusters a number of autopomorphic peculiarities, that is evolutionary modifications which occurred only in the habilis line. These, in neurological outline, include a certain expansion of the cerebral mantle, the specification of the Broca area, the complexity of the parietal lobe, the appearance of the Wernicke area and the complexity of meningeal vascularity (Tobias, 1983:110; 1987:747; 1988:309). With this trend of transformations of an anatomic kind and operative ability, the concept of 'pre-cultural behavior' is exceeded, and humans appear with their cultural abilities. Correspondingly, the skill of speech makes it possible to hand down culture. It is necessary to infer that inside the hominid lines, only one among these species evolutionarily outdistanced the others, being genetically selected towards neotenic forms, with bigger and more developed brains.

Neoteny, as an anthropogenetical factor first suggested by Bolk in 1926, is considered to be a series of slowdowns in morphogenesis and maturity processes. This thesis was resumed by Washburn and Schultz, who pointed out the prolonged period during which the young remained dependent, thus reaching an adult stage late (Washburn and DeVore, 1961:96, 99; Schultz, 1961:69, 71). Neoteny as an anthropogenetic factor has been stressed by Huxley, Novák and others (Novák, 1986:261). The selection of bigger and wider brainmantles must have permitted the development of culture.

We consider culture as an additional ability to process information beyond mere knowledge. Essentially the process leading to culture means that the cerebral working must progressively reach the ability of maintaining two or more planes of thought at the same time and whilst comparing them, giving and/or making sense of the whole situation, as well as of every single element of that situation. The cultural level is to be led back to the investment of meaning which mankind has given to things, actions and events, reflecting on the very events of life. Culture involves a delicate mechanism of reflection which leads humans to interpret what they encounter. For anthropoids, on the other hand, objects keep their actual objectivity, which an animal perceives, without any further signs of interpretation. In the chimpanzees under training, just a few clues show the possibility of carrying on two alternate lines of thought (Gardner and Gardner, 1988:65; 1989:433; Premack, 1978:95, 103, 111), for instance the ability to understand the conditional 'if'. Yet we cannot speak of culture since the step of going beyond, through interpretation, is missing.

Any further production of meaning is an idiotypical mark of humankind. According to our interpretation, culture does not really appear as an original improvement of technological abilities, at a practical-factual level, but is related to the ability to approach and compare two (or more) thoughts in relation to an object, and to give a meaning to the things and events of life through an interpretative mediation. Culture, far from appearing a practical premise, is regarded as the ability to foresee something else, a sign of reality for humans, thought and interpreted by them. This ability points to humans becoming 'cultural beings'. With the promotion of two parallel lines of thought, humans meet the object no longer as a counter-object, but they regard it as a phenomenon and see it from a new perspective.

I would like to produce two elementary examples, for a better understanding of this concept. The presence of a line, of a linear wall on the ground, can become a partition line for young people playing. The line on the ground acquires a partitioning and organizing function, which originally does not belong to it as a natural fortuitousness, but is mentally made up by Man. Another example is given by ochre. Ochre is a red-colored mineral, and psychological research has proved that the red color is recognized and seen by alloprimates, as well as by humans. However, only humans are able to produce thoughts about it, and to see the object (the ochre) as a transvaluational, abstract form, which has become cultural. They have the ability to provide it with a meaning and also a set of values and behaviors consistent with the given interpretation.

The meaning and development of values allotted by humans impose themselves as a deepening and a negation of the immediate form of knowledge. It does not matter whether the given meaning is right or wrong, culture is interpretation and different cultures came into being because of different ways to approach and link the events of life.

As the 'cultural moment' follows the intellectual reflective ability, it follows that the cultural interpretations must have been different among different human groups since the very beginning, and for this reason no cultural interpretation can be led back to a single origin. This is a logical, necessary inference. But we think that the possibility of some interpretative constants must have existed early, being provided with varieties of form and content later. Such changes of cultural expression can be explained in relation to a 'differential placing' and to a 'differential importance' of some constituent items inside a cultural complex. Besides, whenever an interpretative element becomes of outstanding importance within a cultural set, other interpretative elements may turn out to be of minor importance and group themselves around it. On another occasion I used the example of the passage from a mother-centered structure to a patriarchal structure of societies (Santangelo, 1987:107, 123). The possibility of a 'reciprocal sliding' related to the components of the events of life, the priority of an element in relation to another one, and so on, underline the change of cultures with the passing of time as well as the development of different cultures. The repetition of the same habitual actions during the course of generations can also result in drifting to set interpretations just as we know that a repeated quantity becomes quality. In addition, the successive human colonizations must have operated in a diversifying sense. For example, colonization of America occurred in a few waves of migration (Greenberg, Turner and Zegura, 1986:477), but later American cultures developed differently in their most characteristic elements (language, beliefs, kinship, economy) and these differences were accomplished within the same continental area.

It is largely open to debate at which biotypological human level the ability for culture can be assumed. After Tobias' work we can date the beginning of culture from Homo habilis on. This statement permits a logical inference: mankind was conditioned by nature, but Man is a cultural being. In the same way, it is incorrect to talk about 'natural peoples', whereas they are certainly 'cultural peoples'. Our interpretation of the concept of culture marks the greatest distance from those theories which speak of culture as a means of practical effectiveness or as a form of continuous adaptation which reaches its climax in humans and enables them to master the environment. These theories do not explain the qualitative jump of the human mind into culture; culture, however, being considered as a process with a practical valence, is seen as a continuum whose starting point lies in the animal scale and which also belongs to the animal scale.

Following this interpretation, the use chimpanzees make of sticks in termitaria is part of a cultural practice. The action of cleaning potatoes, begun by chance by Imo, a female macaque, has been defined as being proto-cultural and this habit was later reproduced by the community. Certain intellectual improvements seem to be cultural, but actually they are not, since they are limited to individual objects, no interpretation is put upon them, whereas interpretation is fundamental with respect to culture. Culture 'par excellence' is e.g., a taboo, which provides interpretative links -

with childbirth or with hunting as well as with other elements belonging to the realm of experience, and a taboo does not necessarily have an adaptive practical value. After what has been said about Culture, producing a manufactured object becomes a less qualifying moment. Making objects calls for a concept of dimension, symmetry, and linearity (Chiarelli, 1988:185; 1989:196, 198). These abilities are preliminary to culture. They are abilities needed by a mind to become cultural, but they are only applications. Moreover, humans began to master the environment only after the development of an advanced technology and this has developed only late in history.

Culture, as a form of interpretation, involves technology but it is not to be identified with it. Culture, in a sense, is necessary for the development of technology. The construction of elementary tools can help the dynamics of supply, but does not overcome the substantial harmlessness inside nature. One cannot say that the human relation to nature changed in importance during the paleolithic ages, even if humans were already cultural beings. This is valid for Homo erectus, who promoted the Levalloisian technique and it is also valid for the Homo sapiens neanderthalensis, who has left us evidence of culture, though he possessed only limited stone tools (Howell, Butzer and Aguirre, 1962; Broglio, 1986:73). One could say the same for the last hunter/gatherer groups nowadays, which show amazing cultural actions as well. The fact that these groups have largely resorted to magic, which is cultural promotion and interpretation, confirms 'in a negative way' both substantial insufficiency in technology and real defenselessness in relation to nature.

It is clear that one can distinguish between the abilities for culture itself and technological abilities as a possibility developing from and along with culture. Technology is a possible result of mental operative abilities, at a practical level, which then develops into culture as an integral part of it. As soon as sufficient intellectual growth occurred in Homo, the development of the ability to reason about any contingent issue, the persistence of mental concepts applied to the operative aspect of concerning things, involve the development of technology as a necessary collateral process, which is an essential part of culture.

At this level of operative ability, according to a scheme of dialectic transformations, the complexity of a tool reveals itself as a sign of intellectual operative organization and can become 'one of the indicators of culture', since it can transform the environment. During protohistoric ages the factual operative ability was able to tame some forms of nature in the sense that the environment nature was selected in its faunal and vegetal component - and thus Nature was modified and adjusted for humans, according to their will and interest (Bargatzky, 1986:200; 1988:389).

At this level of technological operativeness, and referring to this 'appropriation', the relationship between humans and nature is to be revised. We must consider, moreover, the great impact of scientific and technological skill which occurred a few centuries ago, starting with Galileo and Bacon and the moment when a capitalist system of production was established. Technological skill and organization promoted this stage, but it is unnecessary to have an advance in neurological structures in order to explain this technological jump. This process started only 300 years ago, and the capacity of the human mind has remained the same for a much longer time.

Summing up, culture, at its very beginning, is to be considered as an interpretation of reality, investing it with meaning and thus going beyond mere knowledge. The growing intellectual ability of Homo has made it possible to maintain contemporaneously and to compare more planes of thought, hence giving a meaning (it does not matter whether right or wrong) to the things and events of life. Technology is not to be identified with culture, even though it is part of culture. The lithic industry did not free man from the constraints of his natural environment. Not even today are the aborigines (Homo sapiens) living in marginal territories free from the constraints of their own environment. They live according to a cultural form. On many occasions they resort to magic (an eminently cultural aspect) but they do not possess enough technology to modify the environment and master it.

Technology is an aspect of intellectual ability and is part of culture in general, but the first effective impact of technology upon nature resulted late. Culture, however, represented the very early advance made by Man and characterized his becoming human.

## References

Bargatzky, T. (1986). "On Adaptation and Equilibrium: A Critique of Biological Analogy in Cultural Anthropology." *Zeitschrift für Ethnologie*, 111(2):193-203.

Bargatzky, T. (1988). "Kulturökologie." In H. Fischer (ed.). *Ethnologie. Einführung und Überblick*. Berlin, D. Reimer, pp. 375-392.

Boné, E. (1983). "L'acquisition de la station etc. et de la locomotion bipéde chez les Hominidés." In C. Chagas (ed.). *Recent Advances in the Evolution of Primates*. Cittá del Vaticano, Pontificia Academia Scientiarum.

Broglio, A. (1986). *I Neandertaliani*. Museo Preistorico e Archeologico, Ferrara, A.C. Blanc.

Chiarelli, B. (1984). *Origini della Socialitá e della Cultura Umana*. Bari, Laterza.

Chiarelli, B. (1988). "Manufatti litici e livello intellettivo." In *Anthropologia Contemporanea*, 11(3-4):185-186.

Chiarelli, B. (1989). "Spatial Coordination, Gestural Communication. The Origin of Language and Cerebral Lateralization in Man." In *The Mankind Quarterly*, 29(3):195-210.

Count, E.W. (1965). *Phasia: The Humanization of Primate Phonic Communication*. Symposium on Animal Communication, Burg Wartenstein. (Working paper.)

Deacon, T.W. (1989). "The Neural Circuitry underlying Primate calls and Human Language." *Human Evolution*, 4(5):367-401.

Denes, F. (1978). "Asimmetrie Anatomiche." In *I Due Cervelli. Neuropsicologia dei processi cognitivi*. Bologna, Il Mulino. pp. 13-54.

Fabbro, F. and Bava, A. (1989). "Asimmetrie dell'Encefalo Umano. Filogenesi ed Ontogenesi." *Anthropologia Contomporanea*, 12(3):81-157.

Gardner, R. and Gardner, B. T (1988). "The Role of Cross-fostering in Sign Language Studies of Chimpanzees." *Human Evolution*, 3(1-2):65-79.

Gardner, R. and Gardner, B. T. (1989). "Prelinguistic Development of Children and Chimpanzees." *Human Evolution*, 4(6):433-460.

Geertz, C. (1973). "Il passaggio all' umanità." In S. Tax (ed.). *Horizons of Anthropology*. Aldine Publ. 1964. Italian trl. *Orizzonti di Antropologia*. Brescia, Morcelliana, pp. 25-36.

Geschwind, N. (1974). *Selected Papers on Language and the Brain*. Dordrecht, D. Reidel.

Greenberg, H., Turner II, C. G. and Zegura, S. (1986). "The Settlement of the Americas: A Comparison of the Linguistic, Dental, and Genetic Evidence." *Current Anthropology*, 27(5):477-497.

Howell, F. C., Butzer, K. W. and Aguirre, E. (1962). *Noticia preliminar sobre el emplazamento acheulense de Torralba (Soria)*. Madrid, Ministerio de Educación Nacional.

Jerison, H. J. (1973). *Evolution of the Brain and Intelligence*. New York, Academic Press.

Kroeber, A. L. and Kluckhohn, C. (1972). *Culture. A Critical Review of Concepts and Definitions*. Peabody Museum, Cambridge Mass, 1957. Italian trl. *Il Concetto Di Cultura*. Bologna, Il Mulino Ed.

Levy J. (1978). "Implicazioni psicobiologiche dell'Asimmetria Cerebrale." In *I Due Cervelli. Neuropsicologia dei processi cognitivi*. Bologna, Il Mulino Ed., pp. 351-381.

Mac Lean, P. D. (1973). *A Triune Concept of the Brain and Behavior*. Toronto and Buffalo, University of Toronto Press.

Marks, J. (1989). "Genetic Assimilation in the Evolution of Bipedalism." *Human Evolution*, 4(6):493-499.

Mazzi, V. and Fasolo, A. (1977). *Introduzione alla Neurologia Comparata dei Vertebrati*. Torino, Boringhieri.

Novák, V. J. (1986). "The Contribution of Behavior to the Evolution of Human Society in Adaptation." In V. J. A. Novák, V. Vančata and M. A. Vančatová (eds.). *Adaptation, Behavior and Evolution*. Praha, Czechoslovak Academy of Sciences.

Premack, A. J. (1978). *Why Chimps can read*. Ital. trl. *Perché gli scimpanzé possono leggere*. Roma, Armando Ed.

Santangelo, A. (1985). *La transizione all'umano e il concetto di comportamento pre-culturale*. Milano, La Pietra Ed.

Santangelo, A. (1987). *The Garden of Eden. The Way to Homo Sapiens: Precultural Behavior and Transition to Culture*. Milano, La Pietra Ed.

Santangelo, A. (1989). *Man: Inheritance and Cultural Advancement*. Milano, La Pietra Ed.

Schultz, A. H. (1961). "Some Factors Influencing the Social Life of Primates in General and of Early Man in Particular." In S. L. Washburn (ed.). *Social Life of Early Man*. Chicago, Aldine De Gruyter.

Senut, B. (1989). "La locomotion des pré-hominidés." In G. Giacobini. *Hominidae*. Milano, Jaca Book, pp. 53-60.

Susman, R. L., Stern, J. T. and Jungers, W. L. (1986). "Locomotor Adaptations in the Hadar Hominids." In E. Delson (ed.). *Ancestors. The Hard Evidence*. New York, A. Liss.

Tanner, N. M. (1985). *On becoming Human*. Cambridge, Cambridge University Press.

Tobias, P. V. (1983). "Recent Advances in the Evolution of the Hominids with Especial Reference to Brain and Speech." In C. Chagas (ed.). *Recent Advances in the Evolution of Primates*. Città del Vaticano, Pontificia Academia Scientiarum, pp. 85-132.

Tobias, P. V. (1985a). "Punctuational and Phyletic Evolution in the Hominids." In *Species and Speciation*. Pretoria, Transvaal Museum, pp. 131-141.

Tobias, P. V. (1985b). "Single Characters and the Total Morphological Pattern Redefined: The Sorting Effected by a Selection of Morphological Features of the Early Hominids." In E. Delson (ed.). *Ancestors. The Hard Evidence*. New York, A. Liss, pp. 94-101.

Tobias, P. V. (1987). "The Brain of Homo Habilis: A New Level of Organization in Cerebral Evolution." *Journal of Human Evolution*, 16:741-761.

Tobias, P. V. (1988). "Evidence for a Dual Pattern of Cranial Venous Sinuses in the Endocranial Cast of Taung." *American Journal of Physical Anthropology*, 76:309-312.

Tobias, P.V. (1989). "The Status of Homo Habilis in 1987 and Some Outstanding Problems." In G. Giacobini (ed.). *Hominidae*. Milano, Jaca Book, pp. 141-149.

Vančata, V. and Vančatová, M. A. (1987). "Major Features in the Evolution of Early Hominoid Locomotion." *Human Evolution*, 2(6):517-537.

Washburn, S. L. and DeVore, I. (1961). "Social behavior of baboons and early man." In S. L. Washburn (ed.). *Social Life of Early Man*. Chicago, Aldine De Gruyter.

# PHYLOGENESIS: REFLECTIONS ON EVOLUTION

Antonio Guerci and Oscar Torretta

### I. Introduction

Jean-Baptiste-Pierre-Antoine de Monet, knight of Lamarck, offered the first solution to the problem that Buffon had posed to the scholars of natural history: the derivation of all organic phenomena from the operations of a system in motion. In fact, Lamarck, as his friend Buffon, defined nature as the system of laws and forces that govern the motions of matter. Until that time the biological scientists believed that each species had been created separately by God and all were arranged by Him, from the lowest to the highest, along a Great Chain of Beings.

With the new evolutionary theory, nature is no longer fixed and immutable; species need not correspond to a predetermined model, instead variability is the most important event. Darwin's theory of natural selection linked together two basic components of the evolutionary process, variation and adaptation, by showing how the environment selected those variants adapted to it (see Dubos, 1973). The beauty of this theory is that it demonstrated that all adaptations could be explained as the result of natural selection, and that evolution really was but a single phenomenon.

Currently, two opposite and contrasting perspectives, creationism and evolutionism, try to offer different solutions to the old problem of the origin of human beings and their collocation in Nature. In these theories are reflected the hopes of human beings to comprehend the origin and the scope of their existences and consequently of the meaning of Nature.

With this exposition we do not mean to give either a historical or a retrospective outline of the different passionate theories on transformism supported or fought until the present day. Despite researchers' objectivity, all these observations have led to an especially Neo-Lamarckian tendency in the latin countries, and a Neo-Darwinist in the Anglo-Saxon ones. Gaylord Simpson's statistical works seem to extend Bergson's metaphysics into facts, matching apparently opposite opinions. Simpson (1949) considers Evolution from three points of view: speciation, phyletic evolution and quantum evolution.

*Speciation*

Speciation is a specific differentiation, it appears to be a minor term influencing the limited context of races, sub-species, species, but it does not rise further along the plant or animal classification scale. In fact, according to Simpson, the environment in which living creatures evolve presents some alternate, reticulated areas, more or less propitious for adaptation; species' variation, when it occurs, is always sub-zonal, it forms a local adaptation from separation and segregation, caused either by chance or by a change provoked by environment.

Starting from a branching autonomous, reversible, unstable direction, speciation only produces details on the context of morphologic variations concerning color, size, proportions, or individual vital resistances. This specific differentiation occurs in populations of average extension which are not very isolated.

*Phyletic evolution*

Phyletic evolution which paleontologists have best observed, occurs in genera, subfamilies and families, in large isolated units. The low and continuous action of phyletic evolution seems to extend to the areas where adaptation is followed by a post-adaptation which is secular, with few changes. Phyletic evolution develops on a linear direction which is forked and branched according to a stable pattern.

*Quantum evolution*

Quantum evolution (because of the principle of 'all or nothing') can brutally and swiftly create suborders and orders. Its interzonal and preadaptive action, often preceded by changes that are not propitious for adaptation, occurs in restricted populations, at linear, primordial levels constituting important hierarchical, morpho-physiological stages.

When Evolution forces these passages linking the different levels, then it becomes essentially quantum and creative. It does not simply harmonically modify an already known theme, such as the diversifying evolution of specific differentiation, it exceeds a degree of the organic scale, with even more strength than phyletic evolution. It is exactly in this passage from an organic type to another that, according to Simpson, the fundamental element of evolution lies. The adaptive and diversifying evolutions are just secondary sides of the organic variability; whether sometimes they are not regressive, such as for some speciations, they often remain digressive as in the case of phyletic evolution.

The first important stage of quantum evolution is represented by living molecules. These have been able to develop in the sea or perhaps in meres. The micro-dimension of these primitive infra-viruses must be similar to that of the genes inhabiting multi-cellular beings to which they are always curiously analogue. The ultra-virus, the gene, the living protein macro-molecule born in its watery environment, they all must have been, and are still, orientated, namely anisotropes: *fluent and free in one sense, solid and solidary in the other.* This particular condition of the living substance, constituting the first hierarchic stage, is of capital importance since it is a structural phenomenon that we can find at all evolutionary levels.

Certainly there is something more than a simple analogical relationship among the protein chains, the quantum and specific structure of a cell, that of a tissue, of an organ, of a system, of an individual and of a human being. In fact, these different biological units are always characterized by an anisotropy, that is a kind of polarity, of 'dis-symmetry', a real crystalline building. This morphologic orientation of the living substance, its kinetic behavior impose the thought of the probability of an aim, in other words a certain tele-finalism. This process is called quantum by some people and creative by some others. Nonetheless, many scientists agree on the absence of the vital-force entity, since all biological phenomena come down to banal physico-chemical actions under the influence of catalytic substances that are more and more known. However, by contrast with the unbelievable and almost absolute casuality of chance, a more powerful conception tries to solve the paradox that divides materialists and spiritualists.

## II. The inventiveness of nature

A living being comes into the world, lives and dies. This prodigy is similar to the existence of a limited area which, in a plane, continuously modifies its morpho-physiology when a body passes through it. This passage manifests itself through an apparent continuity made of a succession of variable sections. In the same way, life, of which we know just a few aspects, in its development seems to be a manifestation of the fourth dimension in our three-dimensional world. This fourth space (revealed by Einstein's 'Length') seems to contain imperishable entities where past, present and an aleatory future simultaneously coexist.

After the living molecule, the first biological unit which we can hierarchically suppose is a flagellum, a prototype of the moving cell. The most generalized unicellular model, that is the least specialized and therefore the most evolved, is at the same time both animal and plant.

The tissue opposite this perfect original self-sufficient being represents the multi-cellular biological unit and the first elementary hierarchical coherence. There are some 'tissue' plants and 'tissue' animals. They are without any doubt the earliest in the scale of the living beings. It is above all in the vegetal context that the 'being-tissue' acquires its own character with the thallophytes branch. Caulerpa with their morphology trace a root, a trunk, branches and green leaves that outwardly appear as those of a plant, nonetheless inside we can find a uniform tissue without cellular walls. The real tissues specialized in assimilation or conduction cells occur in mosses. But they are not 'organ' plants because, like the superior plants, they are not vascularized.

As for the 'tissue' animals, those which most spectacularly represent this group in the evolutionary hierarchy are without doubt sponges. Sponges are a typical evidence of 'tissue' animals and may remind us of unicellular beings or protozoa in many ways. In its digressive phyletic evolution, the plant definitely blooms at the floral stage below the organ's, while the animal passes it, marking by its passage a closed deviation, coelenterata and echinoderms.

The advent of vessels (xylem) in the vascularized cryptogames has permitted an organic synergy of the plant tissues, through the existence of sap circulation. In phanerogams, a variety of gymnosperms, the flower is still bare; it acquires all its splendor only with mono- or dicotyledon angiosperms. The flower, a standard organ, is an artistic masterpiece characterized by radial symmetry. That marks the organic step of evolution; coelenterata fundamentally have this radial symmetry that is similar to the flower.

Cnidaria, the fresh water hydra, have a corollated mouth provided with eight tentacles. Hydrozoa are polyps that, like plants, free medusas - 'flower' animals - by gemmation. With their stems and their tropic filaments, which are analogous to leaves without chlorophyll, siphonophora imitate a superior plant such as a phanerogam in their morphology. Bryozoa, whose etymology means 'moss animal', have a shaky position, but their appearance of little aspens corresponds well to the diversifying fantasy of Nature that seems to enjoy herself particularly at this stage of evolution.

The 'organ' animal is given vegetal stillness by the statics of the coral-reefs or the colonies of madrepores, of which several fossils are left. Ctenoids, instead, with their radial symmetry in eight meridians, are 'organ' animals. The climb towards annelids develops in parallel with the impasse of ctenoids. Therefore in the evolutionary hierarchy, annelids precede the ramification of marine echinoderms that crown the specialized stage of 'organ' animals.

These metazoa, like for instance the starfish provided with five arms, have a pentamerous-radial symmetry that a bilateral one overlaps. While radial symmetry is evident in the starfish, it becomes less evident in the sea urchin. As in a fruit, the agent of ingeniousness has the upper hand in development. Holothurians, in the shape of cucumbers, reach these echinoderms which look like fruits, just as coelenterata look like flowers. The analogy certainly is superficial, but the reason for the inexplicable fantasy of Nature probably lies in the rigid specialization at the stage of organ common to all the superior plants and to these inferior animals.

In the context of plants, evolution will never surpass the 'organ' stage. It will reach adaptive mutations that can modify species. However important they may be, from a practical point of view they are just secondary divergences of the specific differentiation and of phyletic Evolution.

Motionlessness of cellulose and the lack of nervous system in plants are enough to fix this stage. Although there is a special nervous circulation in plants, as some Hindu authors' works seem to prove (see Martiny et al., 1982:163), it cannot be anything but a dead end. The plant arrested at the 'organ' stage achieves its most important function, that is to make possible aquatic life, then the terrestrial one of herbivores and finally that of carnivores.

The passage to quantum Evolution can be realized only by 'system' animals, that have a nervous system linking organs at distance, while 'organ' animals have still got an autonomous, rough nervous system.

So the organs of the human body, through an ancestral memory, keep a kind of extra-nervous, psychological independence, specified by experimental perfusion. Organs present a comparative morphology that links them tightly to plants. There are several examples: the respiratory tree, the arbor vitae within the uterus, the floral appearance of the tubes, of pelvis, kidneys which look like beans, the heart in the shape of an acorn of chestnut, the skull, meninges and the brain that resembles half of a nut. The liver, spleen, breasts, genitals might remind us of other comparisons. These analogies may make us smile. Why not recognize instead in these museums of relics a historical evidence of Nature? Can we not suppose, most likely, that there can be some constructive mechanism common to both progressive and digressive evolution? When the organ disappeared, it was time for the first 'system' animals: annelids. The system is the connection between different organs being part of a whole. This connection, when it is not humoral, is quicker and more complete and involves in the extreme the coming into being of the nervous system. Annelids have a body with a bilateral symmetry. Radial symmetry, whether it still exists potentially, modifies its morphology so that a segmentation in consecutive rings called metamerism appears.

Metamerism marks the stage of the nervous system in evolution, just as radial symmetry marks the stage of a humor-organ. With flatworms, there appeared some perfecting elements that, afterwards, along other evolutionary lines, attained a better result. In roundworms we can find an external covering of chitinous nature that foreshadows a further perfected stage of 'system' animals. With arthropods, there is a setting up and the blossoming of the 'system' animals. The annelid is an intention at the beginning; the arthropod is a realization at the arrival. The 'conquest of space' realized by the insect happens thanks to the formation of a bodily rigidity which the other invertebrates lack and which we can notice in the chitin carapace of arthropods.

These present a remarkable instrumentation, but only with the insect stage we can witness the birth of the robot civilization of the 'system' animals. The individual then cannot fulfil himself as an isolated creature but in the collective spirit of the honeycomb, the ant-hill or the termitarium. In order to find again the evolutionary thread of the 'individual' animals we have to go through the insects' genealogical branch towards the primitive trunk of metameric animals.

The link between 'system' animals and the individual is the pre-chordatum. The little amphioxus, whose appearance is the intermediary between a worm and a fish, has a remarkable position in the history of vertebrates. Its notochord, with a cephalic predominance, is the starting point in the group of pre-chordata. After the amphioxus there are the inferior vertebrates. Vertebrates' most precious innovation is an inner skeleton made of bones and cartilage; its main feature is its backbone together with its spinal cord and it is characteristically divided into segments, so that this group is named after it. Vertebrates can be easily ordered into five classes which form a hierarchical, chronological, evolutionary scale.

Fishes represent the inferior step, after which we have amphibians which are half-way between the liquid habitat of their precursors and the terrestrial one; finally reptiles achieve this emigration. From these, according to a transformist terminology, two other classes seem to derive, birds and mammals. These two classes have made some remarkable progress compared to the previous ones: birds and mammals are warm-blooded and have a superior nervous organization - both these progresses are of fundamental importance.

Birds and mammals are both deeply concerned with their little ones' well-being. This affective outpouring clearly shows that individuality, which until now dominated the species, goes back into the individual. All these physio-psychological developments have occurred without the existence of a morphological correlation between them. This succession is, on the other hand, more taxonomic than genetic, it is a series of hierarchical levels rather than an vertical chronology.

The differences between reptiles and modern amphibians are fewer than between the latter and fishes, from which derives the touching meaning of this living fossil, the coelacanth, whose fins are already four limbs. Reptiles' radical innovation is not of anatomical nature, but lies in the egg. Thanks to it, reptiles can carry their puddle of native water with them, which was impossible to amphibians. Reptiles were also able to get into the desert - where amphibians cannot survive - and have chosen it as their habitat. This shows that they were the first to find the way to the large, parched spaces. They have populated the earth with the race of monsters: Dinosaurs. At first sight, they seem to have developed a marked capacity for adaptation. The incredible size of these dragons was also their Achilles' heel, since it constituted a specialization which made them vulnerable. They were strictly adapted to the hot, damp environment full of water where they had developed and that had not been subjected to any modifications for a long time. These gigantic, proud lumps of animal matter, which were static and acromegalized, would have soon disappeared at the first threat of a change in climate.

But being warm-blooded constituted the great 'life work' of Nature; far from being an isolated incident, it represented the essential physiologic stage that had to be crossed by the animals destined to raise it to the superior step of quantum evolution. This step was achieved by mammals when Primates came into being.

The babies of apes and baboons do not have the prognathic snout typical of their parents; they look like grown-up miniature anthropoids. It is almost a law of evolution, that the young, generalized form paves the way for an old, specialized one.

During the miocene stage of the Tertiary, anthropoids were widespread, as is witnessed by the large amount of fossil remains left. They lived all over Asia, Europe and Africa, continents which enjoyed a tropical, damp climate. This multitude of big apes, inhabiting the whole area of the Ancient World, constituted the living kingdom from which mankind, probably, gradually emerged. Dryopithecus and Australopithecus seem to have been the closest to the first ancestors of humanity. But during the Miocene, nothing urged the passage. The eden of the virgin forest provided frugivorous anthropoids with the necessary nourishment. Hence, These animals spent all their time on the trees, in the distracting variety of lights and shades.

During the pliocene stage of the Tertiary, when the climate became warm and dry, the savannah took the place of the forest and its facilities, and the struggle for life started. Anthropoids who no longer had interest in being completely arboreal, freed their forehands. Musculature was stressed, nomadism became compulsory, and now nourishment was mixed, thanks to the contributions of small game and sometimes to cannibalism.

The Pleistocene stage of the Quaternary was, as a whole, cold and dry. However long and hot the intermediary periods may have been, it was the climate of the multiple glaciations (Günz, Mindel, Riss, Würm) that caused the fight against the hostile environment to start. It was exactly then that the cerebral faculties of hominids could become human. To adapt oneself or to perish, this was the law of the caveman during the Mousterian and lower Paleolithic; he had to wear animal skins, to create his home around the subdued fire, to feed his family by hunting, to defend himself against all the aggressive living creatures.

The original hominid, or Neanderthal Man, and the species closest to him, lived during the last interglacial era in a huge area, extending from southeastern Asia to western Europe and south Africa. After the last interglacial era and the last glaciation, during the Holocene stage of the Quaternary, the temperate climate, cold and damp, appeared. A definitive progress was marked then by the presence of a new type of hominid, the Cromagnon Man, quite similar to the present humans, but generally with thicker bones and constituting, in his human person, the species of *Homo sapiens sapiens*.

The face has diminished in comparison with the skull and becomes orthognathous, the frontal lobes have developed, the auditory meatus passes above the zygomatic arch, mastoid is oblique downward and forward. H. Vallois (1976) has clearly proved that these following generations of the different human species do not constitute divided but interpenetrated stratifications.

In the caves in Palestine, Neanderthalians and Cromagnons were contemporary. These first humans, belonging to the present species, have civilized the upper Palaeolithic, during which industry is characterized by stone blades, the lance, the bow together with the products of a particular kind of engraving and painting. This human type has spread all over the Ancient World and is by now made up of several different races.

Human races of the upper Palaeolithic show some undoubtable connections with the present races. They probably are secondary differentiations of a type of an undifferentiated man, founder of a stock and probably mongoloid and further on negroid and europoid. We can have an idea of the founder of the stock looking at the new-borns who, in spite of the different races, have all some common features: yellow, sometimes reddish skin, hair often black and flat, a vaguely mongoloid face, indifferentiated dimorphism. Most transformists trace back humankind to a single stock. Scantiness of evidence, however, compels us to stop our reflexions on the new-borns of Palaeolithic whose long gestation has led, through prehominid, to the form we know today: modern humans. Nonetheless, in every human, according to a radial symmetry and intersexuality, an ancestral recall, creates a 'right' man, a 'left' man, an 'anterior' man, a 'posterior' man and perhaps some supplementary 'oblique' segmentations which we have not yet determined. Metameres have lost their apparent morphology, but a certain hidden physiology persists in every metamere.

## III. Conclusion

We believe that evolution is developing towards a stage of organization of the human species, which in the future will build morpho-physiologically either the tissues and the organs, or the systems of Society.

Every biologic unit has two attitudes. The cell without doubt ignores the molecular units of which it is composed and, in a direct but confused way, has a sense of the tissue. The tissue itself does the same: its community ignores the cellular units and has a sense of the organ. The organ overlooks the tissue and has a sense of the system. The individual is neither interested in the billions of cells, nor in the organs, nor in the systems that compose him. On the contrary, he has a mystical sense of his species.

For this reason we suggest that evolution will lead to a conscious interaction between the individual and the society. Interaction that at the moment can only be vaguely perceived.

The essential basis of this biosociology should be the recognition of the anisotropic character of Man living in society, who must be, like every biological unit, free and fluent in the sense of his personality, but solidary and solid with respect to the group.

### References

Dubos, R. (1973). *L'homme et l'adaptation au milieu*. Paris, Payot.

Martiny, M., Brian, L. and Guerci, A. (1982). *Biotypologie humaine*. Paris, Masson.

Simpson, G. G. (1949). *The Meaning of Evolution. A Study of the History of Life and of its Significance for Man*. New Haven, Yale University Press.

Vallois, H. V. (1976). *Les races humaines*. Paris, P.U.F.

# THE THEORY OF INNER ENTROPY - ITS RELATIONS TO GENETIC ENGINEERING AND THE CONCEPT OF NATURE

Jörn Greve [1]

## I. Introduction

Genetic engineering (biotec) formally is a logical procedure to optimize, e.g. bacteria, for economical purposes by linearizing the globularly compiled genetic code (DNA). As in a reasonable strategy bacteria taken as objects for this form of cultivation is a technically mediated domestication.

In the line of objects being selectively changed by humans this is the most recent to be artificially transformed. Biotec seems to be 'soft' and viable because DNA-insertion took place in bacteria since the Archean 4.000 million years ago. But when setting on an artificial genetic drive its special (inner) entropic conditions have to be considered, as in all technical processes, thus the morphological level of organization might be a predictor of future destruction. On the other hand biotec will be of high therapeutic value for diseases with hormone deficiencies like, e.g., in renal anemia treated by recombinant erythropoietin. The obvious result of this efficient treatment will be that more chronic renal patients will survive. This technique is producing its own conditions and its own requests. Biotec is thereby autopoietically setting on its progressive development and will be a highly effective factor to structure human social rules not only by a future DNA - 'screening'. Thus this technique will totalize life-world with a loss of ecological and philosophical alternatives and meaning (Sinn). Because biotec is an outcome of growing economics it might be as well a socio-pathological phenomenon of rationalism. This dialectical rebound is not usually included in the overall idealized concepts of Man and Nature.

---

[1] Thanks are due to Russ Shurig (Toronto) for his invaluable advice and help in preparing this paper.

## II. Genetic engineering (biotec) as an invention of nature

The basic operation of Biotec seems to be quite simple as demonstrated in fig. 1: A certain part of the genetic material (DNA), which is functionally and economically needed, is broken out of the strange nucleus and then inserted by carriers (called plasmids or viroids) in others, who are then working as a kind of host with totally changed functions. By this artificial rationally structured and purpose-related mutation, the mutant will own the faculties due to the implanted DNA. This process can be interpreted as an invention of nature, because man is reproducing with his skills and tools nature-similar and even identical substances by using analogous procedures. His method is to handle nature's objects fragmentarily or digitalized, which gives him a dream-like illusion to amass in short-time relations the same as nature produces in long terms. At the same time nature is taken as the mere object of man's creative action by transforming her as if his culturally and technically elaborated code is corresponding to her 'holistic respiration' (Odum, 1971). So man's creations are limited by his need to produce for his specific desires. Man's yields form the sense in his actions without respecting anything but his own advantages, which are performed in biotec by genetically transformed bacteria or embryonic organs.

Agriculture also deals with mutants and domestication. It is an accumulative selection of the natural mutants since neolithic times. Since that time man has been choosing productive variants for crops, wool and meat. Thereby he is resetting with his domesticated objects the original bio-ecological state, which has already been diminished and emptied by preceding hunting and gathering activities.

Following the trend of genetic variation he puts in his selecting information and is taking nature as a mere receiver of his information formed by his yields without asking for her capacities and codes to receive his progressive amount of digitalized information.

Biotec accelerates this process by reinforcing the genetic drive to produce mutants with arbitrary and possibly unexpected changes. The time rate of growth is disturbed as in cancer.

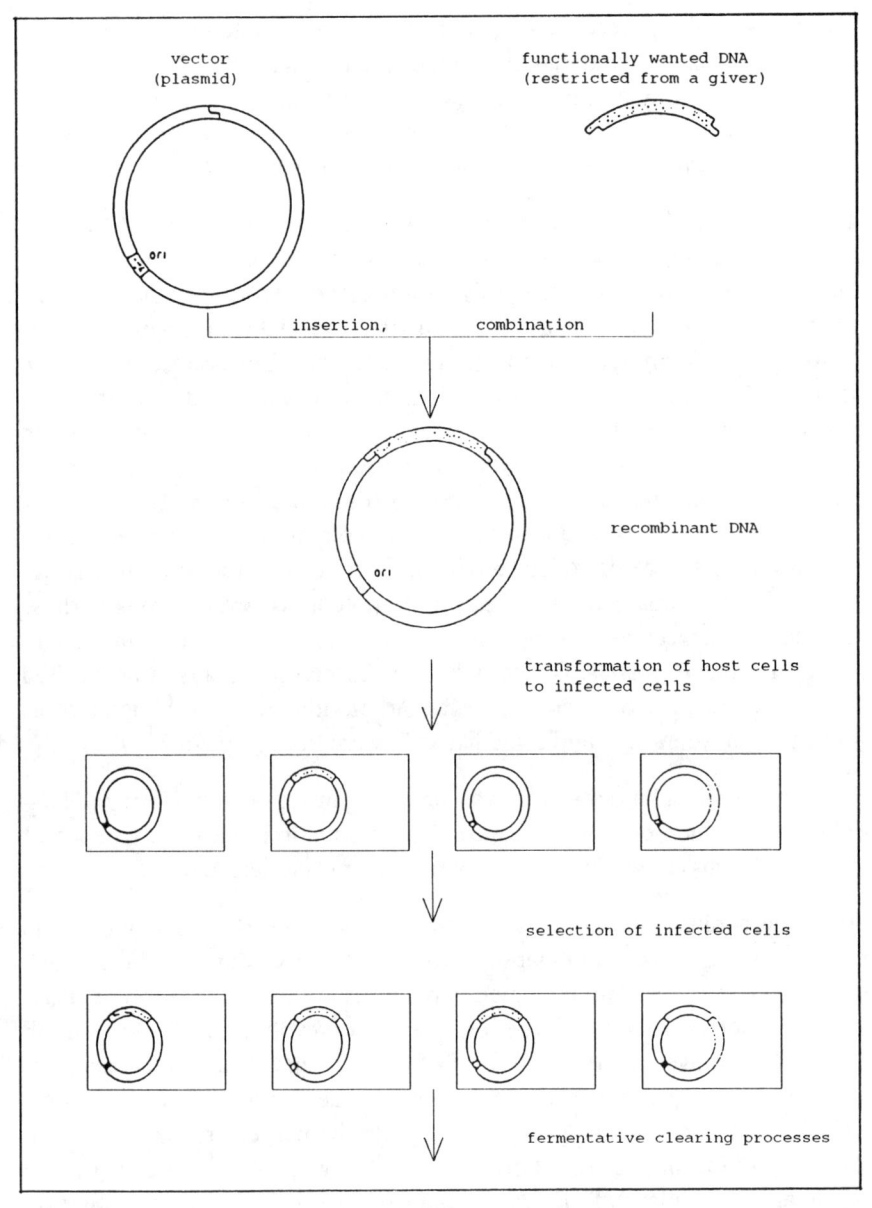

**Figure 1.** Basic operation of genetic engineering (adapted from E. L. Winnacker(1985).

The gross modal procedure in genetic engineering could be described as a double linearization and digitalization of the genetic code. The first is done by selecting and by cutting off the wanted part out of the giver-DNA and then secondly by implanting this fragment in the nucleus of the host by special 'infectious' carriers (plasmids), which will again split the DNA.

This approach of invention shows a new kind of purpose, related to order and information, of biological structure by means of microtomizing and linearization. Structuring like this can also be found in other rational processes (Weber, 1972, pp. 688-868) and especially in science, as the history of epistemology demonstrates since the Renaissance (Foucault, 1966:50-350), and as generative grammar, taxonomy and codification of law and ethics show. So there is an accumulative storage of information and order accompanied by its spreading connected with the civilization process and a simultaneous reduction of spontaneous, localized, self-maintaining and consensual interaction in smaller communities. For ecological evaluations it has to be reflected why this kind of re-structuring nature via biotec is accompanied by destructive potentials even though these rationalized processes are imitating nature and only add information to perform other functions. Biotec only imitates nature because this method has happened since the times when the 'arbor vitae' was unfolding its roots 4.000 million years ago, and algae like cells were taking up viroid DNA.

It is the time eukaryiotic life was emerging with cells enclosing DNA-substances, which even enables sexual differentiation and the existence of humans. In this context biotec is only repeating what nature does.

But if an evolutionary clock is supposed to associate the sprouting of the 'tree of life', genetic manipulation is touching the roots of the whole image of life, because time and interspecies relations are distorted by an artificial human order projected over the total picture of 'evolution'. The basis of all 'living' (lebendiges Sein) in the form of bacteria and virus and consecutive derivations is as well touched as the pathogenetic symbiosis. But this critical view of biotec is not taking into account the immense force of reparation that throws out all sort of inborn errors in the genetic structures since the Archean. The (plasmid) DNA-outcome of biotec is not only similar to nature's products, it is all the same. But fragmented and isolated DNA might be more reactive.

And as we know from iterated processes in fractal mathematics a little variation in sequence and formular structure will change the whole apparition. But until now the model of Chaos Theory can not be translated to 'real' data, so it produces with scientific methods the same illusion as technical processes do. It only seems to verify the desired prediction of what is not predictable. The same problem of a technical mediatory illusion might be transferred to the rationalized scientific and economic interpretation of an already artificialized world; Because human perception is a socially structured representation of reality reflecting the morphological division of 'world' as a fixed rule of anthropocentrism. But 'where is the rub? What dreams may come ?' Telling us, e.g., biotecs will bring us mortal awakening? How should human biotechnical artifacts kill or transform nature? Why should this special form of domestication on the level of bacteria be destructive that it would drive onwards man's own self-destruction?

### III. Entropy-production as an intention of man to survive in masses

Three Phases of ecological destruction are to be stated in cultural evolution: exploitation - (agri)cultural modelling - and artificial deformation as replacement of nature by synthetics (table 1).

The most irritating fact is the acceleration of this development. It is related to the progressive and at least explosive increase of human populations bearing a similar encephalic index as today. So it could be suggested that rationality is an output of brain structures to succeed in man's re-invention of nature with a successive flood of artifacts. But brain structure and output might also be the result of growing sociopathological aggregations accompanied by self-domestication.

| phase | extension | results | socio-technical means |
|---|---|---|---|
| I (addition?) exploitation | 150.000 years | overcome of niches first extinction of game (mammoth) | tools of 1. - 3. generation division of nuture |
| II ecological cultural modelling | 9.000 y. | extinction of game and prim. forests, replacement by domesticated objects | tools of - 5. generation energy transfer, industr. (bronze, pottery) division of work/skills |
| III artificial deformation | 300 y. | artificially induced growth of net production waste, entropy, manipulation of the genetic drive | globalized economical flow of energy and information, microprocesses division of identity |

**Table 1:** Phases of ecological destruction in length of time.

As transcultural comparisons of psychiatry show, not only psychotic diseases increasingly tend to chronicity. An enlarged incidence of psycho-somatic 'syndromes' is also to be stated. These changes can be related to socio-technological progress. Furthermore there has to be stated the progressive production of technical artifacts correlated to the industrial exploitation of nature and chemotechnical synthesizing since the last three hundred years. But these artifacts can only be called waste, the products of entropy, if they can not be integrated in the ecological context. Man's rational and selective faculties to structure information and to perform his functional order in nature only reveal their destructive potentials, if buffer-systems and recycling chains are flooded and broken. These destructive potentials are facultative, mass-related but inherent in the amount of order and information stored and accumulated within the (bio-)technical processing as an 'inner entropical' quality. This inner quality is related to the future outcome, which will be predictable as possible/probable amount of (outer) entropy. Ecological entropy is a measure for the state of a material and its masses containing low energy and high probability and few information for being re-cycled. In the ecological nets and circles the amount of already produced entropy is a term to explain man's successive replacement of nature. Growing waste deposits are an already detectable and measurable form of 'outer' entropy.

'Inner' entropy is a predictive term. It means the stored potentials and accumulated information in a technical and industrial process to produce entropy. It will be a measurement of technology assessment to calculate the former outcome of waste and social consequences related to a specific industrial process and its sprouting. So the amount of 'inner entropy' could be used as a measurement to assure future sustainable development. Biotechnics do not seem to be destructive or contain many entropical faculties. They seem to be 'soft' as they could be used for recycling waste by specialized bacteria. Further biotecs will add the pool of genoms (DNA-settings) that are wasted and less resistant by enduring domestication and agricultural processes. The trouble is that negative effects of this technique could arise by its industrial sprouting, but we can not predict its destructive probabilities by a traditional concept of entropy, because very little subsidiary (fossil) energy is needed and the waste-outcome will be but probably useful ashes and 'some' arbitrary DNA-plasmids.

The inner structure of a technical system and its specific order in relation to biospheric buffer systems might be the answer to this dilemma. This kind of *inner entropy* could give hints to the specific (negative) potential of energy and information stored in the details of a procedure. The structures of a productive process can be detected by the Tayloristic order itself, as a division of work and the accumulated information in a (bio-)technical system, which then reveals its probable ecological contra-function in form of non-correspondence to the biosphere as a measure of future ecological destruction. This (inner) morphological-functional description will also show the special conditions of the division of work as a progressive dichotomic sprouting of 'lifeworld'. So the amount of 'inner entropy' might be a term of socio-ecological alienation or 'Entfremdung' within these special morphological grids (Shurig, 1989:26), which will also show the blows striking the different levels of the biosphere. So inner entropy and structures of order in a process are a scale to prescribe the future flooding by synthetics and the pollution of bio-sphere as well as a progressive division of 'lifeworld'. All these morphological factors and traces have to be taken into account to get an understanding of the influences created by a new technological approach and why its inner structures will promote special social and of course ecological consequences.

## IV. Genetic engineering and economics as totalizers of social life until the perversion of ethics

Recombinant remedies already produced by biotechnology are needed to treat, e.g., renal anemia, because in the end stages of renal diseases there is a lack of a hormone called erythropoietin, which usually pushes on the corporal production of blood. Blood transfusions will be the only alternative for the application of recombinant erythropoietin. But blood transfusions will lead to a sensibilization against strange albuminous substances. So the chance of holding the expected transplanting of a kidney will be lower in end-stage renal patients if they get blood transfusions. This will not be the case if they obtain the recombinant remedy, then they will also be independent of blood transfusions. The effective therapy and its progression will give renal patients better chances to survive. The more survivors there are, the more recombinant remedies will be necessary and there are no ways to produce them with another technique. And no doctor will refuse a recombinant remedy which is nowadays excessively expensive. So biotec is programming its own conditions, its special request and progressive yields.

Because it is possible to produce a kind of human 'DNA-screening' by genetic engineering, which also enables man to eliminate and select what is weak or not worthy for his economic or socially totalizing purposes, there will be a total change in social structures. And there is no doubt that this development will continue until a sort of 'genetic design' is reached. Genome analysis might be used to identify individual dispositions and predict humans to react in an allergic, panic, depressive, schizophrenic or possibly highly adapted way.

Having effective recombinant remedies means to be confined in biotec's highly selective consequences. And because it deals with that matrix which is included in all living beings as well as in humans, it will radically transform the appearance of life on all morphologically descriptive levels producing also a rebound in biosphere. The result is a totally ambivalent situation produced by this technique that is re-structuring the DNA-setting in a form of new design. This effect leads to a dilemma of ethics and a negation of logic in a sense of perversion, because we can not deny medical effectiveness and the biotechnical restoration of the environment, which has been alienated by domestication and emptied by hunting and gathering since Neolithic times. Since then, even the genetic pool for resistance against pathogenic microbes is going to be abolished.

Why are humans woven in all these microtomizing processes which they can not get rid of and which are transforming all economical and juridical rules as in a totalized process? Is it the only fate of rationalizing processes leading man to this end of an endless totalizing outcome which will limit and absorb all grades of freedom as Max Weber has imagined already before the Second World War? Or are economics and rationalism in form of industrial and technical processes a sociopathological phenomenon growing up with man's distributive ecological problems in form of progressive disseminations? So one aspect of rationality might be to incorporate order of destruction as a sign of totalized rules of mastery symbolized by technical progress.

Rationalizing means to structure and to form order. But order has its 'inner entropy' which can be shown in a simple example, which may have immense consequences for the concept of nature and man: Imagine that we have a crowd doing nothing at all. It contains peaceful 'ambiente' of going around and there is but an accidental composition (fig. 2a).

Then there might be a motive for solidarity or meditation arising in the crowd. Those people who are attracted will form a circular pattern of varied positions to contemplate or to withdraw (fig. 2b).

But then there comes the order to march or to organize (fig. 2c), which contains a rapid spreading of information. The result will be a linearized pattern of monomorphic elements with possible highly constructive but as well destructive potentials formed by higher order in the mass of people which now is made totally uniform by the information of the command to fulfill its potentially con-/de-/structive faculties.

a) a-functional "ambiente" with probalistic composition

b) "mechanical" solidarity (DURKHEIM) with varied positions

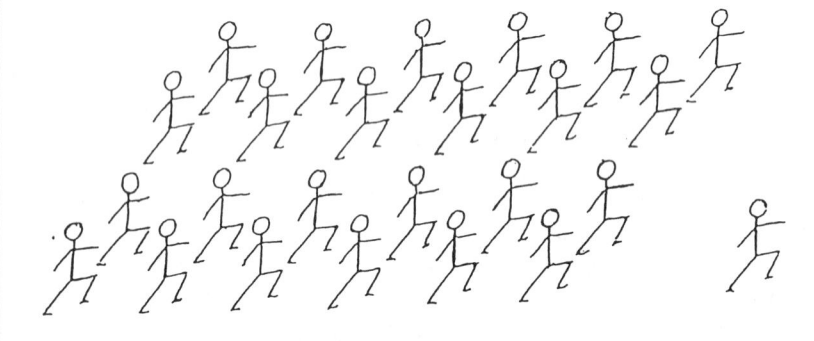

c) hierarchical systemic pattern with monomorphic elements

**Figure 2.** Gross socio-morphological patterns of order.

The concept of *inner entropy* shows a dialectical potential of socio-functional construction and latent ecological destruction. Especially more 'isolated' systems might tend to be pathological. It does not matter whether organizations are in terms of system theory allopoietic (mechanical) or autopoietic (biological and socio-cultural), but they may change their ecological attributes if they tend to isolate themselves and to store information and potential destructive energy.

There is also a dependence on the 'critical masses' of systems or processes to be stated which can be registered as the amount of possibly produced outer entropy in the form of waste in relation to population density and the capacity of ecological buffer functions.

The concept of *inner entropy* could predict the probability of a product or the process of production containing higher structured order with high potential energy and low correspondence towards the ecological context. The description of these ecological attributes is obtained by its specific functional-structural compounds in relation to the environmental setting and its temporal changes. Its systemic informative-functional characteristics can probably be measured in 'bit' and its multiplicators are the tendencies to sprout under industrial productions or to isolate itself within their progressive systemic differentiations.

In biotec the aspects of inner entropy are enclosed in the object of denaturation (DNA) and in the special procedure of production by linearization and thereby splitting the albuminous nucleotid substances. Because in industrial circumstances biotec works under really 'closed' conditions the possibility of a pathogenetic mutant to escape is only unlikely - which means, however, it can happen every time. And the free market will allow anybody to act as a Frankenstein.

But the main point is the faculty of this technique to analyze forms of life at its basis of reproduction in form of the DNA, which is representing genetic as well as pathogenetic order. As biotec is slicing the genetic code it produces an artificial order outside biological creativity, which is not integrated in a long term selection process. This procedure will accumulate potential or latent distortions detectable as amount of inner entropy, which will cause rebound effects at all morphological levels. Thus DNA-analyses will also produce their own order including a high selectivity in social interaction.

This may signify even more for man's fate than the possible danger of uprooting the 'arbor vitae'. Because identification of the 'identic' actually destroys the authentic identity by uncovering the sense of originality and its unity as senseless - as genome analysis will demonstrate.

Furthermore, there will be another offspring as a longline-process that is included in the mere procedure, which enriches the nutritive brine of the microbic cultures with molecular fragments in that cellular 'aestuarium'. These tiny fragments may cause allergies and even cancer coming out of the 'closed' production which needs ventilation and decontamination, because even nucleotide fragments tend to recombine! So the hope to solve the cancer problem by this technique is doubtful, because in the same time it will augment these problems. This technique can produce diseases whilst curing them: On one hand you can identify specific cancers and their possible remedies by this technique but on the other hand the fragments of its outcome might produce them.

The rub of Hamlet's dream is the dreaming state. Concluding all these arguments, the concept of inner entropy contains practical and theoretical implications which could explain the impact of humans on nature, because nature obviously tries to keep down inner entropy by 'pumping disorder out' as Odum (1971:37-60) stated already.

Man, on the other hand, tries to survive with the final aspect to restore his social and economical orders under conditions of overpopulation which promotes mastery to enslave humans by humans and urges slavery of nature which is herself no longer sufficient to serve for man's comfort. So man only becomes an opponent to nature by ending his and nature's self-maintaining original equifinality by the accumulation of order which he idealizes as rationality (table 2).

| Bio-ecological | Agricultural technical (social) |
|---|---|
| **MEANS** ||
| Continuous input (sun) | Growing input (subsidiary energy) |
| Isothermic processing (quantum use) | Hyperthermic processes |
| Cyclical interdependencies Self-maintenance and-regulation (Bertalanffy, 1951) | Progression of 'independence' increasing net production (Odum, 1971) growth and globalization |
| Conversion of energy (flow) | Accumulation of energy, output |
| Continuous disorder pump out (Odum, 1971) | Progressive disorder production (warmth, free energy, dissipation) |
| Communicative information and additive storage - integration | Accumulative storage of information exchange and destruction |
| **QUALITIES** ||
| Equifinality (Bartalanffy, 1951) | Heterogenous determination |
| 'Holistic respiration' (Odum, 1971) | Structures of rationality |
| Autopoietical (Maturana and Varela, 1987) | Allopoietical (rules of mastery) |
| **MAJOR RELATIONS AND MORPHOLOGICAL CHARACTERISTICS** ||
| Maintenance of interspecies relations by defining niches | Overpopulation with exponential growth, monospecial selection and bursting of niches |
| Variety (richness) | Standardization, self-similarity, Purification and totalization |
| Limited to biosphere (carbon c.) | Destructions by capital cycle |

**Table 2.** Antithetic characteristics and systemic incompatibilities of the bio-ecological and agricultural technical (social) means.

## V. Selectivity - totalization and no ending...

Fifty years before Darwin Goethe suggested that there was a kind of primitive 'Urform', from which all forms of differentiated plants derived. This is an idealization to see the 'arbor vitae' as a linear progression of growing complexity - because all seems to culminate in the 'emergence of man'. This concept of nature is also inherent in all evolutionistic, systemic and holistic approaches, which only glorify man's actual 'civilized' state. Civilization spreads with progressively selective rationalism, which man himself projected in nature as selection theory. No one would reject the idea of selective mechanisms in nature but they are only one aspect of an overwhelming creativity.

On the other hand stressing selective theory means also to focus man's rationality. Idealized rationality as a lightspot illuminates the motivational background to spread man's cultural behavior by means of technological progression, which is a purpose-related active deformation of nature for structuring social rules of mastery in masses. Its mere idealization eliminates the negative dialectical aspect of order and hierarchies as potential destructive energies which could be described in terms of inner entropy.

*One might say that evolutionary theory as an idealization itself constitutes the rise of motivational structures of a socio-pathology to reinforce man's imperialistic economic behavior.* Nearly all philosophical constructions contain that higher informative structure, which are compressed and lined out in their special context of idealized scientific and philosophical order as a paradigmatic differentiation of institutionalized thinking in specific logo- or 'Noo'-spheric categories (Shurig, 1989). This context might be interpreted as the output of unsolvable ecological, distributional limitations with disproportionate relations. It has to be pointed out that this process started already with Greek philosophy, when urbanization with high subsistential rivalry and growing population density expanded in the Bronze Age. This time in the history of ideas represents also the starting point of all salvation/damnation religions with a hierarchy of more abstract anthropomorphic images of the gods.

The impact of man and nature itself in this context only seems to be a consequence of higher structured social order in dependence to overpopulation. And *man only can endure this self-created pathology by idealizing his critical existence.* The outcome of that historical process is a growing difference between nature and that which man is interpreting to be the concept of nature. As in teleologically orientated selection theory its 'logospherical' appearance is nothing more than a mirror image of what man is producing in his 'lifeworld' as an inflicting counterproductivity by the enhancement of the capital cycle e.g. via biotec. And even the 'holographic' paradigm is nothing more than an inverted image for what is not possible to be reinstalled.

Inner entropy as the detectable amount of information stored in a technological process, and outer entropy as measurable outcome in form of waste and greenhouse-effectors, together represent the dimension of alienation and distance between biosphere and 'lifeworld'. The resulting ecological artificiality corresponds to the social differentiation in form of growing institutional interdependencies (Shurig, 1989).

Already at a general descriptive level beside all morphological categories the structural and functional differences between bio-ecological and socio-technical attributes are so amazing (table 2) that any positivistic anthropological concept of man must be a plot of tautologies because his attributes serve only his advantages and cultural yields to survive with higher standards of civilization. Man has to state his negative assumption of being potentially self-destructive and in an ecological way 'entropical'. This is already reality, if he is crowded and organized in higher social levels - otherwise he will fulfill the dialectical fate of rationalism performing his own endless ending. In terms of ethnology: *Man has to be ethnocentric* otherwise he would be ashamed to be the producer of his own fate.

Regarding the attributes of incompatibility in biological and cultural systems man can be sure of mortal awakening (table 2). Biotec, because of its 'softness' could help us to survive, but inner entropy aspects show that it is a procedure with high structured order transforming an object (DNA) which itself is structuring the order of life, so the effect is a total one. It is totalizing and directing the life of man and of nature in succeeding alienation to the primary context.

As a result of this endless alienation process even space, time and motives or 'naturalistic' patterns for dreaming are repelled. Psychotherapy will convert us to accept the frightening chimeras as dreamlike transformations which assure us of our mere existence and that technological evolution will only produce its own goodness. If we do not follow this tranquilization one has to look at a rather unsolvable sequence of needed *solutions*:

1. Reduction of social differentiation and of globalized hierarchical economic structures under the compulsion of overpopulation.

2. A critical approach towards idealizing cultural progression and an exclusion of anthropocentrism and economized standardization.

3. To respect and re-create the autonomy of ethnic groups, reduce generalizing social order, repulse economical aspects of internationalization and growing institutionalization.

4. All religions, even those with a low degree of order are promising better dreams, but their ideas all become rules of mastery and their organized worshipping serves only man's image of his own holiness and not that of earth being the only subsistence of man.

### VI. Conclusions concerning the quest of ultimate reality and meaning

The results of ecological research and evaluation show an impact of genetic engineering on the concept of nature because there are no connecting links between economically mediated accumulation, globalized spreading of waste and entropy production and nature's tendencies of self-maintenance. The reality of this impact ultimately means that the process of civilization will end in a totally artificial world of highly organized order with high destructive potentials even in the sense of self-destruction. In this process, identity and natural surroundings as patterns of religion and dreaming are abolished by mainly linearized structures, which formally show an analogy to purpose-motivated rational human communicative actions (Habermas, 1985, I:294-350).

The dissolution of natural patterns is perfect and total, they are replaced by cultural-technological artifacts and symbols with accumulated information. This abolishment of natural origin is enhanced by biotechnical procedures especially because their demands are prescribed in social development. The outcome will be a one-way lane of no escape which is reinforced by economics as distribution rules for consumptive demands of men in masses. The resulting distribution problems can only be managed by rationalized optimizing as in capitalistic economics and in science-mediated technological progress. This process of feeding time, space, and energy into the production of waste overwhelms primary nature and her original spirit and meaning. A glance of hope is rising if we take into consideration that our dreams represent an inverse picture of reality. Dreaming is a work to perform and to change reality. 'Dreamtime' as an ethnological term or 'the dreaming parts of the real things' (Lorenzo, an Ojibwa Indian I met in Toronto in 1989) will effect a double rejecting historical reality.

As essential of ultimate meaning remains an existential interpretation which means to endure a civilization which is not compatible with dreaming nor with any reasonable concept of nature. Because capitalistic economics are taking its system as an open one where nature is not included as a value, this progressive technical expansion will be limited by its own costs of reparation as genetic engineering already demonstrates. This process is perpetuated by monetary rules to pay the costs of lost natural resources with an increasing amount of money, work and waste. There is to be stated a chaotic outcome if this endless iteration is not stopped ....

## References

Bertalanffy, L. von (1951). *Theoretische Biologie*. Bern, A. Kerne Verlag. (Eng. tr. General System Theory, 1956).

Foucault, M. (1966). *Les mots et les choses*. Paris, Editions Gallimard. (German, 1974. *Die Ordnung der Dinge*. Frankfurt/M., Suhrkamp Verlag.

Habermas, J. (1985). *Theorie des kommunikativen Handelns, I and II*. Frankfurt, S. Fischer Verlag. (Engl., Boston, Beacon Press.)

Maturana, H. and Varela, F. J. (1987). *Der Baum der Erkenntnis*. 2. Auflage. Bern, München, Wien, Scherz Verlag. (1984. *El arbol del conocimiento*.)

Odum, E. P. (1971). *Fundamentals of Ecology*. Philadelphia, W.B. Saunders Comp.

Shurig, R. (1989). *Understanding Institutions Morphologically*. Toronto, Morphology Institute.

Weber, M. (1972). *Wirtschaft und Gesellschaft*. 5. Auflage. Tübingen, J.C.B. Mohr Verlag.

Winnacker, E.L. (1985). *Gene und Klone*. Weinheim, VCH-Verlag.

# ART, NATURE, ARTIFICIALITY: THE ARTIFICIALITY OF NATURE IN WESTERN ART

THOMAS HÖLSCHER

## I. Introduction

The paper tries to investigate to what extent nature as represented in Western art turns out to be not so much 'natural' as 'artificial'. It questions the main doctrines of Western theory of art: imitation (imitatio naturae) and invention (inventio). The former being usually related to nature and the latter to the works of art or the creativity or subjectivity of the artist, the question is put forward as to what it may mean to correlate imitation with artificiality and invention with nature. This way of looking at things immediately reveals a considerable distortion in the ordinary interrelation of both pairs of concepts, especially considering what art is really doing. Thus a thorough reinterpretation of what Jacob Burckhardt coined as the famous formula of the Italian Renaissance seems to be at stake: instead of 'The discovery of nature and man' 'The invention of nature' (and perhaps even of man). The paper restricts itself to painting (from the 15th century on) and to a few selected examples for the sake of a paradigmatic insight. It concentrates on Leonardo da Vinci's renderings of nature in some of his drawings and paintings on the one hand and on computer-generated simulation of nature on the other, with excursions into the graphics of Mandelbrot-Sets, Magritte and C. D. Friedrich. This limited field of exploration is to be the framework for establishing valid relations concerning the different kinds of artificiality of nature, thus making them reflect and clarify each other.

## II. Computer simulation: Nature as hyperartificiality

Examples of nature being totally artificial and yet giving the impression of total naturalness (in a realistic, naturalistic sense) can be found in the most recent field of image-production, namely in computer generated digital pictures (plates 1-3). This imitation of nature, no longer based on any natural model or prototype and yet extremely similar to nature, is called simulation. Simulation is thoroughly artificial. It creates artificial realities (or worlds) that are artificial to such a degree that they do not appear artificial at all. What we have here is a second reality parallel to the 'first' one, of a striking undiscernible resemblance to the latter. In the strictest sense, those pictures-by-simulation are not based on any model, photographical or other, but solely on a computer-program written in mathematical-logical symbols, containing the purely scientific optical and physical information. This logical-mathematical language is translated into pictures by the computer. Such pictures are exclusively 'calculated' i. e. the product of calculation processes. No input of data taken from the outer reality, for example by camera, is involved. One speaks of a 'synthetic camera' as opposed to a real one. By this method artificial realities or natures of every kind can be generated, and in no case solely the given reality is reconstructed, from photos for example. These artificial imitations of nature, these hyperrealistic inventions of nature are the key to simulation. Indeed, what we have here, is a borderline- or bastard-genre of pictures: which therefore are, strictly speaking, no actual replicas or images and even less are they the originals in themselves. Hence, we have something 'in between' resp. something 'different' than originals/replicas. It is a puzzling, totally indefinite ontological status, exactly corresponding to the artificial nature manifested by them: a 'real nature' that does not exist, a possible nature in existence, a kind of mental naturalism.

## 1. Computer-generated landscape: Fractals as artificial nature

The series of three mountain landscapes by Richard Voss (plates 1-3) is entitled 'Changing the fractal dimension'. The computer program hereby used is based on the so-called 'fractal geometry', which has proved highly appropriate for the modelling of natural forms. It was developed by the mathematician Mandelbrot (Mandelbrot, 1982), who was interested in the geometry and measurement of irregular forms i. e. not classical, idealized forms (like circle, ellipse, triangle). Taking coastlines, for example, if they are to be measured in their intricately fractured real course instead of any idealized corrections, he found that the smaller the chosen measure is the longer the coastal piece to be measured turns out to be. The particular ratio of the measure's and the coastline's lengths amounts to the 'fractal dimension' of the coast. The latter represents a fractured dimension, an entity between a one-dimensional line and a two-dimensional surface, hence the name 'fractal'. It ensures mathematizability of complex entities, considerably surpassing the possibilities of the ideal forms of Euclid, who could not proceed in any way but in a reductive manner. This applies not only to static forms like jagged coastlines, mountains, cracks in materials, but also to highly complex dynamic formations like clouds or various currents i. e. to their irregular courses that are difficult to grasp. Being mathematizable means being mathematically modelable. The fractals' core principle is that of 'self-similarity': each form being composed of smaller ones being similar (but not equal) to itself and so forth ad infinitum. What is the reason behind the success of fractal models in relation to complex forms of nature? Is it that *the* mathematics of reality, i. e. the mathematics being identical with nature would have finally been discovered? Or is it not after all a case of subtle confusion of model and reality?

Here again we come across our ontological problem concerning image and artificial nature: is it that nature is artificial because nature and artificial model coincide, or is it artificial even though both do not coincide, a difference between nature and model or image remaining which cannot be set aside? The elementary procedure which the mountain formations by Voss are based on (even in a more refined application) consists of the following rule: subdivide a triangle into four smaller ones by randomly breaking its sides and iterate the procedure - to the limit of the computer's resolution or calculation time. The result is an object which is, like a piece of crumpled wrapping paper, getting more and more peaks and crinkles: a fractal formation or - 'a mountain'. The modifications in the mountain scenery by Voss are based on a changing parameter of the 'crumpling', on a changing of the 'fractal dimension' (which is precisely that of the mentioned measure's length in relation to the jagged coastline).

## 2. Artificiality and 'Einbildungskraft' (imagination)

But how do we now explain the striking resemblance between this synthetic, artificial nature and that authentic one we are familiar with, since, after all, even the fractal model and nature do not seem to coincide? Expressing it somewhat abstractly, but adequately, concerning the functional level of the relation between computer and humans (the so-called 'interface'), we are dealing with the question of all questions: how does a purely syntactical formation (as in the case of every computer product) attain semantics? It is certainly because the syntactical mountain induces us to construe it in a semantic way in the first place, due to our experience with mountains. But how does this work? Here we hit upon the problem of association, of projection, of interpretation, and this in the very deepest philosophical sense, hence the most general problem of 'hermeneutics'. All this is very much connected with 'imagination'. One must simply grasp the right notion of 'Einbildungskraft', a notion which would allow us to mentally connect the naturalness and artificiality of nature like the artificiality and naturalness of the human mind (i. e. the faculty of semantics), in each case separately and both together. In fact, the question of the artificiality of Western nature seems to me to be linked most closely to the question of a sufficiently understood 'Einbildungskraft': which leads to Western Culture's 'innermost heart of things'.

Above, I was not totally correct in strongly distinguishing static from dynamic fractals. All fractally modelable formations are dynamic: the fundamental morphogenetic processes seemingly being more clear in clouds than in coastlines and mountains is due only to the shorter duration of their changes. Of course, mountains too, - even including Goethe's 'Granite': the 'most unperturbable', which he wants to contrast with the human heart as the 'most perturbable' - and the courses of coastlines, are determined by the morphological processes of their formation and erosion. The series by Voss (plates 1-3) may be read as a morphogenetic-evolutionary line to more and more form, to an ever increasing differentiation of form. It is instructive that the last step of the development is already about to lead out of the field of what we are able to imagine effortlessly and unambiguously as 'mountains'. One step more in the rule-induced splitting up of the forms - and the impressions 'mountains' fades. This means that syntax (computer) and semantics (human 'Einbildungskraft') are not behaving to each other in a converging, not even parallel, even less identical manner but rather like the arms of a parabola: from the divergence of the one to the divergence of the other infinite with local, respectively temporal points of contact in the finite. After all this partial coming together of morphogenesis and 'Einbildungskraft' alone is remarkable enough.

### 3. Mandelbrot-Sets: Cycle of nature-art-science (I)

The main field of application of fractals is formed, however, by the so-called 'Mandelbrot-Sets' (plate 4). It is a matter of the same iterative processes as in the 'mountain'-generation, only this time applied to complex numbers. The latter ones experience, similar to the formula of circle or ellipse in their corresponding figures, a visualization as correspondingly complex 'pictures' on the computer. What we have here are, above all, purely mathematical structures, whose peculiar aesthetic appeal, transgressing into 'art' and 'beauty', is, on the one hand, due to a skillfull aesthetic preparation, having nothing to do with mathematics, though, on the other hand, unconceivable without the highly developed capacities of calculators and programs. Their highly artificial beauty, which distinguishes them from all known art, even the abstract kind, as well as from nature, is again on the whole based on the characteristic of self-similarity, which manifests itself here in a superabundance of forms, all interlocked and similar to each other into infinity. Yet this artificial beauty is not an end in itself nor purely decorative, but serves strictly as a better investigation of the inherent mathematical structures. The totally new discipline of 'experimental mathematics', another strangely paradoxical enterprise, is dealing precisely with this. Furthermore, these aesthetic formations serve the closer knowledge of phemomena of reality by simulation, from physical phase changes (ice to water to steam) to social catastrophes. Here it is always a matter of complex dynamic systems and morphogenetical processes, depending on chaotic phenomena, where the modeling of fractal mathematics is appropriate. Accordingly we have a cycle consisting of a move of mathematical-scientific phenomena to an aesthetic area and, vice versa, art as being of a cognitive potential turned back into nature studies: a cycle of nature-art-science in the medium of the artificial. This artificiality is of an abstract, 'artificial' kind. I myself, however, want to pursue the 'natural', realistic artificial and thus break off at this point.

## III. Leonardo's artistic studies of Nature: Hyperartificiality as second naturalness

### 1. 'Copse of Birches'

Let us turn to the main exponent of Western artistic nature studies: Leonardo da Vinci. Leonardo wanted painting to be the purest representation of nature. Again and again he is conjuring up the old formula of 'imitatio naturae'. Nature should be the supreme mistress. Simultaneously, he wants painting to be science. He would like himself to be transparent like a mirror, but a mirror with a conscience. He has absolute confidence in pure vision, raising the eye to the highest ranks as a means of cognition, but emphasizing simultaneously the superior significance of the 'head', of thinking over the 'hands' as a means of execution in painting. Thus Leonardo is a concept-painter choosing nature as his actual subject and ultimate aim. He wants to create once again all of nature in its whole manifold variety by his own power in painting. He wants to penetrate it cognitively by means of painting, in order to give nature back to itself in painting, mentally penetrated as such. Consequently, he wants to totally reconstruct nature in painting. He wants to reflect upon it thoroughly, much more in the sense of a mirror than by speculation. Only in this way was he, as an artist, within the bounds of his painting, able to emulate the Creator, or better, the creative principle of nature as above: all selfish creative ambition would have led him away from his goal. What he was interested in concerning imitatio was above all the virtuosity of the artistic devices required to produce it. They aim at the most possible transparency, striving to draw attention to themselves this way and not through deformation or other 'creative' peculiarities. And he intensifies them up to that point of hyperartificiality at which they, and above all the artificiality of nature effected by them, appear even natural again, as a kind of second naturalness.

The red chalk drawing of a 'Copse of Birches' (plate 5) does not have any overtly artistic ambition at first. It is a nature study of the kind Leonardo endlessly drew. The empty white space presumably should have been supplied with an explanatory text, as is the case with a similar sheet.

Probably it was intended to be a sheet of demonstration for Leonardo's 'Treatise on Painting'. Directly connected with this sober didactic goal Leonardo, however, goes one considerable step further. While the text may have dealt with certain questions of painting technique, the drawing intention is not the demonstration of the object as object, but of the artistic devices, of their artificiality as projected on the object, thereby transforming it. In this simple drawing the point is already a 'meta-level' and we must try to grasp more precisely the different light it is cast in by this. 'Copse of Birches' is only a study, not a finished picture, still less a thoroughly composed landscape painting, only a segment of landscape. Nevertheless, this detail of nature has been executed like a picture and placed with carefully chosen proportions into the empty space of the sheet. The text may even have been added later. By the manner of its positioning into the empty sheet this piece of nature unmistakably gains a certain character of appearance. What is appearing here in the manner of a floating island, that is no detail, no separated part, no 'piece of nature, is, as it were, a partial nature 'whole' in itself.

The drawing is of an extraordinary wealth of differentiation. What one supposes at first glance to be an 'impressionistic' quality reveals itself, however, as a supremely artificial interlocking of trunks, branches, even leaves, drawn almost miniaturistically distinct, with a fluctuating, gently breathing and pulsating overall figure. Focusing on the four or five front trees out of the whole, densely interwoven even into its depths, we can find a subtle back-and-forth movement of foliage matter, which is at the same time one with its changing degrees of density. A slight plastic relief arises, yet remaining elastic, formed as it is by a soft swell of wind, shadows and glimmering light. The light acts as a medium of fluctuations - totally different from Impressionism - here being structured; but also being different from the often prismatic geometrical light of the Quattrocento. This permanent fluctuating interweaving imparts to the picture its hypnotic character, as has been noticed (Pedretti, 1980:32). One seems to look on the rhythm of this nature as through a plane of glass, yet seeing nothing of a sterile herbarium, nothing that keeps one rigidly at distance, on the contrary even finding an intensification of the hypnotic, the enigmatic quality of this nature. The effect of 'behind glass' here is not like being 'sealed off', not artificial such as being vacuum-packed in transparent plastic foil. Also, ideas like a fly enclosed in amber are far from Leonardo's intention here. Rather, the fluctuating little wood seems to be viewed like flowingly moving ferns seen through the equally fluctuating and at the same time transparent medium of softly flowing water. Incidentally, this is one of Leonardo's favorite ideas (Pedretti, 1980:42), not to speak of the paramount significance of water for his image of the world as one sole 'complex-dynamic' formation. Even the psychodramatic compositional logic of the 'Last Supper' has been rightly connected with the 'form of movement in water and air', as they were studied by Leonardo (Gombrich, 1976:54). Processiveness does not detract from clarity, clarity does not block processiveness. The fluctuating quality is attached to its solid counterpart, the hypnotic or 'visionariness' to the real, the transitory to the clear, all of it being the result of that barely perceptible intensification of the real, the clear, the firm - meaning intensification in itself, not increasing beyond itself - constituting the true hypnotic. The kind of artificiality involved here is not a fixing one, but a process-like artificiality; it could be called a morphogenetic artificiality or, to use an older expression: an artificial organic. Nature appears as in a magic mirror; concentrated to be sure, but not magically spellbound: alive. This life of nature, this natural life, appears therein mirrored in itself, moving in itself perfectly, as independent, self-contained, life-pulsating nature, which, in spite of its being independent of its outside beholder, does not confront the latter as alienated or reified. It is this kind of autonomous process of nature, moving in itself, as described today by the Chilenean biologist Humberto Maturana, for instance (Maturana, 1982), which Leonardo had in view. One could say as well that it is a new and different kind of the absolute, an absolute-as-life, i.e., as living nature, and this means once again: as a complex-dynamic real entity.

Subject and medium are understood in a process-like manner, as by the example of the transparent flowing water. This double characterization means for our drawing that even the form of the image starts to flow, the picture in itself tending towards the transitory. The picture itself becomes a phenomenon of process, of movement with Leonardo, thereby adopting features of a 'similacrum', thereby increasingly entering the state-of-artificiality of freeing itself from all fixing prototypes or originals: this is certainly not only due to a special hovering, floating mode of appearance in this drawing placed, as it is, into the more or less accidental emptiness of its white sheet. The significance in the development towards picture and nature as simulacrum, which has shown itself here, is best assessed in its most consequent realization, namely in Magritte.

## 2. Magritte: Image and original of nature, both, as simulacra

'La Condition Humaine' (plate 6) is a title leaving no doubt that matters of principle are dealt with here. What we see is a landscape painting in front of the landscape itself, apparently being its model. Image and original merge almost indiscernibly. At first it looks as if the age old dream of 'imitatio naturae' had become true: the image literally turned into that transparent window pane, which painting-theorist Alberti in the 15th century was so enthusiastic about. Yet, here we have a more subtle stratagem. Obviously the canvas on the easel stays preserved as canvas. Yet, if image and original, work of man and work of nature merge into one another, then it means, both are artificial or both are natural, both are originals or both replicas. At the same time, both remain to be distinguished in a rest of difference. This plunges us into confusion. Again, we have arrived at our ontological bastard. The moral of Magritte's picture reads, in deceptive simplification: there are solely images, simulacra.

## 3. Leonardo's mountains as mental image. Science of painting as dynamic-morphogenetic view of nature

In Leonardo's drawing, 'Snow-covered Mountain Peaks' (plate 7), the turning of the '(never surpassed) optical truth', as has been said (Clark in Pedretti, 1980:10), into a kind of hyperreality immediately strikes the eye. Again this change into the artificial, happens implicitly, subcutaneously. The same is presented in the light of something other, without any external modification taking place in the same. I cannot circumscribe it but paradoxically: a transcending of nature into nature has been performed here, a reflection of nature in nature. The idea of these mountains comes to the fore compared with real nature, an idea, however, real in itself. There could be talk of a 'transubstantiation' of the mountains into their concept-form, of the exposure of their mental image, whereby the mental, for its part, retains a natural characteristic and the conceptual stays identical with the mountains' realness. Here we have the case of something different and simultaneously identical, and vice versa, being very similar to Magritte: namely the case of a 'double' as an indicator for simulacra.

At first sight it may appear astonishing that this can happen with such a massive and immobile formation as mountains, without any rhythm of fluctuations and flows like in the 'Copse of Birches' (plate 5). However, precisely mountains, assumed as the most constant, if not eternal on this earth, in nature and world, are Leonardo's favorite objects for the demonstration of this dynamic view on nature. Mountains, like everything else in nature, are permanently coming into and going out of being, many different processes working here, above all the effects of water, Leonardo's favorite element. Also, many chaotic processes are included. Like no one before, Leonardo answered to the maxim of the most recent disequilibrium thermodynamics by Ilya Prigogine (Prigogine, 1979, 1982) and of Mandelbrot's fractal mathematics: namely, order-from-chaos. This maxim represents the core of his dynamic-morphogenetic view of the world, in regard to his thinking and research as well as his 'science of painting'. It does not suffice, therefore, to relate him to the dynamics of Newtonian physics (Damisch, 1972:188-96, 215-26). At the end of his life, Leonardo tried to find out something about the fundamentally chaotic processes by planning a great series of very different drawings supposedly dealing with the 'Deluge', while in fact dealing with the 'End of the World' (plate 8). This ending of the world is made up of purely morphogenetic processes of nature, not unlike our 'big crash' in physics. It is not improbable that Leonardo intended to give a résumé of his idea of nature in the form of a huge representation (maybe in a cycle of frescoes) of a 'Chaotology', instead of a 'Cosmology'. There is even speculation on a plan of a counter-project against his rival Michelangelo, correcting his Story of Creation in the Capella Sistina (Gombrich, 1976:55f).

## 4. Leonardo and computer-simulation of nature: Cycle of nature-art-science (II)

Looking at the drawing of the mountains (plate 7) once more, we become aware of the many differentiated states, one can almost speak of 'phases', of the mountain formation: the mountain-ranges rise from the valleys, where water is toiling away, and by the force of these same waters they are decaying again, finally being destroyed. In the main range we have the emphasized contrast of almost whole parts with other ones breaking into manifold forms, in which is expressed an exact morphogenetic time vector from left to right. What we find here is a mini-model of the fractal-series of mountains by Voss (pl. 1-3). Finally, there are the areas of snow and ice, contrasting with the naked rock, but also as physical states of the water attacking it, in order to destroy it at last by bursting it open. And all this - to close the circle - demonstrates the conceptual and mental image of nature, which has been our subject: artificiality and morphogenetic complexity interlocking in Leonardo's thinking. Therein we find embodied the cycle of nature-art-science in the medium of the artificial, as it is peculiar to him.

What distinguishes Leonardo's cycle from the one of computer-simulation and Mandelbrot-Sets can possibly only be approached in the closer study of the relation of morphogenesis and imagination. The background landscape in Leonardo's 'Virgin and St Anne' (plates 9-10) offers richly illustrative material concerning this relation. The landscape evokes a synthetic impression, often described as 'visionary'. The artificial is here due to its being composed of most varying elements out of reality, forming a unity which is totally characterized by the 'reality'-properties of these elements, without actually occurring in reality that way. This makes it astonishingly similar and even comparable to the fractal mountain landscape by Voss (plates 1-3) likewise simulating a nature which does not exist as realistically as possible. The morphogenetic trait of the mountains-drawing (plate 7) has been intensified here to become a spectacle of nature's forces at work. We see the interlocked processes of chaos and order in action, in a desert of water, of mountain cliffs and of ice, i. e. a kind of turbulent melting pot of the different physical states and stages of forms in nature. This is the natural-historical basis for the observed 'visionariness'. Simultaneously we can find here an increasing processualization of the mental, of the transcendental itself, compared to the mountains-drawing (plate 7) and even going beyond the processualization of subject and medium in the drawing of the 'Copse of Birches' (plate 5). Leonardo seems to have thereby touched upon the time essence of 'Einbildungskraft', i. e. upon its point of non-difference with morphogenesis.

When speaking of the 'visionariness' of this landscape, results like the above are all too quickly reinterpreted backwards into a context of false metaphysics of subjectivity, artist and creation. Leonardo, however, means the artificial of nature as exactly found in its artistic character. The latter he conceives of as 'order-from-chaos' - morphogenesis, setting it against applications of the theological paradigm of creation to human artistic affairs. He pursues a double strategy: against the 'non-artistic' of nature on the one hand, and against the ancient concepts of human artistic ability designed by the theology of creation on the other. As an alternative to the rejected views he does not propose any reductive identification with one of the areas of the human and the natural, but a specific interlocking of both of these. One has to keep this in mind regarding Leonardo's opinion: that the 'Invention of Nature' amounts ultimately to an exposition of the 'inventiveness of nature' itself, respectively that the artificiality of images of nature amounts to the artificiality of nature itself. However, Leonardo remains within the initially outlined field of a partial coordination of morphogenesis and imagination, while computer techniques in general are going far beyond this field: the decisive question arising out of this is whether the large areas of purely syntactical artificiality, which are thereby being developed, can be matched semantically i. e. by activities of human interpretation. Depending on the kind of adaptation taking place, more and more daring forms of interlocking naturalness and artificiality could arise. And despite all diagnose concerning 'posthistoire', the dynamic potential of Western culture does not yet seem to be exhausted at all.

## IV. C. D. Friedrich: Artificial naturalism as theological one

One should not, however, be deterred or discouraged too easily by so much artificiality - not even the sympathizers of a society devoted to the search for 'Ultimate Reality and Meaning' to whom this lecture has been given.

For this reason I would like to present, as an epilogue, C. D. Friedrich's painting, 'Morning Mist in the Mountains', from 1808 (plate 11). Again it is a representation of nature and again undoubtedly, it is as highly artificial as it is highly naturalistic. Again it is a mountain scenery. Therein it resembles Leonardo, yet still more strikingly the final piece of the fractal mountains by Voss. Here, to be sure, the mental, or if you like the 'conceptual' core, upon which the artificial illusion of nature depends, results from ideas of Christian doctrine, permeating the whole nature: for Friedrich the representation reaches its peak in the little cross on top of the mountain. It looms into a small spot of blue sky between dense clouds, as a sign of Christ revealing always a new heaven for the faithful: the faithful rallying in the form of spruces round the rock as church, which is obscured by the mist of the limits of human rational understanding.

## References

Damisch, H. (1972). *Théorie du nuage. Pour une histoire de la peinture.* Paris, Le Seuil.

Gombrich, E. H. (1976). *The Heritage of Apelles. Studies in the Art of the Renaissance III.* Oxford, Phaidon.

Mandelbrot, B. (1980). *The Fractal Geometry of Nature.* San Francisco, Freeman.

Maturana, H. (1982). *Erkennen: Die Organisation und Verkörperung von Wirklichkeit. Ausgewählte Arbeiten zur biologischen Epistemologie.* Braunschweig, Vieweg.

Pedretti, C. (1980). *Leonardo da Vinci. Nature Studies from the Royal Library at Windsor Castle.* Catalogue by C. Pedretti. Introduction by Kenneth Clark.

Prigogine, I. (1979). *Vom Sein zum Werden. Zeit und Komplexität in den Naturwissenschaften.* München, Piper.

Prigogine, I. and Stengers, I. (1980). *Dialog mit der Natur. Neue Wege naturwissenschaftlichen Denkens.* München, Piper.

**Plate 1.** Richard Voss 'Changing the Fractal Dimension' 1983, part I, 10" x 14". In: Cynthia Goodman, *Digital Visions. Computers and Art.* New York 1987, pl. 69.

**Plate 2.** Richard Voss 'Changing the Fractal Dimension' 1983, part II, 10" x 14" In: Cynthia Goodman (1987), pl. 70.

**Plate 3.** Richard Voss 'Changing the Fractal Dimension' 1983, part III, 10" x 14". In: Cynthia Goodman (1987), pl.

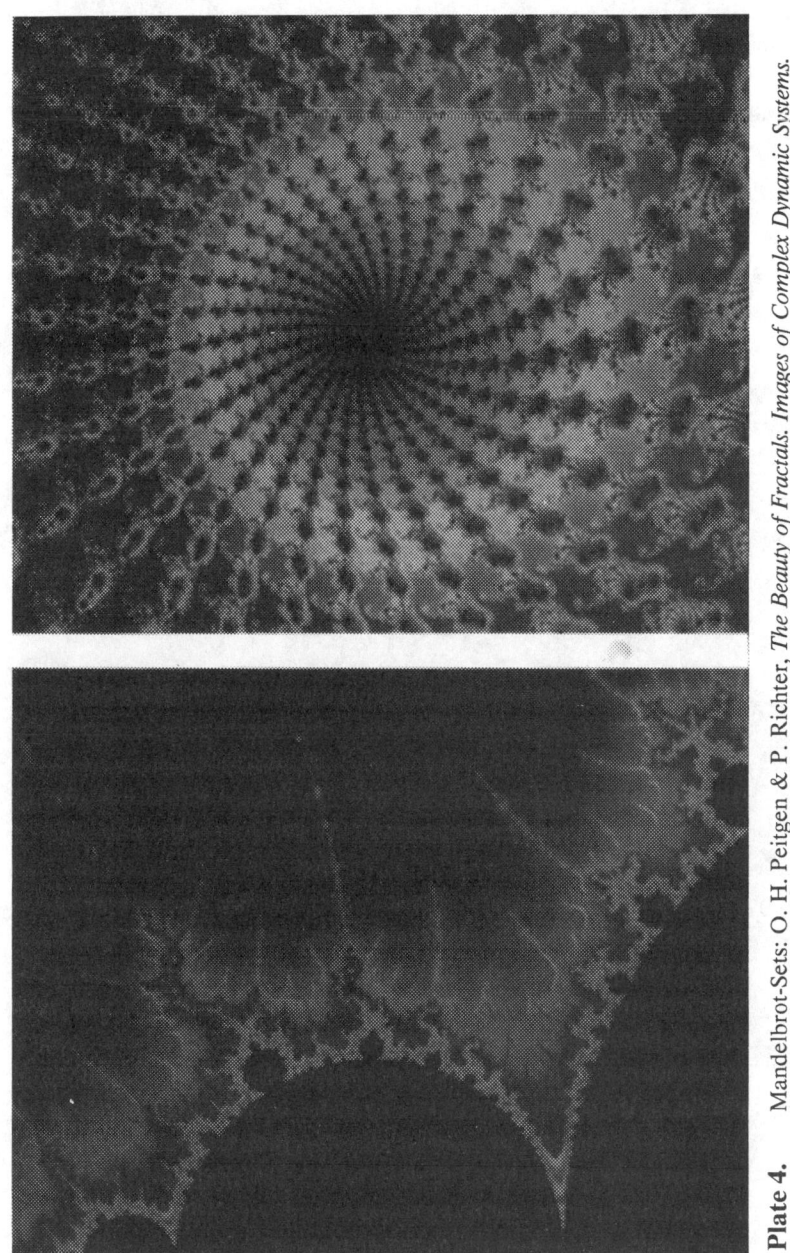

**Plate 4.** Mandelbrot-Sets: O. H. Peitgen & P. Richter, *The Beauty of Fractals. Images of Complex Dynamic Systems.* Berlin etc. 1986. GEO No. 6, June 1984; *Scientific American* Aug. 1985.

**Plate 5.** Leonardo: 'Copse of Birches' ca. 1498-1502, 193 x 153 mm, red chalk; Pedretti 1980. No. 7A (RL 12431 r), plate III.

**Plate 6.** René Magritte: 'La Condition Humaine', 1933, 100 x 81 cm, Priv. Coll.

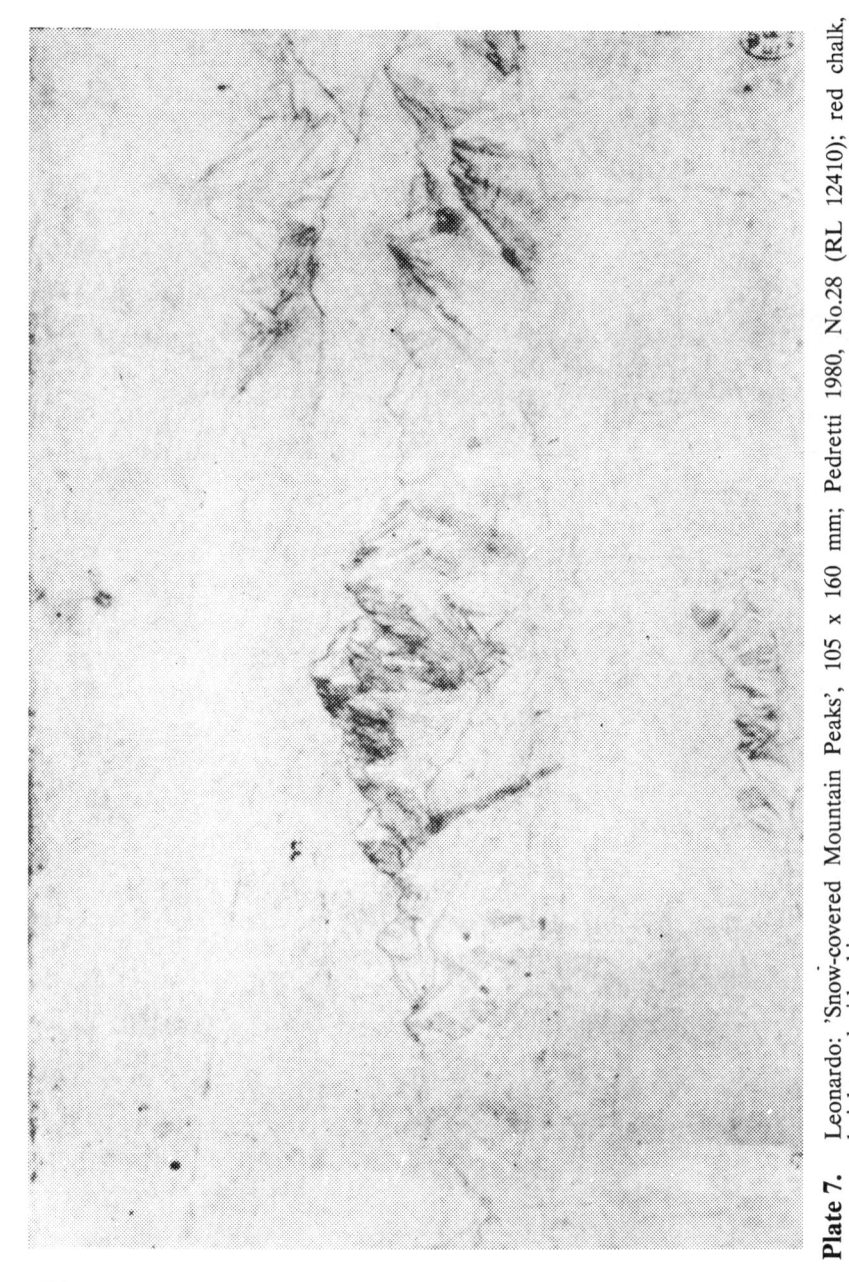

Plate 7. Leonardo: 'Snow-covered Mountain Peaks', 105 x 160 mm; Pedretti 1980, No.28 (RL 12410); red chalk, heightened with white.

**Plate 8.** Leonardo: 'Mountain range burst open by water, the falling rock producing enormous waves in a lake; with a note' ('Deluge'- Series), 162 x 203 mm; pen and two inks (black and yellow) over black chalk; Pedretti 1980, No. 42 (RL 12380).

**Plate 9.** Leonardo: 'Virgin and St Anne', 1510, Louvre Paris, 16 x 112 cm; detail.

**Plate 10.** Leonardo: 'Virgin and St Anne', 1510, Louvre Paris, 16 x 112 cm; detail.

**Plate 11.** C.D. Friedrich: 'Morning Mist in the Mountains', 1808; Rudolstadt, Staatl. Museen Schloss Heidecksburg: H. Börsch-Supan/ K.W. Jähnig, *Caspar David Friedrich. Gemälde, Druckgraphik und bildmässige Zeichnungen.* München 1973, Cat.-No. 166, plate 5.

# CONTRIBUTORS

### Thomas Bargatzky

Born 1946. Dr.phil. (Hamburg 1977); Dr.phil.habil. (München 1988). He is Professor of Anthropology at the University of Bayreuth and has held positions at the University of München, University of Tübingen, and University of Heidelberg. He has carried out fieldwork in Western Samoa. His publications include "Culture, environment, and the ills of adaptationism", *Current Anthropology* (1984); *Einführung in die Kulturökologie* (1986); and "Upward evolution, suprasystem dominance, and the Mature State", in H.J.M. Claessen and P. van de Velde (eds.), *Early State Dynamics* (1987).

### Gerhold K. Becker

Born 1943. Lic.phil. (Pullach/München 1969); Lic.theol. (Frankfurt 1973); Dr.phil. (München 1979). He is Chair of Religion and Philosophy and Director of the Centre for Applied Ethics at Hong Kong Baptist College. He has held positions at Hochschule für Philosophie (München) and University of München. Among other things, he has done research on Hegel, Heidegger, Hume, Descartes, Kierkegaard, and Ernst Troeltsch. His major works include *Theologie in der Gegenwart* (1978); *Neuzeitliche Subjektivität und Religiosität* (1982); and *Die Ursymbole in den Religionen* (1987).

### Ulrich Berner

Born 1948. Dr.theol. (Göttingen 1974); Dr.theol.habil. (Göttingen 1980). He is Chair of Comparative Religion at the University of Bayreuth and has held positions at the University of Göttingen, University of Hamburg, University of Bonn and University of Bremen. His publications include *Untersuchungen zur Verwendung des Synkretismus-Begriffes* (1982); "Inkulturationsprogramme in indischer und afrikanischer Theologie", *Saeculum* (1986); and "The image of the philosopher in late Antiquity and in early Christianity", in H.G. Kippenberg, Y.B. Kuiper and A.F. Sanders (eds.), *Concepts of Person in Religion and Thought* (1990).

### A. Martin Byers

Born 1937. B.A. in history/anthropology (McGill University 1966); M.A. in cultural anthropology (McGill University 1969); Ph.D. in archaeology (State University of New York, Albany, 1987). He teaches at Vanier College, Saint-Laurent, Québec. His publications include "Structure, meaning, action and things: The duality of material cultural mediation", *Journal for the Theory of Social Behaviour* (1991); and "The action-constitutive theory of monuments: A strong pragmatist version", *Journal for the Theory of Social Behaviour* (1992).

### Franz X. Faust

Born 1953. Dr.phil. (München 1983); Dr.phil.habil. (München 1992). He has taught Anthropology at the University of München, Fundación Universitaria de Popayán (Colombia), and Universidad del Cauca. He has carried out extensive fieldwork in Colombia. His publications include *El Sistema Medico entre los Coyaimas y Natagaimas* (1986); "Etnogeografía y etnogeología de Coconuco y Sotará", *Revista Colombiana de Antropología* (1990); and *Kultur und Naturschutz im kolumbianischen Zentralmassiv* (1992).

### Jörn Greve

Born 1939. Dr.med. (1978). He is a neuro-psychiatrist (State Examination 1965), and works in the field of social medicine. His publications deal with social integration of the handicapped, psychiatric and neurological rehabilitation and socio-ecological themes. Among his works are "Photographische Bewegungsanalyse neurologischer Störungen und ihre Bedeutung für die Rehabilitation" (with B. Brill), in K. Schimrigk and A. Haaß (eds.), *Therapie und Therapiekontrolle zentraler Bewegungsstörungen und Arzneimittelinterferenzen* (1985); "Evolutionary aspects of the magic, animistic, and psychotic", in C.L. Cazzullo et al.(eds.), *Schizophrenia - An Integrative View (1984);* and "Präventivmaßnahmen aus sozialmedizinischer Sicht", in K. Aurand et al. (eds.), *Umweltbelastungen und Ängste vor Gesundheitsschäden (1993)*.

### Antonio Guerci

Born 1945. Ph.D. in biology (Genova 1971). He is Professor of Physical Anthropology at the University of Genova and also Director of the Institute of Physical Anthropology and Coordinator of the Museum of Ethnomedicine. He has published widely on physical anthropology. Among his works are "Antropologia e fisiologia", *Antropologia Contemporanea* (1979); *Biotypologie humaine* (with M. Martiny and L. Brian, 1982); and "La medicina popolare nel Mezzogiorno. Considerazioni di etnomedicina comparata", in Guida (ed.), *Salute e malattia nella cultura delle classi subalterne del Mezzogiorno* (1990).

### Thomas Hölscher

Born 1944. Dr.phil. (München 1985). He has taught art history at the University of München and University of Innsbruck. His current research focusses on electronic image processing in relation to the traditional media of the visual arts. His publications include *Bild und Exzeß. Näherungen zu Goya* (1988); "Das Vergnügen an der Kunst. Michael Baxandalls 'Ursachen der Bilder'", *Merkur* (1991) and "Was ist ein digitales Bild?", in F. Rötzer (ed.), *Die Malerei im Rückspiegel der Medien* (forthcoming).

### Rolf Kuschel

Born 1939. M.A. (Copenhagen 1969); Ph.D. (Copenhagen 1988). He is Associate Professor of Social Psychology at the University of Copenhagen and has done extensive field research on Bellona Island in the South Pacific, and in Nepal. His publications include *Animal Stories from Bellona Island (Mungiki)* (1975); "Cultural reflections in

Bellonese personal names", *Journal of the Polynesian Society* (1988); and *Vengeance is Their Reply. Blood Feuds and Homicides on Bellona Island* (2 Vols.) (1988).

## Catherine E. (Read-)Martin

B.A. (Reed College, Oregon); M.A. and Ph.D. in anthropology (University of California at Los Angeles). She is Professor of Anthropology at California State University at Los Angeles, where she has also acted as director of Women's Studies, Canadian Studies, The General Education Honors Program, and The Academic Advisement and Information Center. She received the Outstanding Teacher of the Year Award for 1990-91. She has done research on human evolution, animal behaviour and symbolism, ethnobotany, and childrearing in different cultures. Her publications include "Australopithecine scavenging and human evolution: An approach from faunal analysis", *Current Anthropology* (1975, with D. Read); "Children's games and creativity: Art and the child", transl. for *Umjetnost I dijete* (Zagreb 1989); and "The evolution of the Brain", in D.D. Curl (ed.), *Chiropractic Approach to Head Pain* (forthcoming).

## Patricia J. O'Brien

Ph.D. (University of Illinois-Urbana 1969). She is Distinguished Professor of Anthropology at Kansas State University, Manhattan. She is presently the editor of the *Plains Anthropologist*. Her current research interests are Central Plains Tradition and the question of the political character of Cahokia, near St. Louis. Her publications include "Prehistoric evidence for Pawnee cosmology", *American Anthropologist* (1986); "Evidence for the antiquity of women's roles in Pawnee society", *Plains Anthropologist* (1991); and "Early State economics: Cahokia, capital of the Ramey state", in H.J.M. Claessen and P. van de Velde (eds.), *Early State Economics* (1991).

## Antonio Santangelo

Born 1928. Dr.med. He is a physician and is engaged in the field of paleoanthropology for more than thirty years. He has taught as a part-time lecturer at the Università Cattolica del Sacro Cuore, Milano. His publications include *Epopea Ominide* (1985); *The Garden of Eden: The Way to Homo Sapiens* (1987); and *Anthropology and the Processes of Civilization: The Birth of New Values* (1992).

## Gerd Spittler

Born 1939. Dr.phil. (Freiburg 1966); Dr.phil.habil. (Freiburg 1977). He is Chair of Anthropology at the University of Bayreuth and was Professor of Sociology at the University of Freiburg. He has done extensive fieldwork in Niger and Nigeria since 1967. His major works include *Herrschaft über Bauern. Die Ausbreitung staatlicher Herrschaft und einer islamisch-urbanen Kultur in Gobir (Niger)* (1978); *Verwaltung in einem afrikanischen Bauernstaat. Das koloniale Französisch-Westafrika, 1919-1939* (1980); and *Les Touaregs face aux sécheresses et aux famines. Les Kel Ewey de l'Aïr, 1900-1985* (1993).

**Oscar Torretta**

Born 1951. M.A. in physical anthropology (University of Massachusetts 1986); Ph.D. in geography (Genova 1990). He is currently external researcher at the University of Genova. He has carried out fieldwork in Burma and Brasil. His works include "La sopravvivenza degli Yanomami", in *L'età dell'Acquario* (Torino 1987); "Enfermedad de Chagas en una población indígena", *Anales de Antropología* (Mexico City 1991); and "Contributi antropologici nella displasia congenita dell'anca", *Acta Congr. Naz. Soc. Ital. Ortopedia Pediatrica* (1991).

**Fred W. Voget**

B.A. (University of Oregon 1936); Ph.D. in anthropology (Yale University 1948). He is Emeritus Professor of Anthropology at Southern Illinois University at Edwardsville, and currently is Adjunct Professor of Anthropology at Portland State University, Oregon. He has taught at the University of Nebraska, University of Arkansas, McGill University, University of Toronto, Northwestern University, Sir George Williams University (Montreal), and the University of München. He carried out fieldwork among the Crow and Wind River Shoshoni, and among Canadian Iroquois at Caughnawaga (Québec) and Six Nations in Ontario. He is author of numerous books and articles, among them, *Osage Indians I: Osage Research Report* (1974); *A History of Anthropology* (1975, Ital. transl. 1984); and *The Crow-Shoshoni Sun-Dance* (1984).

Stanisław Kowalczyk

# An Outline of the Philosophical Anthropology

Frankfurt/M., Bern, New York, Paris, 1991. 289 pp.
ISBN 3-631-44156-8                                    pb. DM 84.--

What is the nature, origin and destiny of man? These questions are vital not only to the philosophy. This book is an attempt to unite the classic thomistic philosophy with the phenomenological method. The first part of the book contains methodological remarks connected with the transition from the phenomenology to the metaphysics of man. The second part of the paper gives a phenomenological description of man: his corporeity, main attributes and activity – external and internal. The final part of anthropology is the metaphysics of man. Human being is the substantial self, the personal "I", a psycho-somatic reality endowed with mental faculties. The book discusses also the problems of death and immortality, the relation between an individual person and social community.

*Contents:* Currents in personalistic anthropology, love, freedom, labour, conscience, religious experience – Person and personality – Creationism and evolution – Human soul – Humanism and personalism

**Verlag Peter Lang  Frankfurt a.M. · Berlin · Bern · New York · Paris · Wien**
Auslieferung: Verlag Peter Lang AG, Jupiterstr. 15, CH-3000 Bern 15
Telefon (004131) 9411122, Telefax (004131) 9411131
- Preisänderungen vorbehalten -